After the
New Economy

After the
New Economy

Doug Henwood

THE NEW PRESS

NEW YORK
LONDON

Published in the United States by The New Press, New York, 2003
Distributed by W. W. Norton & Company, Inc., New York

LIBRARY OF CONGRESS CATALOGING–IN–PUBLICATION DATA

Henwood, Doug.
After the new economy/Doug Henwood
    p. cm.
Includes bibliographical references and index.
ISBN 1-56584-770-9 (hc)
    1. United States—Economic conditions—2001–. 2. United States—Economic
conditions—1981–2001. 3. United States—Economic policy. 4. Electronic commerce—
United States—History. 5. Stocks—Prices—United States—History. 6. Corporations—
Corrupt practices—United States—History. I. Title
HC106.83.H46 2003
330.973—dc21

                                                                2003044234

The New Press was established in 1990 as a not-for-profit alternative to the large, commercial
publishing houses currently dominating the book publishing industry. The New Press operates in the
public interest rather than for private gain, and is committed to publishing, in innovative ways, works of
educational, cultural, and community value that are often deemed insufficiently profitable.

The New Press
38 Greene Street, 4th floor
New York, NY 10013
www.thenewpress.com

In the United Kingdom:
6 Salem Road
London W2 4BU

Book design by Doug Henwood
Composition by LBO Digital

10   9   8   7   6   5   4   3   2

for my parents,
Harold and Victorine Henwood

Contents

Acknowledgments

Though books usually have a single name on the cover, writing one requires lots of help from others. I'd like to thank, among many, Laura Starecheski for her excellent research work; my good friend Philippa Dunne for her many forms of collaboration; Colin Robinson for being the best publisher one could ask for; and André Schiffrin and the staff of The New Press for both their professional skills and their role as splendid officemates. Thanks also to Jared Bernstein, Patrick Bond, Heather Boushey, Tom Frank, Branko Milanovic, Christian Parenti, Michael Perelman, Kim Phillips-Fein, Nomi Prins, Max Sawicky, Michal Seligman, Gregg Wirth, the members of the lbo-talk listserv. And, most of all, thanks to my wife, Liza Featherstone, who not only made this a better book with her comments on the manuscript, but who makes life worth living as well.

After the
New Economy

Introduction

For a while in the late 1990s we had a New Economy. It was the wonder of the world. Computers had unleashed a productivity miracle, recessions were things of the past, ideas had replaced things as the motors of economic life, the world had become unprecedentedly globalized, work had become deeply meaningful, and mutual funds had put an end to class conflict. Even to conventional minds, a lot of that sounds embarrassing now. But commentary on the era usually treats it as a mix of collective folly and outright criminality—never as something emerging from the innards of the American economic machinery. And now we're forgetting about it, our amnesia encouraged by the frequent reminders that we're in a state of permanent war.

There was something aberrational about the late 1990s, for sure, but the New Economy moment was a manic set of variations on ancient themes, all promoted from the highest places. Presidents and treasury secretaries restructured economies, encouraged by Wall Street analysts and Alan Greenspan. Techno-utopianism is an old theme in American culture. Bill Gates's fantasies of the frictionless economy—spun out, it's said, with the assistance of thirteen ghostwriters—were the latest incarnation of an old elite desire to put workers and the ugly things that sometimes come with them out of sight. We've been hearing about postindustrial society for at least thirty years; if it had come about, would we have to worry about global warming? Dreams of an end to the business cycle often flower at the end of long booms; long-term stock market investors could take them as reliable sell signals. Office foosball machines didn't really change the nature of work, and they've gone the way of Casual Fridays. Class divisions never disappeared; only 401(k)s did. Sure, poverty fell and incomes rose after years of stagnation and decline, but those developments now look like the lucky by-products of an unsustainable bubble.

Although this book is relentlessly critical of claims for a New Economy, I want to make it clear from the start what it's not. It's not an attack on technology itself, nor is it a plea for a return to "community" and "place." I like technology and use it all the time. Anyone scanning the bibliography will quickly see that much of the material cited was nabbed from the web, as were almost all the raw statistics. I publish a newsletter that would be impossible to produce without today's gadgetry. I also don't endorse the critique of globalization that urges a return to the local. "Technology" and "globalization" should be neutral terms; whether they're good or bad depends on how they're used—whether to enrich the lives of billions of humans, or to enrich a small band of executives, financiers, and promoters. That band has left the U.S. economy much the worse for wear. They've got a lot to answer for.

1 Novelty

The U.S. economy likely will not see a recession for years to come. We don't want one, we don't need one, and, as we have the tools to keep the current expansion going, we won't have one. This expansion will run forever.
—the late, prestigious MIT economist Rudi Dornbusch (1998)

Between 1996 and early 2001, you could hardly have opened a newspaper or turned on a TV without hearing about a wondrous New Economy.[1] The raving cooled considerably along with the NASDAQ's long swoon (as the graph on page 4 shows), but, sadly, it's not dead yet, despite all the scandals. This book is an exercise in kicking the thing while it's down, to make sure it won't get up again.

The canonical New Economy discourse was relentlessly, almost deliriously, optimistic. It goes something like this. Finally, after a long wait, the computer revolution is paying off economically. It used to be, as the economist Robert Solow famously put it, that that revolution was visible everywhere but in the statistics. But with the takeoff in the U.S. productivity stats in the mid-1990s, Solow's quip was ready for retirement. It took some time for people and organizations to learn how to use computers (broadly defined, of course, to include all kinds of high-tech electronic gadgetry), but now they've finally learned. All that hardware, now linked from local area networks to the global Internet, along with a political re-

gime of smaller government and lighter regulation, has unleashed forces
of innovation and wealth creation like the world has never known before.
Flatter hierarchies and more interesting work are the social payoffs; rising
incomes and an end to slumps the economic payoffs. Quality replaces
quantity, knowledge replaces physical capital, and flexible networks replace rigid organizational charts.[2]

Along with these qualitative claims came some quantitative ones as
well. Allen Sinai, president of Primark Decision Economics and a prominent televised talking head, told *Bloomberg* magazine, "The nineties have
been the best decade for the U.S. economy going back to the 1850s. We
woke up to the idea that spending and borrowing our way to prosperity
was wrong. We raised taxes and took
a turn toward a budget surplus. We
took advantage of our unique free-
market system of incentives that
encourage entrepreneurship, and
which put us in the lead in high
tech. Our society responded, and
all kinds of good things happened"
(quoted in Goldman 2000).

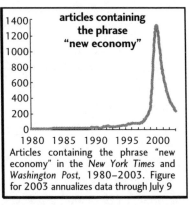

Articles containing the phrase "new
economy" in the *New York Times* and
Washington Post, 1980–2003. Figure
for 2003 annualizes data through July 9

Later chapters will deal with
the qualitative claims; hierarchy, for
one, never went away, and asserted itself brutally when the bubble burst.
Sinai's enthusiasms can be easily dismissed at the outset. Almost everything
he said deserves a clarification, if not an outright correction. Measured
by GDP growth rates, the most conventional and fetishized number in
all of economics, it's hard to see how the 1990s were "the best decade
for the U.S. economy going back to the 1850s"; nineteenth- and early-
twetieth-century growth rates were pretty ripping by modern standards.

According to economic historian Angus Maddison's (1995) figures, U.S. GDP growth averaged 3.9% between 1850 and 1914, though wild booms and busts oscillated violently around that average; the 3.4% average of the 1990s is considerably lower, little different from the growth rates clocked in the much-maligned 1970s and well below that of the 1960s. But Sinai isn't alone in this claim; in congressional testimony in the summer of 2000, Lawrence Summers—who was a distinguished economist before he became Bill Clinton's last treasury secretary (and, later, companion of right-wing talk show host Laura Ingraham)—said, "We are growing faster than ever before" (quoted in Fidler 2000).[3]

"We"—the identity of this first person spurious of elite discourse is never made clear—never stopped spending and borrowing; the expansion that began in 1991 was the most consumption-intensive expansion since World War II. And while the federal government stopped borrowing for a while in the late 1990s—though the George W. Bush administration has returned to the trough—households and businesses have most certainly not, nor has the U.S. as a nation collectively stopped borrowing abroad. To take just one extreme example, the *Wall Street Journal* (Zuckerman 2000) reported:

> While home buyers once needed a 20% down payment—and thus needed a degree of financial well-being—today over 40% of new-home mortgages are with down payments of less than 10%, according to SMR Research, a financial-research firm. "At least a quarter of all new mortgages go to people who are basically broke, and the figure could be much higher," says Stuart Feldstein, president of SMR.

Rampant borrowing continued through the recession that began in March 2001, with low interest rates prompting enormous home-equity withdrawals.

And the issue of the private sector's unique and ineffable contribution to technological development is one of the most mystified aspects of U.S. economic life. Yesterday's favorite miracle, the Internet, was initially a project of the Pentagon, as was the computer itself; the government picked up the basic R&D tab for decades, when neither Wall Street nor private industry showed any interest. In fact, capital only became interested when the start-up costs had all been borne by the public sector and there were finally profits to be made. Much of the software that runs the net is "open source"—with the code freely circulated among developers, a nightmare to commercial software publishers who want to copyright everything and keep it secret. And biotech, the successor miracle that mostly survived the bust, also owes its existence to federal largesse, with basic research having been funded for decades by the National Institutes of Health and other public entities.[4]

Of course, good American individualists don't like to talk about the public sector, since their hero is the plucky entrepreneur. This entrepreneur's contribution is further called into question by the unpleasant fact that the stodgy social democracies of Scandinavia are among the most wired countries around. In early 2003, the World Economic Forum proclaimed Finland the most tech-savvy nation in the world.

Fact-checking the likes of Allen Sinai is pretty unrewarding work, even though someone has to. But fact may never have had much to do with it. A good bit of the New Economy discourse was a product of fantasy, a symptom of American triumphalism—very much like the globalization narrative that Paul Smith takes apart in *Millennial Dreams* (Smith 1996). Fantasies and symptoms are notoriously immune to rational refutation.

Claims about New Eras have plenty of historical precedents, as do their association with great bull markets in stocks (see Shiller 2000, chapter 5, for a review). Perhaps the first episode, at least in modern history, was one that occurred around 1901. This, like the recent one, was jacked up with New Century fever; similar enthusiasms erupted in the late 1920s and late 1960s. The latest episode struck sometime in the mid-1990s; Shiller (2000, p. 97) cites several pioneering newspaper and magazine articles from 1996 and 1997. The mythmaking got quite a shot in the arm when it was endorsed by Alan Greenspan as he retreated from his December 1996 "irrational exuberance" speech. What a difference from 30 years earlier. Then–Fed chair William McChesney Martin publicly expressed anxiety that speculation was getting out of control in the mid-1960s, in a way reminiscent of the 1920s, and he cited as evidence "the spreading conviction among the public that 'a new economic era' had begun" (quoted in Shiller 2000, p. 224).

It's remarkable how similar the language of the various New Eras has been. The early days of the telegraph were laden with fantasies of universal peace, love, and understanding, very similar to some of our more fervent web enthusiasts—and even "web" metaphors themselves were common (Standage 1999). And the language and thinking of the 1960s New Era taste curiously like the more recent vintage, sharing both a journalistic source, *Business Week,* and the trope of Euro-envy. In 1965, *BW* patriotically enthused (quoted in Grant 2000b):

> Some European central bankers and economists have been watching the U.S. economy with utter amazement, some apprehension, and not a little jealousy.
>
> By all their rules, the U.S. economy should have started long ago to show the signs of strain that are the inevitable prelude to a bust. Yet, despite an expansion that has carried gross national product up a startling 30%, or 150 billion, over the past $4^1/_2$ years, the economy remains generally free from inflationary pressures and imbalances. And the businessmen who run the show fully expect their trouble-free prosperity to continue.

> The underlying factor behind this remarkable performance, so baffling to the
> European traditionalists, has been a sharp rise in productivity.

The magazine went on to cite the splendid acceleration in productivity growth since the 1950s, and to quote a Milwaukee CEO as saying "I see no end to the gain in productivity."[5] Unfortunately, productivity gains topped out just six months after those words were published, slid into the early 1970s, recovered a bit, then lapsed into the much-lamented productivity slowdown that would extend into the mid-1990s. Inflation bottomed out at year-end, and the great and troublesome inflation of the late 1960s and 1970s was almost upon the land. The next year brought the first post–World War II financial panic, the credit crunch of 1966, and the beginning of the slide in corporate profit rates that lasted into the early 1980s. CEOs and journalists should note the biblical correlation of pride and imminent falls.

The Gildered Age

Speaking of scripture, you can actually push the birth of the most recent New Era back a little farther than Shiller did. *Baffler* editor Tom Frank (personal communication) says that the earliest claim he could find for the existence of a "new economy" was a 1988 speech by Ronald Reagan at Moscow State University. In it, Reagan said:

> In the new economy, human invention increasingly makes physical re-
> sources obsolete. We're breaking through the material conditions of exis-
> tence to a world where man creates his own destiny. Even as we explore the
> most advanced reaches of science, we're returning to the age-old wisdom
> of our culture, a wisdom contained in the book of Genesis in the Bible: In

the beginning was the spirit, and it was from this spirit that the material abundance of creation issued forth.

Reagan's invocation of scripture isn't standard in the New Economy literature, but there's no small amount of mysticism and true-believerhood in the doctrine. As Frank pointed out, Reagan's line was straight out of George Gilder—and it's quite likely Gilder's son Josh wrote the speech.

Gilder is a fascinating figure; it's stunning how his seemingly wacky thoughts become conventional wisdom in a decade or less. Most centrists and liberals found his 1981 book *Wealth and Poverty,* with its argument that the poor are spoiled by a generous welfare state (as if the U.S. ever had one of those) and instead need the spur of their poverty, rather implausibly brutal; just a decade later, Bill Clinton won the presidency in part on a promise to "end welfare as we know it," and just a few years later, he signed a bill that did exactly that.[6] And Gilder's late-1980s New Economy claims seemed loopy when he first issued them; less than a decade later, they were painfully ubiquitous.

Back in the summer of 1987, when the Eighties were at their Roaringest, an interview with George Gilder ran on the now-departed Financial News Network. Gilder, looking like he'd just beamed aboard from Melville's *Fidèle* (the flagship of *The Confidence-Man*), argued that the trade deficit was nothing to worry about. Trade figures count only things, said the poet laureate of entrepreneurship, but what really makes the world move today is information: today, capital bounces around on satellites and dances up and down fiber-optic cables. Oddly, Gilder treated the terms "information" and "capital" almost as if they were synonyms.

Two years later, Gilder published *Microcosm,* a book that took as its theme the "overthrow of matter."[7] On the first page of chapter 1, we learn that "the powers of mind are everywhere ascendant over the brute force of things." Though the primacy of the mind over matter is hardly a new idea in Western philosophy, Gilder writes as if it is. His universe consists of ideas and the heroic individuals who think them; his rejectamenta consist of matter and its partisans, the dialectical materialists of the Marxist tradition and the pragmatic materialists of mainstream thought. Society, and with it labor and the state, virtually disappear from Gilder's view, except in the form of the fickle and ever-dynamic "market."

And so do class and history. In a classic passage, Gilder erupts:

> The United States did not enter the microcosm through the portals of the Ivy League, with Brooks Brothers suits, gentleman Cs, and warbling society wives. Few people who think they are already in can summon the energies to break in. From immigrants and outcasts, street toughs and science wonks, nerds and boffins, the bearded and the beerbellied, the tacky and the upright, and sometimes weird, the born again and born yesterday, with Adam's apples bobbing, psyches throbbing, and acne galore, the fraternity of the pizza breakfast, the Ferrari dream, the silicon truth, the midnight modem, and the seventy-hour week, from dirt farms and redneck shanties, trailer parks and Levittowns, in a rainbow parade of all colors and wavelengths, of the hyperneat and the sty high, the crewcut and khaki, the ponytailed and punk, accented from Britain and Madras, from Israel and Malaya, from Paris and Parris Island, from Iowa and Havana, from Brooklyn and Boise and Belgrade and Vienna and Vietnam, from the coarse fanaticism and desperation, ambition and hunger, genius and sweat of the outsider, the downtrodden, the banished, and the bullied come most of the progress in the world and in Silicon Valley.

In compiling this catalog, Gilder forgot the teenage women going blind from soldering circuits in the Philippines, the low-wage workers packed six to a room in the Silicon Valley, the reporters and data-entry clerks paralyzed by repetitive strain injury, and, less melodramatically, the researchers in the nonprofit bureaucracies known as universities and in the once-protected monopoly of Bell Labs (where the transistor was invented).

But that's not to take away from Gilder's talents as a maker of lists, some of the most prodigious since Whitman. Here's a very different, though equally exuberant, lineup from an earlier book, offers richer insight into Gilder's social philosophy:

> The idea that America might find renewal from a mélange of movements of evan-
> gelical women, wetbacks, Dartmouth Review militants, South Asian engineers, Bible
> thumpers, boat people, Moonies, Mormons, Cuban refugees, fundamentalist college
> deans, Amway soap pushers, science wonks, creationists, Korean fruit pedlars, acned
> computer freaks and other unstylish folk seems incomprehensible to many observ-
> ers who do not understand that an open capitalist society is always saved by the last
> among its citizens perpetually becoming first.

That's from his 1986 book *Men and Marriage,* a revision of his 1973 embarrassment, *Sexual Suicide.* It's part of an argument linking a vigorous capitalist economy with a deeply moral philosophy straight out of Jerry Falwell: as he put it, "[T]he new miracles of modern technology are created and sustained by the moral discipline and spiritual incandescence of a culture of churches and families" (Gilder 1986, pp. 112–13). Entrepreneurial vigor is assured when women stay home and nurture while men perform the modern equivalents of hunting, like designing chips or trading stocks.

Much of Gilder's work celebrates the end of scarcity and a new world of endless abundance. But his own personal style is deeply austere: a slender New England WASP, his furniture is so shabby that, it's said, Goodwill wouldn't accept it as a donation. What is all this plenitude for if it's not to increase human comfort?

Gilder's career reads like an anxious escape from the corporeal, with a hysterical optimism compensating for inner desiccation or fears of being overwhelmed by primitive lusts. As he said at the beginning of *Men and Marriage* (ibid., pp. 9–10), in a quote delectable enough to have made it into Bartleby.com: "Unlike femininity, relaxed masculinity is at bottom empty, a limp nullity. While the female body is full of internal potentiality, the male is internally barren.... Manhood at the most basic level can be validated and expressed only in action."

The action of the entrepreneur and engineer, of course. It's embarrassing to read Gilder's grim view of "relaxed" masculinity—empty, limp, and barren. But that's not all Gilder has to say about men: they're also violent, predatory, promiscuous, and badly in need of being civilized by the feminine, which will allow them to channel their energies into capitalist productivity rather than rape and pillaging. There's little hope for warmth, reflection, or nurturance in Gilder's men—that's the province of women.

Having investigated sex, Gilder moved on to another great site of anxiety and turmoil in American life: race, the subject of his 1978 book *Visible Man* (which was reissued in 1995). The title is a deliberate reversal of Ralph Ellison's title, which is offensive enough, but not as offensive as his preferred title—he first wanted to call this book *Sam Beau,* after its protagonist, but his editor pleaded with him to change the title, fearing condemnation for racism. According to Gilder, he "responded weakly that as a child in the South, my hero had actually been known as Sambo; I was dubbing him a more elegant name, touched with French" (ibid., p. xiii). The view of Sambo as hero is unusual, but Gilder is a proven iconoclast. He did call the first chapter "Sam Beau's Tubes," a reference to the first appearance of the star of the book, who's lying in a hospital bed recovering from a stab wound.

Sam's unfortunate position, considered to be emblematic of his race, wasn't the result of "white racism," which "was not a significant problem of American blacks in 1978, and white racism had nothing to do with the problems of my lumpen-hero Mitchell 'Sam' Brewer. To the contrary, his problem was the fantasy world of bizarre expectations and entitlements fostered by constant state indulgence and favoritism towards him" (ibid, pp. xiv, xv). It was "affirmative action and Marxist teaching" that did black Americans wrong. Those and the welfare state, which Gilder found irrationally generous, and fatal to the male authority necessary to keep social discipline, since it provided a check to women independent of husbands.

Gilder never repudiated any of his early positions. There's "an actual difference between male and female brains," he revealed to a *Seattle Weekly* journalist (White 1999). In a 1996 speech (quoted in Bronson 1996), using stats he must have gotten from *The Bell Curve,* he declared:

> Among people of influence in America, racism is dead. Racism has virtually nothing to do with the plight of black America. If you adjust for age and credentials, black women earn 106 percent of the wages of white women. If you adjust for age, IQ, and gender, black full-time workers earn 101 percent the wages of white workers.

The intellectual distance from the 1970s books to *Wealth and Poverty* is actually rather short. By giving women some economic autonomy, welfare undermined male authority, and in Gilder's mind that had all kinds of bad consequences.

But after the success of *Wealth and Poverty,* Gilder reinvented himself as a techie, immersing himself in the electronics business and even enrolling at Caltech to study physics. The first fruits of the reinvention appeared as the book *Microcosm.* He took up writing for *Forbes,* where his reactionary politics and boundless techno-optimism fit perfectly. And as the 1990s progressed, he shifted his interest from the endless miniaturization of everything—how many transistors *can* they squeeze onto a chip?—to bandwidth, the communications networks that tie all the miraculous computers together. Bandwidth would soon be limitless.

Of course, progress in both microelectronics and communication has been stunning, not only over the last decade, but over the last five or ten decades. But what's culturally and politically interesting about Gilder's fantasy of abundance, aside from its contrast with his personal austerity, is how selective it is; there have certainly been no corresponding triumphs when it comes to feeding and housing the world's two billion poorest. And even though at the dawn of 2003 the U.S. economy was four times larger than it was in 1980, and almost ten times larger than it was in 1970, in many ways we feel more strapped than we did in the past. We're constantly told we "can't afford" universal health care or a civilized welfare state. It's one of the paradoxes of capitalism that the richer a person or a society gets, the poorer they often feel.

Even allowing for this selectivity, Gilder's notions of abundance are incompatible with real capitalism. What civilians call "abundance" economists call "excess capacity," and it leads to falling prices and disappearing profits. This is exactly what happened in telecommunications in the late 1990s. Firms like Global Crossing—in which Gilder was a passionate believer, and which he was at first unable to believe that it had filed for bankruptcy—laid thousands of miles of fiber-optic cable. Yet though they built it, no one came: almost all the cable they laid is unused, and unlikely ever to be used. We could all have movies on demand for pennies or less, but if no one can offer the service profitably, it won't be offered.

Alan "Small Is Beautiful" Greenspan

It would be easy to dismiss Gilder as a lone nut, despite his voluminous writings, his posh seats in right-wing think tanks, and the influence of

Wealth and Poverty. Gilder's line became a staple of the business press in the mid- and late-1990s; for example, the cover of the October 3, 1994, *Fortune,* that slick *Pravda* for the American business class, announces that "Your company's most valuable asset" is "intellectual capital," which is apparently far more important than the physical or monetary kind. It would be nice if the business class suddenly realized that the source of all wealth really is human workers, and rewarded them as such, but that's not likely to happen. Saying that it will makes for good cover copy, though.

Another reason to take Gilder seriously is that his line on matter's overthrow has also long been celebrated by Federal Reserve chair Alan Greenspan. As far back as 1988, writing on the *Wall Street Journal* editorial page, Greenspan noted a near-universal trend towards tininess. Chips have replaced vacuum tubes; Thinsulate, fur; terabytes, paper securities; and intangible, knowledge-dependent services, bulky old-fashioned goods. "In fact, if all the tons of grain, cotton, ore, coal, steel, cement and the like that Americans produce were combined, their aggregate volume would not be much greater on a per capita basis than it was 50 or 75 years ago," he argued with the air of someone revealing an important truth. Greenspan's celebration of the immaterial looks especially odd in light of his youthful faith in the gold standard, one of the most curious of the materialist superstitions (this was when he was writing for Ayn Rand's *Objectivist*). In making his argument, Greenspan apparently ignored the evidence of his own agency's industrial production indexes, which showed per capita U.S. manufacturing volume up more than threefold in the fifty years before he wrote these words, and more than sixfold over the previous seventy-five years.

Ten years, and another 26% increase in per capita industrial production later, Greenspan returned to this theme, in congressional testimony in September 1998:

> We have dramatically reduced the size of our radios, for example, by substituting transistors for vacuum tubes. Thin fiber-optic cable has replaced huge tonnages of copper wire. New architectural, engineering, and materials technologies have enabled the construction of buildings enclosing the same space but with far less physical material than was required, say, 50 or 100 years ago. Most recently, mobile phones have been markedly downsized as they have been improved. As a consequence, the physical weight of our GDP is growing only very gradually. The exploitation of new concepts accounts for virtually all of the inflation-adjusted growth in output.

Taking advantage of one of those New Economy miracles, a visitor to the New York City sanitation department's web site <www.ci.nyc.ny.us/html/dos/html/dosfact.html> would quickly learn that the city produces 26,000 tons of garbage every day. This is weight that would be highly pleasing to lose.

Discourses like Gilder's and Greenspan's typically forget that their miraculously weightless blips depend on a vast physical infrastructure of computers and cabling, the manufacture of which is very toxic and the disposal of which is a problem that people have barely begun thinking about, much less managed to solve.[8]

Chipmaking, for example, has one of the highest instances of occupational injury and illness around (Benner 1998, p. 65), and well under one tenth of the many millions of computers—laden with some of industrial civilization's most toxic charms—discarded every year are recycled. All those machines crave electricity, which may look clean at the socket end but which usually involves lots of oil, coal, or uranium at the source. And the studies that Greenspan relies on for his optimistic view of tech-driven productivity all emphasize that high levels of capital spending—the rapid accumulation and deployment of things—are the underpinning of the reported productivity boom (Oliner and Sichel 2000a; Jorgenson and Stiroh 2000). Things that embody high concepts, for sure, but very much thingly things.

Adventures in accounting

It's not just stock touts, manic pundits, and revered central bankers who celebrated the New Paradigm, it was also academics at prestigious universities. One of the boldest is Baruch Lev, an NYU accounting professor who shed his field's reputation for caution, rudely violating Italo Svevo's dictum that there's no room for dreams in double entry. (No marginal figure, in August 2000 Lev won the aptly named Wildman Medal, given by the American Accounting Association, for making the year's greatest contribution to his profession.) Lev dreams in numbers—or, more precisely, he wants to put numbers on "intangible assets, ideas, brands, ways of working, and franchises," as an introduction to an interview with Lev in the New Economy bible *Fast Company* put it (Webber 2000). Lev argues that the 500-year-old discipline, invented by the 14th-century Venetian mathematician Luca Pacioli, is simply inadequate to the ineffable glories of 21st-century capitalism. Today, knowledge, not things, rule. That's a fashionable point of view that assumes our ancestors were dolts, as if the wheel and the power loom weren't productive embodiments of knowledge. Things get interesting when Lev gets specific. He thinks financial statements should recognize four kinds of New Era assets: (1) "assets associated with product innovation," which presumably includes everything from a new microprocessor to a new kind of cereal; (2) "assets that are associated with a company's brand," which let a company sell its products or services at a higher price than its competitors; (3) "structural assets"—not flashy innovations but better, smarter, different ways of doing business that can set a company apart from its competitors; and (4) "monopolies, companies that enjoy a franchise, or have substantial sunk costs that a competitor would have to match, or have a barrier to entry that it can use to its advantage."

These are quite extraordinary thoughts. It's possible to swallow point 1, if we're talking about a real advance; it's a bit harder if we're talking about a fresh variant on Frosted Flakes. But the rest is considerably harder to take.

One of the cornerstones of New Paradigm thinking, and one that's survived the bust, is the curious doctrine that "brand equity"—the financial value that stock markets assign to names like Nike and Mickey Mouse—is a kind of capital, like a lathe or even a piece of software. It's easy to see how even privately held assets of that more conventional sort can contribute to social wealth; unless they belong to a bomb factory, their produce can make people better off (even if the profits they generate are appropriated by a handful of managers and shareholders).

But a "brand," as Naomi Klein (1999, p. 22) put it in *No Logo,* is a kind of "collective hallucination." Branders put a positive spin on these mass delusions. Ad agency Young & Rubicam identified them as "the new religion," a source of "meaning" (Tomkins 2001). Today's brand builders, said Y&R, "could be compared to the missionaries who spread Christianity and Islam around the world." The best brands offer a set of uncompromising beliefs; among those names, Y&R disclosed, are Calvin Klein, MTV, and Gatorade. Religion, though, typically promises salvation, while advertising stimulates a perpetual craving for more—a scientifically crafted realization of Freud's observation that there's no satisfaction in satisfaction. Also mining the spiritual vein, Peter Singline of the consultancy Brand DNA emphasized brands' "spiritual dimensions," claiming that the mystical identification "offers something to the wider community, attaching a belief system to the brand and creating value that transcends profitability" (Burbury 2001). But the whole point of creating the brand is to enhance profitability, not transcend it.

Nike may gain from selling shoes at $150 that cost a few dollars to make—as do its ad agencies and the media where it plasters its swoosh and Michael Jordan for hawking his branded shoes—but it's hard to see how society as a whole does. (I'm leaving aside the fact that there are actual workers who make the swoosh-festooned shoes who simply disappear in the New Paradigm analysis; just because a commodity is hyper-fetishized doesn't mean there are no human toilers lurking behind it.) The vast markup over its costs resembles what economists call a monopoly rent, the extraordinary gain over a "normal" profit (a concept underscrutinized in conventional economic discourse) enjoyed by a nicely situated producer with the market power to gouge buyers. Not that the brand-hawker always succeeds in collecting the superprofit; it's very expensive to create a brand. As Klein (Naomi, not Calvin) argues, those expenses increase the urgency of cutting manufacturing costs to a minimum, which mainly means pushing the wage down to a dime an hour. The vast gap between direct manufacturing costs of maybe a dollar or two a shoe and the final selling price goes to ad agencies and celebrity endorsers. But from the point of view of the consumer, the $100 premium, say, over the price of a modest unbranded shoe is money that could have been spent on other goods or services. It seems like a massive waste of money, but any believer in freedom of religion wouldn't want to gainsay the spiritual experience of purchasing and wearing cleverly branded footwear.

Lev's point 3 is almost too insubstantial to refute; how can even the most creative accountant put a monetary value on a "smarter" way of doing business? But point 4 is a beaut: monopoly is spun as something to celebrate, at least by the accountant's concept of celebration. No longer would the claim of monopoly position attract the interest of regulators or the antitrust division of the Justice Department: it'd be something to boast about on the balance sheet.

Lev has some more curious ideas, perhaps the most curious being that accounting is far too fixated on the "transaction," the exchange of money for a good or service. Rejecting several centuries of capitalist history in which the sale of a commodity for more money than it took to produce it—profit—was the system's reason for being, Lev argues instead that in the New Economy, value is created in far more ineffable ways:

> When a drug passes its clinical tests, huge value is created—but there's no transaction. Nothing changes hands. Nobody buys anything and nobody sells anything. When software passes a beta-test, it suddenly becomes valuable—but there's no transaction. Or think about how value is destroyed: When a big, old company is late in figuring out how to enter the world of e-commerce, huge value is destroyed—but there's no transaction.

Lev is speaking here from the point of view of the stock market, which is what creates or destroys "value" by these criteria. But what he seems to forget is that these movements of value anticipate transactions: the new drug, or the new piece of software, is valuable only because it will result in future sales.[9] If no one buys these products, the value is illusory. So too the destruction of value: if the lumbering behemoth is slow with its website, it only matters if it loses sales to nimbler competitors. Thanks to hindsight, you no longer have to argue the point vigorously, but it's stunning that a prizewinning professor could have been taken seriously making such foolish points in 2000.

New Economy thinking was inseparable from the bull market; it was both its intellectual by-product and its justification. Not to pick on Lev—

though he's an irresistible target—but the relation is nicely illustrated by his claim (Lev 2000) that since the market value of the companies in the Standard & Poor's 500 index was 6.25 the firms' book value,[10] "in the U.S., knowledge assets account for six (!) of every seven dollars of corporate market value" (exclamation point in original). So, you see, knowledge assets drive the New Economy. How do we know this? Because the stock market tells us so. How do we know the stock market is right? Well, it just is.

Shown to the right is a version of Lev's measure of corporate America's IQ from 1945 through 2002. Instead of focusing on just the S&P 500 stocks, it looks at all nonfinancial corporations, using the figures from the Federal Reserve's national balance sheets.[11] By that measure, corporate America

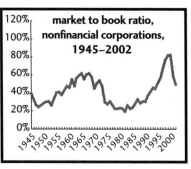

got three times smarter—or more knowledgeable, take your pick—from 1948 through 1968, then came down with a serious bout of idiocy—or ignorance—between 1968 and 1981 (maybe it was all the drugs), only to recover during the Reagan years (maybe it was Ron's personal example), and then achieve unprecedented levels of genius during the Clinton years. Indeed, corporate America's brainpower tripled between 1990 and 1998. But those wondrous times have come badly undone; corporate America was suddenly struck with a serious relapse of ignorance/idiocy in the spring of 2000, and as of press time there were few encouraging signs of imminent re-enlightenment.

When I asked Lev to comment in early 2001 on the southward trajectory of USA Inc.'s IQ, he sent a draft of the closing chapter his book on intangibles (Lev 2001, chap. 6).[12] In it, he denies ever having been a partisan of the New Economy, even though *Fast Company* read him as one of its leading theorists, and he emphasized that in an environment of weak growth and lugubrious financial markets, the careful study and management of intangibles is more important than ever. The judgment of the IQ testers on Wall Street can evidently be overlooked when they're giving bad grades.

Market democracy

The 1990s weren't only technologically wondrous times, they were wonderfully democratic ones too! Along with the extraordinary economic and even spiritual claims for the New Era have come some political claims. In a January 26, 2000, talk at the Columbia School of Journalism, former Citibank chair Walter Wriston said that the net was like a "giant voting machine," which allowed capital to stay where it is well treated and promptly leave places where it isn't. Like Gilder, he used capital and information almost interchangeably, calling this regime an "information standard" that replaces the old gold and paper-money standards. How the volatile preferences of a relative handful of portfolio managers constitute democracy, Wriston didn't say. It's reassuring that something's replacing the voting machine, though, since U.S. election turnouts continue to make new lows; Bill Clinton was reelected in 1996 with the votes of 23% of the voting-age population, the lowest share since 1924. The "winner" in 2000, George W. Bush, got a slightly larger share than Clinton, though the candidate who got a slightly larger share than Bush was officially deemed the loser. At least with money, there isn't much doubt about who wins and who loses, as long as Arthur Andersen isn't the accountant.

The democratization of finance was another popular New Era theme.[13]

Interestingly, one of the foundational moments of speculation, the Dutch tulip-bulb mania of 1636–37, also thrived on a democratizing rhetoric. Once a rare flower, imbued with the exoticism of the East in its first days in Europe in the late 16th century, the tulip was seen as an extravagance, cultivated by "gentleman botanists for themselves or a small number of professional growers for their professional clientele" (Schama 1987, p. 354). But by the 1630s, bulb supplies had increased, bringing down prices, and the tulip developed a mass audience. With the popularization, apprentice horticulturists struck out on their own, with an "aggressively entrepreneurial" culture replacing the "genteel and circumscribed" one. "Marginal entrepreneurs," wrote historian Simon Schama, "who would have found it difficult to enter older crafts and trades, could, with their specialized knowledge, quickly make their way among the bulb men." Shades of the dot.com world in the second half of the 1990s. "[W]eavers and carpenters, millers and smiths and barge skippers had all been caught up in the horticultural craze" (ibid.). By the middle of the 1630s, supply couldn't keep up with demand (a shortage compounded by the fact that the flower is a seasonal item); prices reversed and began a near-vertical rise that made the NASDAQ of 1999 look modest.[14] In late 1636, the trade had evolved into "a pure *windhandel,* a paper gamble," with trading in titles to bulbs taking the place of trading in bulbs themselves. The elite got nervous, and moralizers worried that dreams of riches without labor were corrupting the masses. Schama made fun of these concerns, but the collapse of the bubble, and with it a $7 trillion loss in wealth, prove that it's not morality that makes dreams of effortless wealth impossible to realize, but the structure of speculative markets themselves.

Back to the present. Modern mythmaking held that new technologies overturn old hierarchies, leading to a virtual social revolution—not in the very old-fashioned world of organized politics, of course, but in

the new one of wireless web connections.[15] When I interviewed *Wired*'s
Kevin Kelly, I interrupted his effusions to ask him what relevance they
had in a world where the statistics showed that the gap between rich and
poor—nationally and globally—has never been so wide, a world where
half the population has never even made a phone call, Kelly responded by
saying that there's never been so good a time to be poor, though he didn't
offer any evidence.

Farther up the social ladder from absolute indigence, we hear some
grand claims. For example, we heard constantly that mutual funds and
web brokers have enabled Main Street to prosper at the game that used
to be Wall Street's monopoly. While it's true that a bit over half of U.S.
households now own stock, an all-time record, it's never mentioned that
wealth, like income, has never been so concentrated, and that regardless of
how many households may own some shares, either directly or through
mutual funds, most people have insignificant amounts of wealth. The full
numbers will be presented in chapter 3; right now, it's enough to say that
the top 1% of Americans control about 40% of all wealth, and the bottom
two-thirds have essentially no savings at all.

Net magic

I've noted several times the intimate relations among the bull market, the
Internet, and New Era thinking. Extraordinary stock valuations—literally without any precedent in the 130 years since good numbers began
in 1871—were justified by appeal to an alleged technological revolution.
The more statistically minded pointed to the burst in reported productivity growth that started in the late 1990s. Whether this is a long-term thing
or not isn't yet clear; it's going to take a few more years to tell whether the
productivity slump of the 1970s and 1980s is over or not. But even en-

thusiasts rarely bother to delineate the mechanisms linking the net to the productivity burst. It may be that very unglamorous things—the cheapening of labor through outsourcing, the movement of much of production to low-wage countries, continued unwillingness of firms to share their good fortune with employees, and what the people at *Labor Notes* call "management by stress" (pushing human workers and work arrangements to their breaking point and maybe a little beyond)—are the real underlying mechanisms. It may also be that people are actually logging lots more hours on the job than get recorded in the official statistics. Or it may be that the productivity blip is a statistical illusion—a product of the way output is valued by statisticians. All these propositions will be considered in detail in the next chapter.

But maybe the Internet did have some responsibility for giving birth to both the bull market and New Era thinking. (2000, pp. 19–21), an economist rare for his interest in the influence of psychology and faddishness on financial trends, argued that the proliferation of the Internet into the homes of the many—particularly the more upscale many who trade stocks—promoted the impression that the world had changed utterly. The net (not unjustifiably) gives people a feeling of power, of cosmopolitan reach—sensations that might lead to an impression that it's of great economic significance. But there was no explosion in profitability on a par with the explosion in stock prices or the hype that went with it; it's merely that investors were willing to chase stocks at much higher levels of valuation than at any time in the past. More generally, Shiller points out, new technologies don't necessarily guarantee higher profits; if new gadgetry simultaneously requires heavy spending and renders old gadgetry obsolete, it could as easily depress profits as stimulate them. "What matters for a stock market boom," writes Shiller, "is not...the reality of the Internet revolution, which is hard to discern, but rather the *public impressions* that the revolution creates. Public reaction is influenced by the intuitive plausi-bility of Internet lore…." And there was no shortage of appeals to intuitive plausibility, from high theory to low journalism.

Theoryheads

Perhaps it's wrong to be annoyed that such pampered products of the status quo as Greenspan, Kelly, Lev, Gilder, and Sinai should utter so much nonsense. What's more surprising—and depressing—is to read putatively sophisticated cultural and political theorists seconding them. Pick up a book or essay by a post-Marxoid theorist like Manuel Castells and you read what is essentially Gilder and Greenspan translated from cheerlead-ing journalese into clotted academese—like this passage from an article in *New Left Review* (Castells 1994):

> By this concept [the informational society], I understand a social structure where the sources of economic productivity, cultural hegemony and political military power depend, fundamentally, on the capacity to retrieve, store, process and generate in-formation and knowledge. Although information and knowledge have been critical for economic accumulation and political power throughout history, it is only under the current technological, social, and cultural parameters that they become directly productive forces…. Material production, as well as services, become subordinate to the handling of information….

And this, from the first volume of his far-from-physically-weightless trilogy on the Info Age (Castells 1996): "Timeless time belongs to the space of flows…," which sounds like something out of Deepak Chopra.

Or take the inevitable Jean Baudrillard (1993, pp. 10–11, 33), who was several years ahead of the accounting profs:

Marx simply did not foresee that it would be possible for capital, in the face of the imminent threat to its existence, to transpoliticize itself, as it were: to launch itself into an orbit beyond the relations of production and political contradictions, to make itself autonomous in a free-floating, ecstatic and haphazard form, and thus to totalize the world in its own image. Capital (if it may still be so called) has barred the way of political economy and the law of value; it is in this sense that it has successfully escaped its own end. Henceforward it can function independently of its own former aims, and absolutely without reference to any aims whatsoever…. Money is now the only genuine artificial satellite. A pure artifact, it enjoys a truly astral mobility; and it is instantly convertible. Money has now found its proper place, a place far more wondrous than the stock exchange: the orbit in which it rises and sets like some artificial sun.

Apparently the Asian crisis of 1997, like the Gulf War, didn't really happen.

But the weightlessness discourse infects even highly admirable writers like Fredric Jameson, who argues in his essay "Culture and Finance Capital" (1998) that capital has become both deterritorialized and dematerialized in this "globalized" era. All the weightless postindustrial nostrums are represented: "profit without production"—in fact, the disappearance of production, except for "the two prodigious American industries of food and entertainment"—and "globalization," defined as "rather a kind of cyberspace in which money capital has reached its ultimate dematerialization," as messages which pass instantaneously from one nodal point to another across the former globe, the former material world. Globalization here becomes the triumph of nothingness, and finance capital becomes "deterritorialized," and "like cyberspace can live on its own internal metabolism and circulate without any reference to an older type of content."

It seems very old-fashioned to point out a few facts about this apparently weightless, placeless capital thoroughly unmoored from the real. The world money of the 19th century, gold, though quite tangible, nonetheless circulated without the imprint of any state; today's nonphysical monies need state entities like central banks and the IMF to guarantee and regulate them. Food production has been shrinking when measured as a share of GDP, and the share of household budgets devoted to food has been in a long decline. The alleged economic importance of the entertainment industries is a staple of both left and right discourse, with extravagant claims made about their rank in production and trade, but it's just not true.[16] Motion pictures account for about 0.3% of U.S. GDP—half as large as the primary metal industries, a quarter as large as motor vehicles. Add radio and TV and "amusement and recreation services" and you're almost up to 2%—the size of the chemical industry, but less than an eighth the contribution of manufacturing. Production hasn't disappeared from the U.S., much less the world in general. Despite a long manufacturing recession, there were still more than 16 million factory workers in the U.S. at the beginning of 2003, nearly one in eight employed workers.[17]

And though financial markets seem very fanciful, appearing detached not only from production but even from social relations, they are actually institutions that consolidate ownership and control among the very rich of the world (a point developed in the last chapter of this book). Much of the damage done to Southeast Asia in 1997 and 1998 and to Mexico in 1994 and 1995 was done by allegedly weightless financial flows. Closer to home, bond markets exert strict discipline on the economic policies of national and local governments, and shareholders have been exerting strict discipline on the companies they own. The wave of corporate downsizings in recent years—according to the head-hunting firm Challenger, Gray, and Christmas, 3.9 million were announced by large employers between January 2001 and April 2003—is an example of the kinds of corporate policies they've been pushing on managers for the last two decades.

Drawing on a point made by Ursula Huws (1999), while the physical commodity—the one, in the classic definition, you can drop on your foot—may be diminishing in importance relative to services, many of those services are the commodification of activities that were once performed without the exchange of money (and much of that labor, whether paid or unpaid, is disproportionately performed by women). McDonald's replaces the home-cooked meal, commercial laundries replace in-house washing, and paid child-care replaces the unpaid maternal kind. Services formerly performed by nonprofits, like education, are increasingly the realm of profit-seeking entities, from Chris Whipple's Channel One to the University of Phoenix. By focusing just on the form of the commodity—good or service—partisans of weightlessness overlook the monetized social relations behind seemingly insubstantial wares.

Monetized social relations may be encouraging myths of weightlessness in one largely unappreciated way. As Barbara Ehrenreich (2000) noted in a very fine essay on the growth of domestic labor:

> To be cleaned up after is to achieve a certain magical weightlessness and immateriality. Almost everyone complains about violent video games, but paid housecleaning has the same consequence-abolishing effect.... A servant economy breeds callousness and solipsism in the served, and it does so all the more effectively when the service is performed close up and routinely in the place where they live and reproduce.

Ehrenreich ties the growth in the professional/managerial class's use of domestic labor to the broad polarization of U.S. society—the polarization of incomes, which creates an affluent upper middle class capable of hiring a plentiful supply of poor women, and the polarization of work, "where so many of the affluent devote their lives to such ghostly pursuits as stock-trading, image-making, and opinion polling," which renders physical work largely invisible to the opinion-making class. With our shoes made in Indonesia, our cars assembled in Mexico, and a Jamaican to scrub the toilet, it's easy to think that stuff doesn't matter anymore.

But in saying stuff does matter, and that finance is attached to the earth in important ways, I don't mean to argue that the perceptions of weightlessness and detachment aren't powerful. That's the way many of us experience the world (though Honduran garment workers probably don't), and Jameson is right about its pervasiveness in culture high and low. It's hard to guess how much rational refutation can shake that perception, given how it's reinforced in both cultural products and daily life. But if we want to understand the world, it's helpful to start by acknowledging that things aren't always as they seem.

The people who started and funded dot.coms took the talk about weightlessness too seriously for their own good. Early in the tech boom—like when Amazon.com went public in the lush and hopeful spring of 1997—it was thought that e-tailers could serve millions of customers without building a major distributional system; a small staff of marketers and programmers would contract out all the boring stuff, like warehousing, shipping, and customer service. But e-merchants found that if they didn't do this sort of thing themselves, it was hard to do it well. So they had to get involved in the messy business of building warehouses and fulfillment centers—those that survived, that is.

But the e-tailers didn't founder only on their need for a physical infrastructure; they discovered they needed lots of low-wage workers to pick and pack or respond to customer emails. Amazon.com, one of the few survivors, pays its cubicle-dwellers—college grads, many of them with advanced degrees and even books to their name (ones they've written, not wrapped and mailed)—around $10 an hour with no benefits to pseudo-personalize canned email responses to customer queries and complaints. In return for this lowly wage—20% below the national average in a chic, expensive metropolitan area, a high-tech hotbed—the company required immense, almost cultlike dedication. But of course there was also "a whispered mantra of 'stock options,'" in the words of Richard Howard (1998), an ex-Amazonian who wrote about his brief career there in the *Seattle Weekly*. That story, by the way, was a major hit with Amazon.com employees, as the *Weekly* reported (Collins 1999)—as were the paper's help-wanted ads.

Even in boomtime America, it wasn't hard to find smart, eager young people just out of college to work for the wage of a millhand or meat cutter. But it wasn't so easy to staff the high end. James Cramer (1999), then of the now near-dead financial news site TheStreet.com, whined that:

> [N]o one but the richest companies can afford to staff a new large-scale Web site business.... The market for Web professionals is so thin that you have to pay fortunes to get anybody with a brain and then top that off with a hefty dollop of stock options. And once you get them, they tend not to know as much as you thought they did...! The labor shortages and labor costs for the lowest level programmers and execs are totally out of control.

Of course employers often bellyache in this style, but it does seem that the web economy needed lots of labor, most of it very cheap but some of it very expensive, and a much bigger capital infrastructure than anyone allowed for at first. That's not the way it looked to their bankers, nor to someone clicking on the one-click order button, but there are plenty of things and people behind the disembodied pixels.

Speaking of labor, how did average workers feel about the New Economy? A poll (Conlin 1999) done by *Business Week* at the height of the mania found 79% of Americans agreeing that a productivity-led boom was driving the U.S. economy. That's hardly a surprise, since that's almost all they'd been hearing for years. Peering a little below the surface of the headline number, though, we find that just 21% strongly agreed, with the balance, 58%, agreeing only "somewhat." But what does this agreement, regardless of its strength, actually mean?

Almost two-thirds of those polled—63%—said that the celebrated productivity boom hadn't raised the level of their income, and 62% said it hadn't raised their job security. Just 10% said the boom had made their lives a lot better, compared to 8% who said it had made their lives worse, 43% who said a little better, and 37% who said it had had no impact. Three-quarters felt the rewards of the New Economy were unevenly distributed. Almost twice as many (33%) trusted business less than they had 10 years earlier as trusted it more (18%). Over half (52%) felt business had too much power, and an identical share professed sympathy with the anti-WTO protesters in Seattle. These numbers, striking enough in the context of normal American political conservatism and temperamental optimism, are extraordinary late into the longest and most triumphalist-propaganda-saturated expansion in U.S. history.

It's ironic that this poll appeared in *Business Week,* a once-staid publication that had transformed itself into a hotbed of New Economy cheerleading. When I asked a *BW* old-timer whether he believed any of the line his magazine was retailing, he laughed and said "No." "Then why are you publishing this nonsense?" I asked. "Because it sells magazines," he answered.

Scandal

That was then, and it seems like a long time ago. For a while, it looked like handcuffed CEOs doing the perp walk would acquire the same iconic status in the early '00s that successful IPOs did in the late 1990s, but it hasn't turned out that way, thanks to the generous safety net provided for the American elite. And though it would be deeply satisfying to see Ken Lay breaking rocks, there's a danger in focusing just on crime or scandal—namely that all the respectable cheerleaders for the boom, like Gilder, Greenspan, and Lev, would remain unindicted, because they were guilty of nothing other than credulous exuberance, and central institutions of the American economy, like the stock market (the star of chapter 5), would stay out of the dock as well.

Before diving into the details, it would be useful to explore how the most infamous scandal of all, Enron, emerged from the environment sketched earlier in this chapter. So much of the last twenty years come together in the Enron story—deregulation, financialization, postmateriality fantasies, the links between capital and the state, the increased role for the stock market in the running of big corporations, and professional corruption. Its attitude toward its workers was savage; former chief exec Jeffrey Skilling famously laid down the law: "You must cut jobs ruthlessly by 50% or 60%. Depopulate. Get rid of people. They gum up the works."—just like things (Platt's 2002). Enron should be read as the demise not just of one firm, but of an entire economic model. So far, it hasn't worked out that way, but one must keep hope alive.

Enron "was and truly is an American success story," said the company's lawyer in Manhattan bankruptcy court in December 2001. If trading on political connections and scheming to fleece consumers and investors while hiding behind a lot of free-market rhetoric is what makes an American success story today, then Enron surely qualifies.

Though it grew into a globe-spanning monster, Enron began its life as a modest natural-gas pipeline company. But moving gas through pipe was much too mundane a pursuit for Enron's visionary chair, Kenneth Lay. Lay and his colleagues wanted to liberate the company from the merely physical world and enter the magical realm of the weightless corporation, where value is created not through production but through inventing and trading complex financial instruments and thinking big thoughts. As Lay told *The Economist* in June 2000, "We were a new-economy company before it became cool." And *The Economist* agreed, while worrying a bit about Enron's "hubris."

Enron started slowly, at first just trading gas and electricity. But as the 1990s progressed, and New-Economy thinking reached the irrationally exuberant phase, it got into trading more exotic things, like advertising time, telecommunications bandwidth, and even weather derivatives. (Yes, weather derivatives: through Enron Online, you could bet on—no, *hedge*—your exposure to degree days.) And Enron's culture got more and more cultlike, styling itself "the world's leading company," and alienating even Wall Street bankers with its arrogance. But, fantasy aside, all the exotic instruments and strategies still depended on a troublesome physical world; to have the telecoms bandwidth to trade, Enron also built a big network to fulfill demand that was never demanded. It's not easy to overthrow matter if you're trying to make a profit. You can turn to creative accountants to help you out, but not forever. Almost the only real money Enron ever made was by manipulating California's electricity market during that state's 2001 blackout crisis, but that didn't last very long, and it wouldn't be a very inspiring case study for the Harvard Business School.

Enron is also a fine illustration of the transformation over the last twenty years in how corporations are run. (There'll be more on this in chapter 5, but context demands a bit right now.) From the 1930s through the 1970s, managers largely ran the show, with little attention paid to the stockholders. As the economy soured in the 1970s, and with it profits and stock prices, stockholders woke from their passivity and demanded that the firms be run in their interest rather than that of managers or some broader good. As a result, the interests of managers and board members were supposed to be aligned with those of stockholders, a realignment guaranteed by replacing salaries with stock options.

The doctrine shows a touching faith in the wisdom of the stock market; investors are presumed to be both skeptical and prescient, seeing through managerial scams and correctly anticipating the best corporate strategies. But with the demise of the dot.com bubble and the broader bull market of the 1990s, the stock market's wisdom is in serious doubt. And the crash of Enron shows that making managers and board members think like stockholders dulls their critical faculties; who would want to blow the whistle when the stock was rising by 60% a year?

Enron also was a fine example of New Era retirement planning—no fixed pension, just a portfolio of stock that you hope will fatten as you approach retirement. It didn't work out that way, though; many Enron workers were completely wiped out. Still, many pundits hoped that the disaster wouldn't undermine support for the new pension system. For example, *Financial Times* columnist John Plender (2002) worried that the 401(k) wipeout could compromise the move away from the old "paternalistic" pension system—in which workers were guaranteed a fixed pension, and employers bore the risk—toward the present one, in which employers contribute funds but workers bear the risk.

So Enron had it all. Its accounting practices, though fraudulent, were in many ways conceptually hard to distinguish from Lev's celebration of the intangible. Lay's assetless trading model was right in line with the celebration of postmateriality. The pension system was right in line with New Era pension thinking. And relying on the stock market to judge the company and pay senior managers was right in line with all the trendy talk from professors and consultants. And it all went badly wrong. But instead of being read as a judgment on the idiocy of all these fashions, it's being read as a case of personal corruption—if it's being read at all. Because now

Enron seems so 2002. Like Emerson, America is an endless seeker, with no past at its back, unsettling all things.

But nothing can shake the faith of George Gilder (who would no doubt concur with Ken Lay's characterization of Jesus as a free-marketeer: "I believe in God and I believe in free markets"). As late as December 2002, Gilder wrote in *Forbes* that he trusts Lay and Skilling (and Winnick and Ebbers and the whole crew) more than any politician, judge, or journalist. It's not exactly stiff competition, but still, it's one more reason why Gilder seems like an errant crew member from the *Fidèle*.

Assessing novelty

So was—or is—there a "New Economy"? Or is it as empty a concept as an Enron 401(k)?

In some sense, it's always a new economy; capitalism has generated technical and social innovation from its birth. As the rightfully famous passage from the *Communist Manifesto* put it more than 150 years ago:

> The bourgeoisie cannot exist without constantly revolutionizing the instruments of production, and thereby the relations of productio.n, and with them the whole relations of society. Conservation of the old modes of production in unaltered form, was, on the contrary, the first condition of existence for all earlier industrial classes. Constant revolutionizing of production, uninterrupted disturbance of all social conditions, everlasting uncertainty and agitation distinguish the bourgeois epoch from all earlier ones. All fixed, fast frozen relations...are swept away, all new-formed ones become antiquated before they can ossify. All that is solid melts into air....

That degree of change generates a collective historical amnesia, making it easy for people today to think constant change is a recent innovation.

So if there's always a new economy, is it newly new? It's hard to argue that it is; there are a lot of ancient holdovers persisting into the present. As later chapters in this book will show, the labor market produced plenty of snazzy jobs, like image consultants and systems analysts, but it also produced lots of mundane ones, like security guards and home health aides. Technology may be making some jobs more interesting, but it's de-skilling lots of others—and it's increasing employers' powers of measurement and surveillance over workers. In the late 1990s, income-distribution measures were at their most unequal in sixty years, and world income gaps were chasmically wide. Yes, financial markets and production have been internationalized, but "globalization" has been a feature of capitalism from its earliest days. Yes, finance seems to have become hyperactive, but bubbles too are an old story. And the social philosophy that governed economic policy making in the late 20th century is in many ways hard to distinguish from that of 100 years earlier, though publicists and graphic designers have made it look more dazzling than it was in Herbert Spencer's day.

In fact, it's tempting to read much of the New Economy discourse as largely ideological, whether conscious (as in propaganda) or not (as in the unreflective enthusiasms of partisans or the unanalyzed impressions of less thrilled participants). The enthusiasts' claims often look a lot like preemptive defenses of capitalism against some of the classic indictments of it (not that there have been many of these in the air lately, Tom Wolfe [2000] to the contrary). Find capitalism too controlling? No, it's spontaneous! Too inegalitarian and exploitative? No, it overturns hierarchies! Vulgar, brutal, de-skilling, and mercenary? *Au contraire,* it's creative and fun! Unstable? Nah, that's just its miraculous dynamism at work![18]

Which is, perversely, a way of saying that the New Economy discourse appeals to utopian impulses in these largely anti-utopian times. It would be nice if organizations could be made nonhierarchical, work be made spontaneous and fun, and everyone be cut into a share of ownership. That enthusiasts circulate these ideas and that others accept them is testimony to their persistent appeal. But these things are unlikely to happen under actually existing capitalism. Insofar as the dot.com workplace was "fun," it's because the normal disciplines of capitalist profitmaking didn't prevail in the sector's early days.

But another function of the New Economy discourse was apologetic and/or disciplinary. In an article on union battles with Verizon Communications over the growth of the firm's nonunion operations, particularly in wireless, *New York Times* reporter Steven Greenhouse (2000) described it as "a struggle, stripped to its essentials, [that] pits old-line labor against the New Economy." That's one way to read it. You could also read it as a classic labor-management battle, with a profit-maximizing firm favoring a new nonunion subsidiary over an old, unionized one. But Greenhouse's interpretation—assisted by the phrase "stripped to its essentials," which is pretty devious, given that he's adding spin, not stripping anything away—gives the nonunion strategy the cachet of newness and the inevitability of technological progress, making the unions seem like stodgy holdovers.

And, as Adrian Lucas of the Zurich-based financial software house Actant AG put it in an unpublished interview with the Dutch journalist Geert Lovink, the New Economy discourse "is primarily a form of disciplining entrants to the labour market. By allowing a few very young people to quickly become paper multi-millionaires, the New Economy disciplines an entire generation in the thinking of business, profit and hard work." "Primarily" is overstating the case, and it's not just new entrants that were being disciplined, but Lucas's general point is compelling. Now that that promise has been deferred, the boss is going to have to come up with a new strategy—like maybe old-fashioned fear.

2   Work

...the American approach of working longer for less...
—Alan Cowell (1997) in the *New York Times*

During the late 1990s, we constantly heard that we were in the early stages of a great productivity boom—and one that apparently survived the recession of 2001, in both number and reputation. Exactly what this means is hard to say. Is work disappearing? Getting more meaningful? Are new technologies making life easier? Are we happier for it?

If we are in the early stages of a technorevolution, we're certainly not distributing its dividends in the form of a lighter workload: Americans have to work awfully hard to make ends meet. Several charts on the following pages make this point. While average incomes have risen considerably over the last half-century—rapidly for the first twenty-five years after World War II, far more slowly thereafter—the amount of work necessary to earn those incomes has risen with equal relentlessness. A worker paid the average manufacturing wage would have to work sixty-two weeks to earn the median family's income in 1947. In 1973, it would have taken seventy-four weeks; in 2001, eigthy-one weeks.[1] So, despite the fact that productivity overall is up more than threefold over the last fifty years—and productivity in manufacturing up more than fivefold—the average worker would have to toil six months longer to make the average family income. And the increase in the work effort came at a more punishing pace in the 1990s than it did in earlier decades. Of course, it's not just individual workers who are putting in longer hours; an ever-larger share of the adult population has entered the paid workforce—mainly women, who aren't getting much relief in their household labors to compensate for their increased presence in factories and offices.

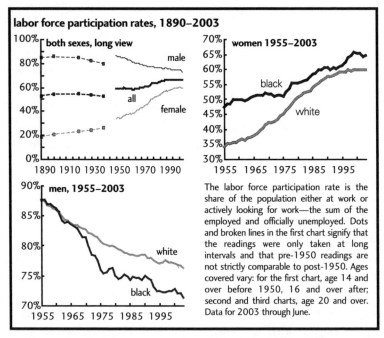

labor force participation rates, 1890–2003

The labor force participation rate is the share of the population either at work or actively looking for work—the sum of the employed and officially unemployed. Dots and broken lines in the first chart signify that the readings were only taken at long intervals and that pre-1950 readings are not strictly comparable to post-1950. Ages covered vary: for the first chart, age 14 and over before 1950, 16 and over after; second and third charts, age 20 and over. Data for 2003 through June.

International comparisons confirm the picture of the U.S. as a workhouse economy. American workers put in more hours per year than workers in Western Europe; only workers in East Asia spend more time on the job than Americans. And our workers don't produce as impressively as people seem to think. Workers in the Netherlands, Germany, France, and Italy all produce more in an hour than American workers, and come in barely ahead of workers in Ireland and Sweden. Nor has the growth in U.S. productivity over the recent past been all that impressive; of all the countries shown in the chart on page 42, the U.S. comes in dead last in productivity growth between 1973 and 1996. It's only over the latter part of the 1990s that U.S. productivity performance ran ahead of that of its peers—though not all that far ahead, if you use comparable statistics, as work by

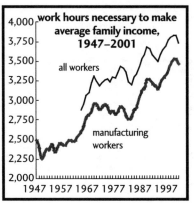

Credit Suisse First Boston economist Julian Callow (2003) shows.

Inside productivity

The central dogma of New Economy thinking—and one that has survived the bubble's demise—is that after an anguishing delay, high-tech devices have finally given us a productivity revolution. Evaluating this claim requires getting uncomfortably deep in statistics.

Productivity measures output relative to input; the more you produce from a given input, the higher your productivity. Over the long sweep of history, improvements in technology, education, organization, and infrastructure have vastly increased the human capacity for pumping out things. How much happiness that has brought with it is an open question.

There are two prominent measures of productivity: labor and total factor (or multifactor). Labor productivity looks at human labor as its only input; a broader measure, called total factor or multifactor productivity (abbreviated TFP and MFP respectively) also include raw materials, energy, and the services of capital equipment among the inputs, as well as the synergies of all these elements operating together (like better organizational and managerial techniques). Both involve big helpings of statistical mysticism, especially TFP/MFP.

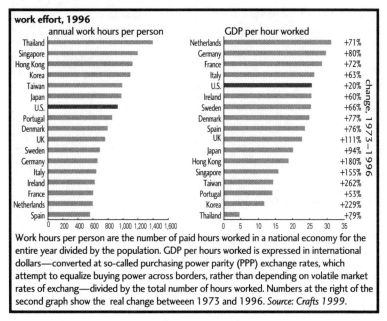

work effort, 1996

annual work hours per person

GDP per hour worked

Work hours per person are the number of paid hours worked in a national economy for the entire year divided by the population. GDP per hours worked is expressed in international dollars—converted at so-called purchasing power parity (PPP) exchange rates, which attempt to equalize buying power across borders, rather than depending on volatile market rates of exchang—divided by the total number of hours worked. Numbers at the right of the second graph show the real change betweeen 1973 and 1996. *Source: Crafts 1999.*

The mysticism begins with defining output. In many economic fables, the commodity chosen for illustration is the nonexistent widget—things typically produced in quantity, one indistinguishable from another. But few things in economic life are like widgets. Instead, output is defined as the "real" monetary value of the goods and services produced. Real means corrected for inflation, but correcting for inflation is hardly as effortless as it might sound. If something—good or service—improves in quality without changing in price, then its price has effectively declined. Or, less optimistically, if it deteriorates in quality, that's conceptually the same as a price increase. (That's why the CPI's airfares index has increased well over twice as much as has general inflation since the industry was deregulated in 1979—fewer nonstops and tighter advance-purchase restrictions are disguised price increases.) If both price and quality change, then you've got two moving targets to hit.[2]

In theory, it's relatively easy to account for quality increases in goods, but it's devilishly hard in practice. If suddenly a ten-ounce tube of tooth-paste becomes an eight-ounce with no change in price, the effect is pretty clear. But not many things are like that. In the 1960s, bigger car engines were considered a quality improvement; in the 1970s, they became a lia-bility as gas prices exploded. But cars are pretty straightforward; they don't change *that* much from year to year. It gets really complicated when you're dealing with rapidly changing gadgets like computers, or things that didn't exist even a few years ago, like MP3 players. If the best PC is twice as fast as last year's best yet costs no more, has its price fallen by half? Maybe, but software writers might respond by jazzing up a program's graphics, which may make it more pleasing to the eye, but not necessarily more produc-tive. And not everyone buys the fastest computer—so how do you come up with a price index for computers in general? Computers aren't such a big deal in the CPI—they account for only 0.21% of the index, about a quarter as much as tobacco products—but they matter a lot when it comes to valuing the capital equipment used by businesses, an important component of the GDP accounts, and, to return to our topic at hand, of the productivity stats themselves. And what is the real value of services like banking, surgery, or lawyering? Are complex derivatives, pointless hyster-ectomies, and compulsive litigation really products that should enter the national accounts with plus signs in front of them?

Indifferent to all these theoretical concerns, the U.S. Bureau of Economic Analysis (BEA), the agency that produces the national income accounts, says that the price of PCs fell 16% per year from 1987 to 1995, an average decline that more than doubled to 31% from 1995–2000, only to return to a more modest 24% for 2000 to 2002. Price declines like this do amazing things to nominal spending. In current dollars, computer spending grew 6% per year from 1995–2000—but 44% per year after price adjustment. This goosed the overall growth rate up nicely: real GDP less computers grew 3.7%, but with computers, 4.0%.

They came up with these numbers using a technique called hedonic pricing (Landefeld and Grimm 2000), which is a mathematical way of trying to account for performance improvements. The most obvious may be speed of calculation, which is quantifiable as instructions per second. Or so it seems: how does the speed correlate with actual performance? Then memory—also quantifiable (though bloated software eats that up). And storage capacity—bigger disk drives, the proliferation of CD and DVD drives. And so on, all built into an equation designed to figure out what 2002's computer would have cost in 2001, 2001's in 2000, and so on. The process, developed in collaboration with IBM (which back then sold hardware, not solutions), isn't applied to many other goods, and has only been in the official stats since 1987. Private estimates for annual price declines in the early mainframe era are as high as 27%, so the recent decline isn't a very fresh development. Hedonic pricing has never been applied to cars, despite massive quality improvements. Gordon (2002) says that were it applied to women's clothing, reported inflation would nearly double, since manufacturers hide price increases behind seasonal style changes. But overall, the BEA says that if hedonic pricing were applied more broadly, "real GDP growth might be revised up substantially" (ibid.). We're better off than we ever realized.

And what about the inputs to TFP/MFP? An hour of labor may be an hour of labor, but should an inexperienced worker's hour be treated as the equivalent of an old hand's? That kind of question seems simple next to defining a unit of capital. Is there any meaningful way in which the contribution of lathes and page-layout software can be expressed in the same metric? Money values are the conventional answer, but then you run into all those thorny problems of price adjustment. Productivity stats are intensely sensitive to the choices of assumptions and techniques.

Why does this all matter? For one, because people think it matters. Alan Greenspan and other central bankers use the productivity stats to make policy, partly out of statistical fetishism and partly out of sound reasoning. The real

Productivity has raced far ahead of pay for decades. The pay measure here includes fringe benefits. Data for 2003 is first quarter.

part is that over time, productivity growth determines the rate of improvement in living standards (conventionally defined), or at least puts an upper bound on them; across space, differences in productivity levels are the reason that people in Michigan are materially richer than those in Malawi—though, as the comparison suggests, there's a lot of politics to productivity hidden behind the numbers.

The chart above shows why productivity growth puts an upper bound on the growth in living standards. During the 1960s, pay and productivity grew in tandem, but they separated in the 1970s. In the 1990s boom, pay growth lagged behind productivity by almost 30%. And that measure of pay includes fringe benefits, which are skewed toward better-paid workers (and may not provide all that much immediate benefit: doctors and drug makers also benefit from health insurance, sometimes more than sick policyholders). Excluding fringes and looking just at direct pay, overall productivity rose four times as fast as the average real hourly wage—and twenty times as fast in manufacturing. With weak unions and strong bosses, productivity growth can just as easily show up in the pockets of creditors, stockholders, and CEOs as it can in fatter paychecks, as it clearly did. Pay caught up a bit on productivity late in the boom—which pinched profits, pricking the bubble. But after 2000, pay returned to its lagging role.

Over the long term, productivity growth and profitability follow roughly the same course. The profit share of GDP was high during the 1950s and 1960s, fell in the 1970s, and rose through the 1980s and 1990s. Productivity followed a similar course. Conceptually, productivity growth determines what an economy can produce over time, but how that growth is distributed depends on social institutions, and the institutions of American society tend to direct the booty upward.

It's all expressed in money, of course; there's nothing that economists don't want to render in monetary form. Economists also think people can and do work pretty much the number of hours they'd like to, and they don't like to talk about overwork or the distribution of income. They much prefer to talk about productivity itself. It is a remarkable fetish.

The Miracle

U.S. productivity growth since 1997 has been hailed as nothing short of a miracle. Its strength can't be denied, though it's hardly without precedent or problems. Heroic conclusions have been drawn from just a few years of evidence. And from those, ideologists have made grand claims for the superiority of the U.S. economic model—with wide wage disparities, no welfare state, an overgrown financial system, and volatile, unregulated, lightly unionized labor markets.

A great deal of the recent productivity blip can be explained by the strength of the economy; when GDP growth is strong, productivity growth often is as well. Employers are usually slow to hire new workers when business is good, and sometimes a bit slow to fire them when business is slack. So, when growth is strong, their preference is to drive

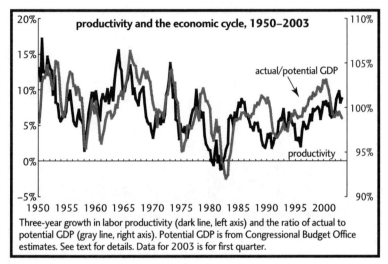

productivity and the economic cycle, 1950–2003

actual/potential GDP

productivity

1950 1955 1960 1965 1970 1975 1980 1985 1990 1995 2000

Three-year growth in labor productivity (dark line, left axis) and the ratio of actual to potential GDP (gray line, right axis). Potential GDP is from Congressional Budget Office estimates. See text for details. Data for 2003 is for first quarter.

the existing workforce a bit harder. Shown above is a chart of productivity growth—over a three-year interval, so as to smooth out short-term volatility and highlight longer-term trends—and the ratio of actual to potential GDP. Estimating potential GDP involves a bit of statistical guesswork; no one really knows what it is. But the best way to think of it is as representing the long-term trend around which actual experience oscillates. After a long expansion, actual GDP is well above its long-term trend; after a recession, it's well below.

At least two things stand out about the chart. First, productivity growth in the late 1990s is strong, but hardly unprecedented over the last fifty years. In fact, instead of looking like a revolution, recent productivity experience is less impressive than it was during the days of rotary-dial Bakelite telephones. And the recent productivity burst looks a lot like earlier productivity bursts—of roughly the same magnitude, and moving largely

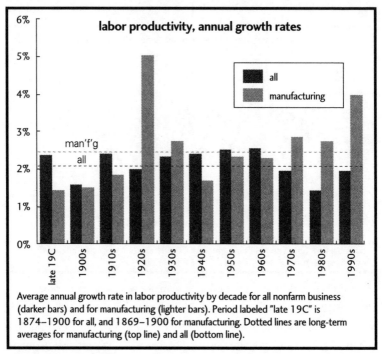

Average annual growth rate in labor productivity by decade for all nonfarm business (darker bars) and for manufacturing (lighter bars). Period labeled "late 19C" is 1874–1900 for all, and 1869–1900 for manufacturing. Dotted lines are long-term averages for manufacturing (top line) and all (bottom line).

along with the trend in the actual/potential GDP ratio.

A longer-term view of productivity also counsels if not skepticism, a bit of sobriety. Productivity growth for all industry in the 1990s was a bit under its 110-year average. Manufacturing productivity growth was admittedly quite strong, a rate exceeded only by that of the 1920s (which isn't the happiest precedent, but we can bracket that anxiety). But the gap between overall productivity growth and that in manufacturing leads to an interesting conclusion: that productivity growth outside manufacturing is underwhelming. Considering that computers and communications technology are supposed to transform knowledge work in a way similar to the way various generations of automation have transformed factory work, this is a surprising outcome.

The broadest measure of all, TFP, picked up in the late 1990s, but not by much. In the official Bureau of Labor Statistics (BLS) stats, it rose from 0.5% per year in the 1980s to 1.0% from 1994 through 1999—still well below the 1.7% average of 1950–1973. Jorgensen and Stiroh have TFP for the late 1990s coming in a hair under that for 1959–1973, but not exceeding it. And this statistic has to estimate the contribution of capital to production. What is that, exactly? It has something to do with how expensive a machine is and how long it lasts, but what is the hourly contribution of a computer to an accountant's output, or a blast furnace to a steel worker's? You can build models out to several decimal points, but they're basically guesses. Still, the official stats have capital productivity growth falling through most of recent history.

Let's go back to the safer ground of labor productivity, and at a finer level of detail. The BLS doesn't publish labor-productivity estimates for the service sector as a whole. But a reasonable guess would be that productivity outside manufacturing grew at an annual average of just under 2% in the late 1990s, a bit better than the 1980s and early 1990s, but well below rates seen from the 1950s through the 1970s—and less than half the rate seen in manufacturing.[3]

The BLS does publish productivity estimates for some industries—about fifty of them outside manufacturing—and those numbers too are underwhelming. But not all journalistic accounts scrutinize the numbers very carefully. For example, a story in the *San Jose Mercury News* (Bjorhus 2000), a newspaper published at the epicenter of New Economy hype, enthused:

> Recent government data suggest that even the service sector is beginning to boost productivity, which is conventionally measured as output per hours of work. Barbershops, for instance, registered a 2.7 percent productivity gain in 1998 and photography studios enjoyed a 14.7 percent increase.

On first glance, these numbers seem literally incredible: what techno-miracle hit the barbering trade? Computerized clippers? And photography? A call to Kent Kunze, the Bureau of Labor Statistics economist who supervises the industry productivity numbers, revealed that these "spectacular" gains are mainly the result of a strong economy. It doesn't take investments in fancy new equipment to get a photographer to take, say, twenty photos a day instead of seventeen—it just takes fewer coffee breaks.

Sadly, though, the tonsorial wonder was largely undone in 1999, with barbershop productivity falling by 12%, bringing it back to 1996 levels. And, worse, the miracle in portraiture was even more drastically undone, falling 14% in 1999, taking that industry back to 1994. But these are both very small industries, employing less than 150,000 between them. A closer look at some of the service industries' performance over the longer term shows that some of the more spectacular gains were made in small industries—like used-merchandise stores (with 208,000 workers) and appliance stores (81,000). Only a few large sectors, like department stores (2.4 million) and telecommunications (1.1 million), scored highly, though telecoms actually saw no great acceleration in productivity growth between the early and late 1990s. Retailing in general seems to have done fairly well. But some of the larger service industries, like commercial banking

(1.5 million), car dealerships (1.1 million), eating and drinking places (8.1 million), air transportation (711,000) food stores (3.7 million), and hotels and motels (1.8 million), did quite poorly. Banking is especially surprising, given the intense automation and branch closures the industry has experienced in recent years. Isn't instantaneous global electronic banking the very model of the cutting edge?

Curiously, as Jack Triplett (1999) shows, productivity in the heaviest computer-using industries—finance, wholesale trade, business services, and communications—has either been increasing very slowly or declining. Commenting on Triplett's findings, Dale Jorgenson and Kevin Stiroh (2000a) concede that "The apparent combination of slow productivity growth and heavy computer use remains an important obstacle for new economy proponents who argue that the use of information technology is fundamentally changing business practices and raising productivity throughout the U.S. economy." Their own study of industry productivity growth shows a stellar performance by high-tech itself, and a less-impressive performance elsewhere. They conclude that despite the explosion in info-tech productivity, there's no sign of "the arrival of phlogiston-like spillovers elsewhere."

Manufacturing numbers

The manufacturing numbers look impressive, but they deserve a bit of scrutiny. If a steel mill that used to use staff janitors starts contracting out for swabbing services, the low-productivity work of janitoring will move from the manufacturing to the services column in the stats, even though fundamentally not much has changed. If the outsourced janitors earn less than the in-house staff they replace, this would appear as a productivity boost whose benefits were claimed by the mill's owners and no one else.

But there are even more daunting measurement issues—arcane, per-haps, but absolutely crucial to the productivity story. Though the pub-lished BLS data won't let us do this directly, we can separate the manu-facturing stats into high-tech and all else. We'll see that high-tech itself is driving the averages upward almost all by itself. Technology's miracle is the production of still more new technology.

The BEA breaks out the contribution of computers to GDP growth, and the Federal Reserve Board includes several measures of high-tech output as part of its industrial production series. Like the BLS, both the BEA and the Fed use a measure of output based on inflation-adjusted monetary value. Most of the time, adjusting nominal values for inflation means marking them down a bit to scrape away the foam of pure price increase. Not with computers and other high-tech equipment, though. Since those prices are dropping like rocks, the growth in the real output of high-tech goods is significantly higher than nominal growth. In the CPI, computer prices fell by an average of 278% per year between 1998 and 2002, so even if the nominal dollar expenditure on computers were flat over that time, real expenditure growth would clock in at almost 400%. For the average product measured by the CPI, inflation averaged 2.4% over the same period, and flat nominal expenditures would translate into a real decline of 11%.

Numbers used to build real GDP are similar to the CPI figures. Be-tween 1990 and the 2000 tech peak, nominal sales of computers rose 78%—but since prices fell by 94%, real computer sales rose 1,783%. Com-puter sales accounted for 1% of nominal GDP growth over the same 10 years—and 12% of real growth.

Within the Fed's industrial production stats are two composite series—high-tech (HITEK2, in Fedcode, consisting of computers, telecommuni-cations equipment, and semiconductors) and all manufacturing except for high-tech (X4HTK2). They show massively diverging paths for the two series. HITEK2's growth has been almost literally exponential over the last decade—30% per year in the 1990s. It peaked at 48% in the spring of 2000, just as the NASDAQ was peaking. Though it accounts for under 10% of total manufacturing volume, that remarkable growth rate has had a remarkable effect on the composite manufacturing index.

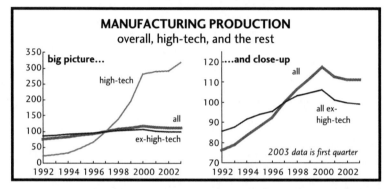

The two graphs above make this point—and two graphs are necessary, because including the HITEK2 index on the first graph so distorts the scale that the rest of manufacturing seems to scrape along the X-axis. The X4HTK2 index grew a sluggish 2.2% per year in the 1990s. But adding HITEK2's 28% annual average to X4HTK2 boosted overall growth in manufacturing to 4.3% per year in the 1990s.

Using those figures, we can estimate productivity for high-tech and the rest, something the BLS's quarterly productivity figures don't do. Shown on page 54 is the result of that exercise (along with a caption that explains the procedure). These are only rough calculations, though they're seconded by Robert Gordon's (2000) more rigorous work. These estimates show no acceleration in productivity growth in manufacturing outside high-tech; in fact, if anything, productivity growth in low- and medium-tech slowed during the 1990s. So the productivity burst of recent years is entirely caused by high-tech. What does it mean when less than a tenth of something can have such an outsized effect on the whole?

Do these numbers mean anything? Can the qualitative changes computers have made in life be expressed in a price index? They've reorganized

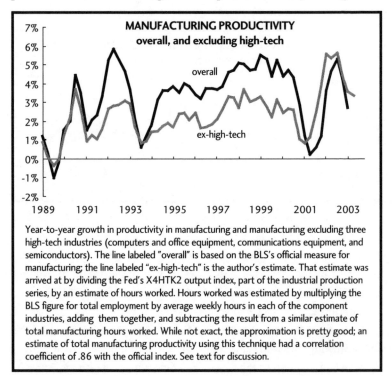

Year-to-year growth in productivity in manufacturing and manufacturing excluding three high-tech industries (computers and office equipment, communications equipment, and semiconductors). The line labeled "overall" is based on the BLS's official measure for manufacturing; the line labeled "ex-high-tech" is the author's estimate. That estimate was arrived at by dividing the Fed's X4HTK2 output index, part of the industrial production series, by an estimate of hours worked. Hours worked was estimated by multiplying the BLS figure for total employment by average weekly hours in each of the component industries, adding them together, and subtracting the result from a similar estimate of total manufacturing hours worked. While not exact, the approximation is pretty good; an estimate of total manufacturing productivity using this technique had a correlation coefficient of .86 with the official index. See text for discussion.

the way we live and work, sometimes to the good, sometimes not. Do they make a 28% annual contribution to the growth of human happiness?

Closely related to the productivity argument is a claim about innovation: that we live in a time of new product development without any historical precedent. This is a remarkably amnesiac claim. The development of the telegraph, for example, reduced the time needed for communication across oceans and continents from weeks to seconds; surely this was a change far more profound than the development of the first Mosaic web browser. Similarly with railroads, automobiles, radio, television, antibiotics, telephones, electricity, jet travel, plastics, indoor plumbing.... Indeed, someone born in 1870 and living the allotted threescore years and ten saw the world change far more than someone like me, say, born in 1952. And, while the number of new products may be larger than ever in absolute terms, the pace of innovation may actually be slower than in the past. Jack Triplett (1999) proves this point by looking at the mundane grocery store. In 1948, there were 2,200 products on sale in the average grocery store. In 1972, the count was 9,000—an increase of 6,800. By 1994, there were 19,000 products on the shelves of the average supermarket, 10,000 more than in the Nixon era. But the grocery universe grew an average of 6.0% per year during the first era, and 3.5% in the second. The sheer number of new things might make it seem like product proliferation has increased lately, but the pace of innovation has actually slowed considerably. Similarly, Triplett argues, New Economy partisans point to vast recent improvement in cars as greatly reducing their effective price—but in fact, the improvement in cars early in the 20th century was much greater than it was at the end of the century.

While much attention has been paid to the great blessings of technology in improving the quality of products and lives, less has been paid to its downside. As New Economy bible *Business Week* confessed in a cover story, "service stinks" (Brady 2000). Customer satisfaction with airlines, banks, stores, hotels, phones, and PCs has declined steadily since 1994, and the number of consumer complaints economywide more than doubled. The complaints are mainly about areas where infotech was supposed to be working such wonders: inaccurate information, slow (or no) response time, and poor training of customer service reps. Perversely, infotech is in good part responsible for this state of affairs: firms identify who their good customers are and pamper them, leaving the rest of us on hold listening to New Age Muzak. More charmingly, companies sell data about customers' history to other companies, meaning that "you can be slotted before you even walk in the door, since your buying potential has already been measured." The approach is probably good for profits; this aspect of the productivity revolution is probably highly welcome to managers and shareholders, but not to many other people except economists.

A mystery surrounding the recent productivity burst is where these apparent gains are ending up. Productivity growth accelerated at the end of the 1990s, with the change between 1997 and 2000 double that of the previous three-year period. But wage growth was strongest in 1997 and 1998, and then slowed over the next two years. Corporate profitability (measured as the profit share of GDP) peaked in 1997, and fell a bit in subsequent years. And many of what seemed like profits during the boom turned out to be accounting fictions. If faster productivity growth doesn't show up in either wages or profits, it's hard to imagine where it's gone, or why it really matters, except maybe to justify the greatest bull market in history and to build capitalism's brand identity.

Professional optimists weigh in

So far, this examination of the productivity revolution has used mainly the silicon equivalent of back-of-the-envelope calculations. Professional economists have thrown far more complicated math at the issue and come up with their own brand of evidence for a revolution. Notably, at the turn of the millennium, several prominent economists who had earlier been skeptical about tech's contribution to productivity—like Daniel Sichel (writing a series of recent papers with Stephen Oliner) and Dale Jorgenson (alone and with Kevin Stiroh)—shed their skepticism and endorsed the notion that there'd been a major uptick in the productivity trend. They're worth a look.

Studies of this sort generally apply what's called a neoclassical growth model to the data. Though things can get very complex in practice, the underlying concepts are fairly simple—or seem simple, until you try turning intuitions into models. Output is taken as a function of two major inputs, capital and labor. Economies grow because some combination of additional machinery and workers are engaged in production. Sounds simple enough, but things almost immediately get complicated. How do you measure capital? The usual answer is "by its monetary value," but that assumes that prices are adequate measure of a machine's "value," and that all these values are commensurate with one another. To return to an earlier example: is a dollar's worth of an accountant's computer the same thing as a dollar's worth of a steel mill's blast furnace? Is a dollar's worth of new computer worth the same as a dollar's worth of last year's? And how do you assign a value to a computer once it's left the retailer's shelf? Is it its replacement value? Its resale value? That's less of a problem with, say, a locomotive, which can last for decades, than with a computer, which may last for years but can quickly look sad and weak next to a new model. (Ever try to sell a used computer? You can hardly give the things away.) But, conversely, a new computer may have more bugs in it than one that's been in service for a year or two. How to account for that?

Even the matter of labor input isn't as straightforward as it might seem. To return to a question raised earlier in this chapter, an hour's labor may be an hour's labor, but how do you value the relative contributions of an experienced engineer and a janitor fresh out of high school? Most economists would say that their pay levels are good measures, but that requires a great faith in the fairness of our labor markets, a faith that most economists freely profess to have.

In other words, to get good measures of the two principal inputs, capital and labor, they must be adjusted for "quality." The contribution of 2003-vintage computers must be reconciled with the contribution of the 2000-vintage. Not easy in practice, but conceivable in principle. What might shock civilians, though, is that the labor input must also be adjusted for quality, so that the contributions of the experienced engineer and the green janitor can be expressed in the same metric. To the more softhearted among us, that seems a bit callous—and it even gets ugly. For example, Robert Gordon (2000) attributes the slowdown in productivity growth in the 1970s to deterioration in average workforce quality, specifically, the "shift toward less experienced teenagers and the rapid inflow of females into the labor force." Yes, teens are inexperienced and even moody, but why should the flow of women into paid work be so corrupting? In an email, Gordon helpfully explained that wages reflect productivity, so if women earn 60% of what men do (which is roughly what they did in thirty years ago, compared with 73% today), then clearly they constituted only 60% as much "effective labor." Gordon did concede effects of discrimination, but he still clearly believes that people are basically paid what they're worth. For their part, Jorgenson and Stiroh assert that the low unemployment rates of the late 1990s brought in a lot of low-quality workers, lowering overall workforce excellence. Economics earns its nickname as the dismal science in fresh ways almost every workday.

Preliminaries taken care of, let's move on to the studies themselves. To measure infotech's contribution to economic growth, you need to put a price tag not only on the input, but the output as well. How much value does a $2,000 computer produce in a year? You can't measure that directly, of course. So instead economists assume that the annual contribution equals the economy's average rate of profit—otherwise, businesses wouldn't invest in them. So if the economywide profit rate is 10%, the $2,000 computer produces $200 a year. It *has* to be this way, because businesspeople are well-informed and rational. If the return on computer investment were less than average, managers would buy fewer of them, and the rate of return would creep back toward the average; if it were higher, they'd buy them by the truckload, bringing returns back to average. It's harder than ever to believe this sort of thing now that we know that accountants were producing some of the 1990s' most striking works of fiction, but mainstream economists believe it anyway.

A closer look at Oliner and Sichel's (2000a, 2000b) work—the intellectual foundation for a lot of Greenspan's New Economy boosterism—shows how intensely sensitive to assumptions and technique these exercises are. For example, in the introduction to their paper, they suggest that a new Pentium-based computer is equivalent to two 486-based computers from three years earlier—but if they can't run new software, the older machines are worth even less than that. Yet in developing their estimates of the capital stock, they assume that PCs have a useful life of five years. The first example implies that computers depreciate very rapidly; the second, much less so. Which is it? It's extremely hard to say. They also assume perfectly competitive markets and that rates of return on capital are the same across sectors and firms. Neither is empirically true; real markets don't resemble the frictionless constructs of theory.[4] They assume "constant returns to scale," meaning that large firms are no more or less profitable or efficient than small ones, which is kind of hard to believe. If you assume rapid rates of technical progress, then the price index you use to estimate "real" investment will decline very rapidly, which implies more rapid rates of real growth. But rapid progress also implies that older equipment is ready for the toxic landfill after a couple of years, meaning that high rates of investment spending are necessary just to stay in place. In their paper, Oliner and Sichel assume that computers earn a return of 4% per year after depreciation; they estimate that computers lose 64% of their value every year they're in service, meaning that they have to earn a gross return of 68% per year. Do they? Who knows? Modest errors in estimating depreciation—less than 10% either way—could make all the difference between doubling the return and sinking it into negative territory. Moreover, Oliner and Sichel develop estimates of the stock of software, with very little clue about how software depreciates over time, or what its actual contribution to the work effort is. New software might have a negative contribution to productivity at first, as users learn the new routines and bugs are ironed out. How do you account for this? Who knows?

Which isn't, of course, to say that all such efforts are worthless. It is a reminder, however, that economics is very imprecise, despite all its pretensions to mathematical rigor. Sophisticated math won't give you good answers if your assumptions are wobbly and your data is questionable.

Undeterred by such concerns, Oliner and Sichel conclude that computers added about 0.6 percentage points to U.S. economic growth between 1996 and 1999. That's hardware only—they estimate another 0.5 points came from software and communications technology. Their Fed colleague Karl Whelan (2000) estimates the contribution at over 0.8. Yet another Fed colleague, Michael Kiley (1999), estimates the contribution between 1985 and 1998 as −.27 percentage points (yes, a negative), mainly because he assumes new computer investments disrupt normal operations of firms—and the increase in computer investment in recent years means more disruptions. In his earlier book, when he was skeptical about the payoff from computers, Sichel (1997) made a great deal out of the support, service, and training costs that dwarf computer expenditures; in this paper, those costs disappear. Jorgenson and Stiroh (2000) estimate the contribution of computer hardware at about 0.5 points, a much smaller number. Which is it? Who knows?

But let's take Oliner and Sichel at their word. Their total estimate is that "information technology capital"—computer hardware and software and communications technology—contributed 1.1 percentage points to U.S. economic growth between 1996 and 1999, a time when growth overall totaled 4.8%—meaning that high-tech was responsible for about a quarter of overall growth. Their estimate for 1974–1990 is that infotech contributed a sixth to overall growth. While this incremental increase may be nothing to sneeze at, neither does it have the feel of an economic revolution. And a good bit of the story is dependent on wonky price indexes. Which makes one wonder how meaningful "real" growth numbers are.

Jorgenson and Stiroh's estimate is lower because they include the household sector in their model, while Oliner and Sichel just look at businesses. To do that, they've got to put a dollar value on the pleasures of the new Xbox and surfing the net on a home computer. How do you value these? Jorgenson and Stiroh assume that the value of their output is equal to the value of the input; you wouldn't spend $200 on an Xbox if you didn't think it gave you $200 of joy in return. Based on such thinking, they conclude that gadgetry at home doubled its contribution to economic growth between the early and late 1990s.

Real GDP has always had a tenuous relationship with the material of real human beings. In poorer countries, the early stages of development might show hefty GDP growth rates at the same time that the average human was actually worse off, as peasants are thrown off the land and migrate desperately to cities in search of work. In all countries, real income gains can go mostly or entirely to the rich, leaving the masses largely unblessed by the statistical increase in wealth. With so much of real growth now concentrated in computers and other high-tech areas—dependent on the quirks of price indexes and quality adjustments—reported growth may have less relevance to the average person in the street than ever.

One in five children in poverty, 41 million people without health insurance—but processor speed is doubling every year and a half!

Gordon's critique

Prestige economics' most prominent critic of these productivity revo arguments is Robert Gordon of Northwestern. Initially, he argued that after correcting for the unsustainably strong economy of the late 1990s, the acceleration in productivity was almost entirely concentrated in computers and other high-tech. Normal benchmark revisions of the GDP data forced him to retreat from the claim a bit. More recently, Gordon (2000) argues that most of it is still concentrated there, with some in other branches of durable-goods manufacturing, but almost invisible in the other 88% of the private economy—services and nondurable manufacturing. Controversially, Gordon strips away the effects of the strong and presumably unsustainable growth of the period; Oliner and Sichel (2000a) say he overdoes the adjustment. But most productivity enthusiasts make no adjustment at all, an oversight that a glance at the graph on page 47 might call into question.

Gordon (2001) points out that Oliner and Sichel's estimates of an increase of almost 1% in annual productivity growth attributable to infotech in the late 1990s depend almost entirely on the acceleration in computer buying during the period, much of it spurred by building the web —jazzed up with Y2K mania. Were computer spending to return to early-1990s averages, much of the miracle, then, would eventually disappear.

Gordon (2000) speculates that the concentrated productivity gains came at the expense of firms that didn't make the investments:

> [C]omputers are used extensively to provide information aimed at taking customers, profits, or capital gains away from other companies. This is a zero-sum game involving redistribution of wealth rather than the increase of wealth, yet each individual firm has a strong incentive to make computer investments that, if they do not snatch wealth away from someone else, at least act as a defensive blockade against a hostile attack.... There is a "keeping up with the Joneses" aspect of hardware and software purchase motivated by competition, employee satisfaction, and employee recruitment.

In the same paper, Gordon contrasts the development of the Internet, and of computer technology in general, with the incredible wave of innovations in the late 19th and early 20th centuries—electricity, telephones, oil refining, cars. In just a few decades, these radically transformed life in far more profound ways than anything in recent history. As he points out, the Internet offers faster substitutes for older ways of doing things—games, the Official Airline Guide, shopping—but few radically new products.[5]

Even the optimists have to concede problems with their findings. Echoing their comments on Triplett's work quoted earlier in the chapter, Jorgenson and Stiroh admit that "a closer look" at their data shows that Gordon has a point in foregrounding the contribution of computer production itself. Productivity acceleration "can be traced in substantial part to information technology industries....The evidence is equally clear that computer-using industries like finance, insurance, and real estate (FIRE) and services have continued to lag in productivity growth. Reconciliation of massive high-tech investment and relatively slow productivity growth in service industries remains an important task for proponents of the new economy position."

Also, all the upbeat studies find that much of the productivity blip can be traced to high levels of investment in information technology

(IT)—"capital deepening," in the jargon. That is, more inputs mean more outputs. If tech were really making us work smarter, we wouldn't have needed all this investment to bring about higher growth rates. With IT spending in a long slump, it will be very interesting to see what happens with the productivity figures over the next few years.

The Wal-Mart effect

The studies quoted in the last section came from academics (and academically oriented central bankers). More practical sorts have come up with some very interesting results. For example, a study by the consulting firm McKinsey & Co.'s in-house think tank (McKinsey Global Institute 2001) looked much more deeply at specific industries and companies. MGI's results are at odds with Gordon's, finding only a minor contribution from the exuberant economy, and shifting the industrial star away from high-tech hardware toward a handful of services (see table). MGI also found that some heavily computer-using service industries—commercial banking and hotels, for example—had rather dismal productivity performance. In fact, MGI found almost no correlation ("barely positive and statistically insignificant") between IT spending and productivity performance. High-tech industries themselves contributed just 27% of the total productivity acceleration. Almost three-quarters—72%—came from three services: wholesale trade, retail trade, and security and commodity brokers.

It's interesting that McKinsey finds so much of the reported productivity burst not in production but in distribution—and not just the distribution of commodities, but the distribution of income and wealth, which is what the brokerage business is all about.

Despite that conceptual unity, the three fields are of course quite different. The brokerage business employs few people (well under 1% of total

employment) and pays very, very well ($156,964 per full-time-equivalent
employee in 2000, by far the highest of any industry, 406% of the national
average). Wholesale trade employs about 5% of all workers and pays them

sources of productivity acceleration (McKinsey estimates)		
annual productivity growth		
1987–95	0.99%	
1995–99	2.32	
acceleration	+1.33	
of which (and share of total)		
wholesale trade	0.37	27.8
retail trade	0.34	25.6
brokers	0.25	18.8
semiconductors*	0.17	12.8
computers*	0.12	9.0
telecommunications	0.07	5.3
net of 53 other sectors	0.01	0.8

Chart reads as follows: of the 1.33-point acceleration in productivity
growth between the two periods, wholesale trade contributed 0.37
points, or 27.8% of the total. Semiconductors and computers are
asterisked because even though they dominate their industrial
categories, their actual categories are formally larger—electronic and
electric equipment and industrial machinery and equipment
respectively. *Source: McKinsey Global Institute 2001.*

26% above the national average.[6] Retail, though, is large and stingy: it employs 18% of the U.S. workforce but pays just 58% of the national average.
The social payoff of productivity accelerations in each of these fields—assuming McKinsey's estimates are right—deserves some thought.

The contribution of the brokerage industry to productivity was mainly web-based trading; how much that contributes to human welfare is debatable. The more people trade, the worse they do (though it makes their brokers happier). Those who shift from phone to online trading suffer a drop in returns (Barber and Odean 2000a; 2000b; 2001).[7]

Wholesale trade consists of warehousing and distribution, which is a bit of an oversimplification. Wholesalers book about one-third of their sales to retailers; the rest go to other wholesalers or manufacturers. Good data wasn't available for MGI to study the sector as a whole, so they focused on a small, important subsector, pharmaceutical wholesaling. It's technologically advanced, and it's likely to be emulated by other sectors. Its strong productivity performance, MGI concluded, was the result of warehouse automation, better organization of work tasks, consolidation among retailers (fewer, bigger chains are cheaper and easier to service), consolidation in wholesale trade itself, and a shift to higher-value drugs— in other words, consolidation, better ways of picking and packing, and more "blockbuster drugs." Are newer drugs worth every penny of their higher costs? Why are drug prices so unlike computer prices, rising relentlessly? Do higher prices reflect quality improvements, or do they explain why this industry is capitalism's most profitable?[8] MGI didn't ask these questions, but they're good ones.

But the real star of the McKinsey study is Wal-Mart, a company that personifies the real New Economy. Technology is important to Wal-Mart's evolution to retailing dominance, but what matters is that this technology enables a ruthlessly efficient corporate food chain, from the woefully underpaid women who staff its stores (it's one of the most potent sex discriminators around) to the woefully underpaid workers at its contractors in China. To MGI, this is using technology "as part of an innovative retailing strategy." An aspect of the Wal-Mart miracle that McKinsey and the business press rarely mention is that it forces its "associates" to work for free. Employees are routinely instructed to clock out and continue working. Store managers earn bonuses based on individual store profits, and it's deeply in their interests to squeeze every dime out of the staff they can. But they, too, often work seventy-hour weeks —with no overtime pay, of course (Greenhouse 2002; Featherstone 2003, 2004). This is a pungent reminder of the difference between the capitalist's definition of productivity (the expansion of profit) and the engineer's (the minimization of inputs, which would include the unpaid hours).

That touches on an issue that's very important to all the productivity analyses: do we have good measures of hours worked? The BLS, for example, assumes that white-collar workers in high-tech put in a normal forty-hour week. But according to a survey by InfoWorld (emailed to subscribers on February 14, 2003), just 11% of tech workers work "regular" hours; 43% "occasionally" put in extra hours, 18% do so "frequently, and 27% are on call twenty-four hours a day. That's one of the beauties of technology—thanks to laptops, PDAs, and cell phones, you can never leave the office, because it follows you everywhere.

Trying to quantify the contributions of computers and other high-tech stuff to economic growth is probably a symptom of statistical fetishism at its most advanced. A lot less energy should be devoted to such imprecise and dubious pursuits and a lot more to asking the kinds of qualitative questions that economists rarely ask. Have computers enriched our lives? Parts of our lives, for some of us. Music sounds better, movies look better—but are the songs and films of any higher quality other than in the technical sense? Computers have made some of our jobs more interesting; I couldn't have produced this book, from concept to camera-ready copy, as completely or as quickly twenty years ago, nor could I have published a credible looking newsletter with up-to-date economic stats without a staff of editors, number-crunchers, and artists. But for lots of people—like the U.S.'s 5 million telemarketers—the computer means sitting in a cubicle and having your output monitored by the boss. Computers have allowed financiers to develop complex new financial instruments and trade them at lightning speed—which is good news for the principals, but is it good for most of society? The net has allowed people around the world to make contact with each other in completely unprecedented ways—but computers have also allowed governments to spy on us and marketers to profile us in unprecedented ways. A gain for human possibilities, and a loss. I said in the first chapter that New Economy rhetoric often serves an ideological or disciplinary purpose. Here's another instance of that, where invoking gee-whiz stats of questionable accuracy forecloses any serious discussion of the broader political and cultural issues. Economists shouldn't be allowed to get away with that.

Work's end?

Some people took the productivity-revolution story to mean that human workers would be rendered obsolete. This gave an extended life to mid-1990s worries about (and book titles like) *The Jobless Future* (Aronowitz and DiFazio 1995) and *The End of Work* (Rifkin 1995). In retrospect, these look like the products of the "jobless recovery" of the early 1990s. That period wasn't as jobless as it's often said to have been; the U.S. economy produced more than 7 million new jobs between 1991 and 1995—but none of these authors are notorious for their careful study of labor statistics. Jeremy Rifkin, at least, has retreated from his pronouncements of work's end; he moved on to other world transforming developments like hydrogen energy (though in another more recent but equally awful book, *The Age of Access,* he did indulge himself the claim that "advances in technology and dramatic increases in productivity" will render "human labor far less important" [Rifkin 2000, p. 263]).[9] End-of-work claims persist in the broader culture; you run across them constantly at conferences and on listservs—and even in more recent books. In his book *Third Millennium Capitalism,* Wyatt Rogers (2000, p. 230) cited Rifkin's baseless assertion that in the future—whenever that arrives—just 20% of job-seekers will be successful, with the other 80% of no economic use whatsoever. Viviane Forrester wrote in her 1999 book *The Economic Horror,* in a passage widely circulated on the Internet:

> For the first time in history, the vast majority of human beings are no longer indispensable to the small number of those who run the world economy. The economy is increasingly wrapped up in pure speculation. The working masses and their cost are becoming superfluous. In other words, there is something worse than actually being exploited—and that is no longer to be even worth exploiting![10]

Forrester might be excused for this view, since she's European; it's tempting to view high European unemployment rates as symptoms of some real structural transformation rather than the natural product of punishingly tight fiscal and monetary policies pursued on the Continent as part of the project of economic union. For someone left of center, it's a far more appealing explanation than the more orthodox one, that chronic unemployment is the result of excessively high wages and excessively generous welfare states. Such explanations are fairly easily refuted: there's no relation between the wage level and the unemployment rate in Western Europe; the Netherlands, with high wages and a generous welfare state, enjoys a relatively low unemployment rate, while Spain, with low wages and a less generous welfare state, has Europe's highest jobless rate.

For the end-of-work thesis to hold water, there would have to be a

employment intensity of growth

	Canada	France	Japan	U.S.
employment				
1960s	2.7	1.1	1.5	1.8
1970s	3.2	0.6	0.9	2.4
1980s	1.8	0.3	1.2	1.8
1990s	1.4	0.4	0.3	1.3
GDP				
1960s	5.2	5.6	10.5	3.8
1970s	4.3	3.3	4.5	3.1
1980s	2.8	2.5	4.0	3.2
1990s	2.5	1.6	1.3	3.1
intensity				
1960s	0.5	0.2	0.1	0.5
1970s	0.7	0.2	0.2	0.8
1980s	0.6	0.1	0.3	0.6
1990s	0.6	0.3	0.2	0.4
1960s–90s	0.1	0.1	0.1	−0.1

The first two panels show the average annual growth rates in employment and GDP. The bottom panel shows the relation between the two—employment growth is divided by GDP, then divided further by 100 as an estimate of how much employment growth would be generated by 1 percentage point of GDP growth. So, for Canada in the 1960s, 1% GDP growth would result in about 0.5% employment growth. Note how little change there's been over time. *Source: author's calculations from U.S. Bureau of Labor Statistics, World Bank, and IMF data.*

decline in what economists call the employment intensity of growth—the amount of job growth generated by a specified amount of GDP growth. But, as the facing table shows, that hasn't happened, either in the U.S. or elsewhere. Economies suffering high rates of unemployment are generally also suffering from low growth rates. There are many causes of low growth rates, but a technology revolution isn't among them.

Jobs of the future

So far, this chapter has been mainly about numbers, and how much we produce per hour of toil. But what about quality? What kinds of jobs is the economy producing?

During the mania, there were a lot of strong claims about the new workplace. It was democratic, creative, and rewarding, and would only become more so. That point of view was most common among the techno-optimists of the libertarian right. But even liberals talked that talk. During the early Clinton years, when he was the great liberal hope within a centrist administration, former Labor Secretary Robert Reich pronounced that "the most rapidly growing job categories are knowledge-intensive; I've called them 'symbolic analysts.' Why are they growing so quickly? Why are they paying so well? Because technology is generating all sorts of new possibilities.... The problem is that many people don't have the right skills" (Bennehum 1996). The "problem" Reich is talking about is presumably poverty and polarization.

Reich, it seems, didn't pay much attention to the projections of an agency he once supervised, the Bureau of Labor Statistics. Every few years, the BLS makes projections for job growth over the next decade. They've always included some of the sorts of jobs that Reich was talking about—the most desirable "indoor jobs, no heavy lifting" (as Bob Dole once said of the vice presidency). But those sorts of jobs have always been greatly outnumbered by much less compelling opportunities.

Listed below are the BLS's projections of fastest-growing occupations between 2000 and 2010; they're not all that different from projections made when Reich was in the cabinet, and bear no relation to his fantasies, or those that filled the pages of *Wired* in its heyday.[11] These thirty job categories

---

the thirty fastest-growing occupations, 2000–2010

combined food preparation and serving workers, including fast food •
customer-service representatives • registered nurses • retail salespersons
• computer support specialists • cashiers, except gaming • office clerks,
general • security guards • computer-software engineers, applications •
waiters and waitresses • general and operations managers • truck drivers,
heavy and tractor-trailer • nursing aides, orderlies, and attendants •
janitors and cleaners, except maids and housekeeping cleaners •
postsecondary teachers • teacher assistants • home-health aides •
laborers and freight, stock, and material movers, hand • computer
software engineers, systems software • landscaping and groundskeeping
workers • personal and home care aides • computer systems analysts •
receptionists and information clerks • truck drivers, light or delivery
services • packers and packagers, hand • elementary school teachers,
except special education • medical assistants • network and computer
systems administrators • secondary school teachers, except special and
vocational education • accountants and auditors

---

alone account for almost one-third of total employment today, and for 46% of the next decade's projected growth. Of the top thirty, those that look like symbolic analysts account for 26% of employment now, and 34% of projected growth. Many don't look very New Agey. It's hard to see from this how "the problem is that many people don't have the right skills."

It is, however, easy to see the polarizing tendencies in today's labor market. Of the top 30 occupations, about 40% of the job growth will be among those in the lowest quarter of the earnings distribution. Another 28% will be in the top-paying quartile, with only 31% in the middle two. Less than a quarter of the top 30 jobs will require a bachelor's degree or higher; 54% will require short on-the-job training. Outside the top thirty, a quarter of new jobs will require a bachelor's degree or more—but almost twice as many will require no more than short- to medium-term on-the-job training. Three-quarters will require less than an associate's degree. Given the correlation of education and income, it looks unlikely that income polarization will be reversing itself soon.

Infotech jobs are a surprisingly small part of the picture. A standard definition of IT jobs includes the categories that the BLS calls electrical and electronics engineers, computer specialists, and operations research analysts. These accounted for 2% of employment in 2000, and will account for 3% in 2010. Since they are slated to increase their share, they're also responsible for a lager share of total growth—10%. A selection of more mundane old economy jobs—retail salespersons, cashiers, telemarketers, truck drivers, and office clerks, who on balance earn a third of what IT workers do—accounts for the same share of growth, and will make up 10% of the workforce in 2010. So the American economy hasn't been producing only burger-flipper jobs. It produces a fair number of high-end jobs, a lot of low-end jobs, but not much in the middle.

And what do people like Reich mean by "skills" anyway? If the ruling class were seriously worried about illiteracy, they'd spend more money on education. While we might all be better off if workers were better trained, there's no sign that employers are demanding such a workforce now.

One problem with analyzing skill is that it's a difficult concept to define and measure. Economists typically use a mix of education and experience to describe the skill of workers, but these are only inexact proxies. At the big-picture level, the rising "education premium"—the earnings advantage enjoyed by those with advanced degrees—is often cited as proof of the rising demand for skilled workers. But comparisons of U.S. regions show that the higher the unemployment rate, the greater the education premium. Since average unemployment rates have drifted upward since the golden age—they averaged 4.6% in the 1950s and 1960s, and 6.8% since 1980—it may be that the rising education premium is just a sign of a slacker labor market. More direct attempts to measure employers' wants offer no support for the skills thesis. To measure the changes in skills requirements in the United States, David Howell and Edward Wolff linked changes in employment in 64 industrial and 264 occupational categories from 1960 to 1985 to their descriptions in the BLS's Dictionary of Occupational Titles. They found that low-skill service industry work grew more quickly than high-skilled—and, perversely, that the more rapidly growing service industries "required higher skills but paid lower wages than the low-growth service industries." The picture was brighter in manufacturing, but it's a shrinking field. For nonsupervisory workers as a whole, the most rapid growth "was in the highest skill segment but in the lowest wage segment." If the "problem" that Reich was talking about was social polarization, then there's not much evidence that skills or their lack have much to do with it. Most of the increase in inequality over the last twenty-five years has come within demographic groups—people grouped by occupation, age, sex, and schooling—and not between them. A better place to look for explanations of polarization would be the erosion of the working class's bargaining power because of union busting, deregulation, and capital mobility.[12]

Why do employers and their mouthpieces keep talking about skills, then? It may be that they mean something other than mental and/or manual dexterity. Of course, formal training does impart certain skills; there are no self-taught neurosurgeons. But work training at less elite levels has proved disappointing; for example, people with (nonprofessional) vocational training in high school find it easier to get jobs, but there's no evidence that they do any better once they're working. And while having a high school diploma is necessary to snag certain kinds of jobs, grade average correlates neither with the probability of getting a job nor with one's pay upon landing one. Studies of the relations among wages, schooling, and scores on standardized tests—admittedly imperfect measures of skills—show that while people with more education make higher scores on the tests, this advantage pales next to the higher wages earned by the credentialed; nothing in the scores can explain why college grads earn 60% more than those with only a high school diploma (Bowles and Gintis 1995).

An elite spin on the Bowles/Gintis thesis was provided by Susan Mayer and Christopher Jencks (2000). Dissenting from the push for higher school "standards" measured by standardized tests, Mayer and Jencks point out that test scores explain less than one-third of the earnings difference between high school grads and dropouts. Employers must want something more than the kinds of skills measured by tests; they provide a helpful list: "Graduates have a better attitude; they are more responsible; they have better people skills." Concluding, they quote Woody Allen's famous observation that "90 percent of life is showing up. Students who finish high school do better than dropouts partly because they have learned this lesson." This is a much less inspiring view of the value of education than the more common excuses, like preparing for self-governance in a democracy or developing a critical intelligence. The real economic value of a diploma is that it proves that you've learned how to report cheerfully for duty.

Writing in the *California Management Review*, Peter Cappelli (1995) asked, "Is the 'Skills Gap' Really About Attitudes?" and carefully answered his own question: "Yes." In the 1970s, Cappelli reminds us, there was lots of worry about bad worker attitudes—the "blue-collar blues," an alienation that expressed itself in strikes, sabotage, and general truculence. By the mid-1980s, though, the complaints were all about "skills"—workers just didn't have what it took to cut it in the modern world. Education summits were convened to address the skills problem—though of course little new funding for primary and secondary schooling was on offer. And with the Oval Office now filled by its most reactionary and illiterate occupant in memory, there's not much hope for an imminent policy reversal.

Employer surveys reveal that bosses care less about their employees' candlepower than they do about "character"—by which they mean self-discipline, enthusiasm, and responsibility. Bosses want underlings who are steadfast, dependable, consistent, punctual, tactful, and who identify with their work and show sympathy for others; those who are labeled "creative" and "independent" received low marks.[13] (A survey of high school teachers about students showed almost identical results.) Workers are rarely dismissed for incompetence, but rather for absenteeism and other irresponsible behavior. An extensive 1991 review of research on personality and job success showed "conscientiousness" to be the best of five predictors, and "openness to experience," the psychologists' odd name for smarts, the least impressive. Employers want the can-do self-starters of classified-ad boilerplate, not adepts at C++ or vector autoregressions.

Another trait that's valued highly, according to the psychomanagerial literature, is a knack for "prosocial" behavior—doing more for others, which in this case, ultimately means more for the boss. Such devotion is especially welcome in these days of employee "empowerment" programs and leaderless teams; workers are expected to be the architects of their own better exploitation (Bateman and Organ 1983, Brief 1986, Cappelli 1992, Edwards 1977).

The challenge to educators is to produce that kind of worker. According to Cappelli, it's not enough to teach students "responsibility, self-discipline, and adherence to rules"; schools must emit graduates with good attitudes—which, as we've learned, means being cheerful, self-sacrificing, and prosocial. Though he is too respectable to say so, Cappelli makes it clear that talk of teaching "values" in the classroom is in part about the most important value of all, shareholder value. Employers, Cappelli and his sources say, should use fear of "losing face" as a motivational tool, and, through "role modeling," use "conformity pressures [to] produce a positive result." It's not enough that employers control your time; they should control your mind and heart as well.

But if that doesn't work, there's always snooping. Ideologists say the new workplace is more spontaneous and less hierarchical than the old one, friendlier to self-expression. For an elite, maybe, but for average workers, today's workplace is a virtual panopticon of computer and video surveillance. As Christian Parenti, author of *The Soft Cage* (2003), put it:

Technologies once reserved for the Pentagon and a few top-of-the-line casinos are now combined and deployed as standard features of the re-engineered American work place. One management study found that eighty percent of all U.S. firms keep their employees under some sort of electronic surveillance. Whiz-bang software and monitoring gear now watch the keystrokes and physical movements of low-wage service workers at establishments like Taco Bell and Target. When that fails cashiers face corporate paid snitches called "mystery shoppers." So too in the office, cameras watch from the ceiling while last year's DoD software silently tracks and analyzes employee output, work patterns and communications. Under such conditions a whole slew of working-class survival tactics are being smashed. The super-wired corporation will not permit: unauthorized break time, excessive fraternizing, fake invoices, on the job theft, pot smoking in the utility room, or for that matter union organizing. The net effect of all this has been to keep American workers on their toes. When the boss is nearly omniscient everyone is open to new types of discipline. Likewise, transparency facilitates new forms of Taylorism. As bugged computers, bar-code-tracked packages and satellite-tagged vehicles proliferate, redundant procedures and jobs can be eliminated and the extra work shifted to a core of intimidated and intensely supervised employees.

If this is what productivity means, can we take a break now?

3 Income

There's never been such a great time to be poor!
—Kevin Kelly, ex-editor, *Wired*

One of the supposed benefits of the New Economy is a new egalitarian-ism. Driven by dynamic markets, not stodgy old welfare states, it has re-portedly given us the toppling of old hierarchies, the erosion of inherited privileges, and the democratization of wealth. In fact, the distribution of income in the U.S. in the early 2000s is about the most unequal it's ever been—and the same can be said of the distribution of world income.

Not, of course, that many people care, or even notice. Back in the 1980s, income inequality used to be a hot political issue. Liberals wor-ried about it, and the idea that the rich were getting richer and the poor getting poorer suffused the popular culture. Conservatives often denied statistical reality—a right-wing media critic told me in the late 1980s that we must "live on different planets" if I thought U.S. incomes were polar-izing. Maybe—but I was the one living on earth: in 1980, the richest fifth of Americans had incomes about ten times those of the poorest fifth; a decade later, that multiple had grown to twelve.

Polarization continued well into the 1990s and beyond—in 2001, the richest fifth had incomes over fourteen times that of the poorest fifth—but with much less political impact. Maybe people have gotten used to it, or maybe enough crumbs reached people below the bulge bracket in the last years of the boom to dull discontent. In the 1980s, real incomes at the middle and lower levels were heading down; in the late 1990s, they were heading up—not as rapidly as those in the upper brackets, but probably enough to soothe. A more cynical interpretation of the disappearance of inequality as a political issue is that liberal pundits became a lot less interested in the problem when there was a Democrat in the White House; it was a lot easier to blame Ronald Reagan than it would be to blame the structural workings of American capitalism. With a Republican back in power, we're hearing a bit more about polarization, but only wimps obsess about inequality when there's a fifty-year war against terror to fight.

Why *should* anyone care about income inequality? Certainly the irrepressible Sylvia Nasar (1999) of the *New York Times*—a rare journalist with formal economics training—has no problem with it. Drawing on the work of economist Finis Welch, Nasar argues that the more egalitarian days of yore were also times of racism and sexism, and "it is hard to believe that most Americans would prefer" going back to those days! Why racism and sexism would be the prerequisite for more egalitarianism she doesn't say; all evidence is that both contribute heavily to inequality. She further argued that "most ordinary Americans...seem to feel that, whatever has happened to the income distribution, opportunities abound—and not just for the rich." Most people may indeed believe that, but Nasar didn't bother to investigate whether it's true. In fact, the U.S. is a lot less mobile than people think; most people don't move far from the station of their birth, and the U.S. is no more fluid than other countries.

But some of us find it disturbing that a lucky handful should worry about renovations on their third houses when hordes of people live on the sidewalks of the richest country in the world. And for a society that's supposed to be democratic, inequality of income and wealth means an inequality of political participation and influence (the poorer people are, the less likely they are to vote, and it's only the well-off who can write $1,000 checks to senatorial candidates). As the table below shows, the affluent are strongly overrepresented among the electorate, and the nonaffluent, underrepresented. Optimists might attribute the nonvoting behavior to a deep contentment with life, but that's a bit hard to believe.

income and voting turnout, 1996					
	percent of			turnout, percent of	
	population	citizens	voters	population	citizens
less than $25,000	26.3	24.6	19.2	40.9	47.2
$25,000–49,999	30.4	30.7	30.5	56.1	60.0
$50,000 and up	34.0	35.3	42.4	69.9	72.5
Columns don't add up to 100% because 9.3% of the population didn't report its income. *Source: U.S. Census Bureau 1998.*					

Leaving aside moral and political objections to inequality, there are medical consequences as well: the lower the class, the worse the health. Going beyond such static measures, even interruptions in income of the sort caused by unemployment have adverse health effects (Kaplan and Lynch 1997). And "sustained economic hardship leads to poorer physical, psychological, and cognitive functioning"—with consequences that last a decade or more (Lynch et al. 1997). Contrary to prevailing wisdom, it's very difficult to pull yourself up by your own bootstraps.

No one can take the crackpot science of *The Bell Curve* (Herrnstein and Murray 1994) seriously when it attributes alleged racial differences in intelligence to genetic differences. But more reputable racialized analyses may also be seeing biological causes in place of social ones—even for purportedly measurable factors like birth weights (theorized to be lower in blacks than whites for genetic reasons) and hypertension (theorized to be more prevalent among blacks than whites, also for genetic reasons). Low incomes, unpleasant occupations, and sustained discrimination may result in apparently physical symptoms that confuse even sophisticated biomedical scientists (Muntaner et al. 1997; Krieger and Sidney 1996). Higher incomes are also associated with lower frequency of psychiatric disorders, as are higher levels of asset ownership (Muntaner et al. 1998).

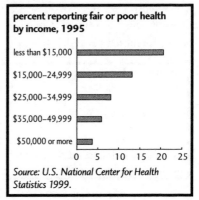

percent reporting fair or poor health by income, 1995

Source: U.S. National Center for Health Statistics 1999.

Distributing income

There have been several long waves of polarization and depolarization throughout U.S. history. Early America, from colonial days through the first years of the nineteenth century, was notable for having a far more egalitarian distribution of income than Europe—if, that is, you overlook the slaves. But, of course, you shouldn't overlook the slaves. While adding them to the calculation of wealth distribution wouldn't bring early America up to the level of European inequality in the mathematical sense, the presence of so large a group of people deprived of freedom and wealth is egregious enough to outweigh the rest.

But even the relatively egalitarian distribution among whites wasn't to last. Right-wingers who love to quote Alexis de Tocqueville on the wonders of the American way of life rarely include this observation by the French visitor: "I am of the opinion...that the manufacturing aristocracy which is growing up under our eyes is one of the harshest that ever existed....The friends of democracy should keep their eyes anxiously fixed in this direction; for if a permanent inequality of conditions and aristocracy...penetrates into [America], it may be predicted that this is the gate by which they will enter" (quoted in Williamson and Lindert 1980).

And enter they did. There was a steady increase in inequality—both in income and wealth—from the 1820s through the Civil War, bringing the U.S. up to European levels of lopsidedness. Though inequality probably dipped a bit during the war, it resumed its rise—at roughly the same rate as before—probably continuing through the outbreak of World War I. (Wars usually lessen the degree of inequality; they require the mobilization of unskilled workers to make armaments, pushing up low-end wages, and wartime inflations can ravage old fortunes.) Inequality quickly returned to prewar levels during the 1920s (Williamson and Lindert 1980; Steckel and Moehling 2000). The driving forces were industrialization, which created great wealth alongside great poverty, and urbanization, which separated workers from the means of production.[1] But aside from those macro relations, wealth inequality also appears to have increased within population groups as well—a feature that would reappear in the next great polarization, the one that began in the 1970s.

The 1929 crash, depression, and another world war ended the long polarization of wealth. Fortunes were destroyed in the 1930s, and the inflation of the 1940s ate away at inherited fortunes. The first few decades after the end of World War II were famously a time of almost universal upward mobility in the U.S. Real incomes across the distribution grew strongly and in parallel, with incomes of the poorer half of the population even outgrowing those of the richer over some periods, resulting in a mild compression of the income distribution (that is, a trend toward greater equality).

Of course, even at its most egalitarian postwar moment, the U.S. remained a polarized society, but it was still widely thought that something had changed to make the new arrangements permanent. In 1955, Simon Kuznets published his famous "inverted U" theory of capitalist evolution: that income inequality rises in the early stages of development and falls as economies mature. Economists came to believe this as a fact of their "science," and you still hear it from development specialists at the World Bank and in academia to excuse the vast increase in inequality in the Third World over the last fifteen years. Recent U.S. experience suggests that Kuznets's U may have another tail to tell.

U.S. income inequality has been on an uptrend since the late 1960s. The point is made most clearly by the graph below of the Gini index, the most common measure of inequality. In a perfectly equal society, the Gini would equal zero, and in a society where one person had all the income, it would equal 1. The index makes little sense as a freestanding statistic, but it's useful in tracing one society over time or comparing different societies at once. Though the Gini could theoretically be anywhere between 0 and 1, the real-world extremes are places like Brazil, where it approaches .600, and Sweden, where it comes in around .220.[2]

The graph here is cobbled together from two sources, and its first half should be taken with a grain of salt, since it's based on ambitious estimates rather than

income inequality
(Gini index)
U.S., 1913–2001

See text for explanation. *Sources: 1913–1946, Smolensky and Plotnick 1992; 1947–2001, U.S. Census Bureau.*

the Census Bureau's rigorous annual surveys. But it does show the polarizing trends of the late 1910s and 1920s, the leveling trends of the 1930s through the 1960s, and the polarization ever since. At the dawn of the twenty-first century, incomes were distributed more unequally than at any time since the early 1930s.

There are several reasons for this increased polarization. At the top end, there's been a tremendous increase in elite compensation, from megabucks sports and film stars to stock-option-laden CEOs. The strength of the

real pay through the distribution, 1973–2002

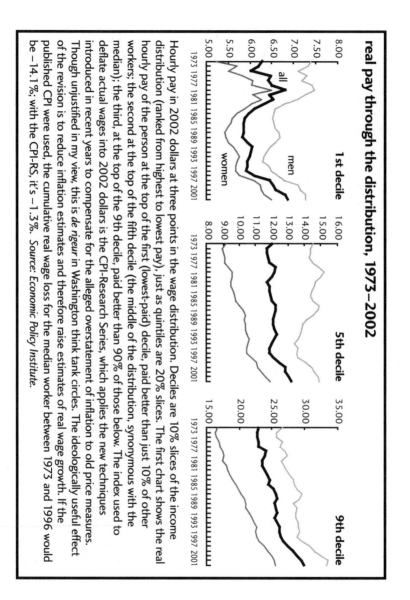

1st decile · 5th decile · 9th decile

all · men · women

Hourly pay in 2002 dollars at three points in the wage distribution. Deciles are 10% slices of the income distribution (ranked from highest to lowest pay), just as quintiles are 20% slices. The first chart shows the real hourly pay of the person at the top of the first (lowest-paid) decile, paid better than just 10% of other workers; the second at the top of the fifth decile (the middle of the distribution, synonymous with the median); the third, at the top of the 9th decile, paid better than 90% of those below. The index used to deflate actual wages into 2002 dollars is the CPI-Research Series, which applies the new techniques introduced in recent years to compensate for the alleged overstatement of inflation to old price measures. Though unjustified in my view, this is *de rigueur* in Washington think tank circles. The ideologically useful effect of the revision is to reduce inflation estimates and therefore raise estimates of real wage growth. If the published CPI were used, the cumulative real wage loss for the median worker between 1973 and 1996 would be –14.1%; with the CPI-RS, it's –1.3%. *Source: Economic Policy Institute.*

stock market between 1982 and 2000—and, somewhat more obscurely, the
long bull market in bonds that has accompanied the decline in interest rates
since their early-1980s peaks—greatly expanded the income of the very
rich who own most investment assets. Income from capital gains doesn't
appear in conventional income surveys, so most official stats understate the
growth inequality. But even those have traced a tremendous polarization.
Capital gains aside, the last twenty-five to thirty years have seen an increase
in the share of total income coming from regular returns on investment
(interest, dividends, and rent), and a decline in the share of labor income
(wages, salaries, and fringe benefits). And labor incomes themselves have
become more unequal. Roughly speaking, from the mid-1970s to the
mid-1990s, real hourly pay for the bottom third of the pay distribution
fell, pay at the middle was pretty flat, and pay at the top rose nicely—with
women doing better than men (see charts on page 85). Real wages across
the distribution picked up in 1996, but they weakened with the rise in
unemployment after 2001. But despite those late-1990s gains, real pay for
most U.S. workers is lower today than it was in 1973.

The standard explanation for the flourishing at the top and the stagnation and decline below is what economists call an increasing return to
skill—that is, the wage premium earned by the well-educated has expanded.
A problem for skills-based explanations is that the major erosion of pay
happened at the bottom end in the late 1970s and early 1980s—before the
proliferation of small computers, the operation of which is the major skill
proponents of this theory like to talk about. And that would fail to explain
the uptick in wages in the late 1990s, a time of heavy technoproliferation
(Howell 2000). It's also hard to reconcile with the fact that the distribution
of educational attainment has long been growing less, not more, unequal.

Even classic statements of this skills argument, like that of Juhn, Murphy, and Pierce (1993), find that the standard proxies for skill like years of

education and years of work experience (proxies being needed because skill is nearly impossible to define or measure) only explain part of the increase in polarization—less than half, in fact. Most of the increase remains unexplained by statistical models, a remainder that is typically attributed to "unobserved" attributes. That is, since conventional economists believe as a matter of faith that market rates of pay are fair compensation for a worker's productive contribution, any inexplicable anomalies in pay must be the result of things a boss can see that elude the academic's model.

Those of us who are not constrained by a faith in the correlation of pay and productivity, or who don't accept conventional definitions of what constitutes productive labor, will want to look elsewhere. Leading culprits are racial, sexual, and other forms of discrimination; the declining power of unions; the eroding value of the minimum wage; cutbacks in social spending (welfare and unemployment benefits act as a kind of floor under the wage—as the floor is lowered, so too are wages, especially at the bottom); persistent labor market turbulence (layoffs, restructurings, givebacks) that put workers on the defensive and weaken their bargaining power; relatively high rates of unemployment, even in good times (not true in the late 1990s, but true for the twenty previous years[3]); and, more controversially, the increasing importance of international trade and immigration.

Income up close

"Boom" is the word typically used to describe the U.S. economy from about 1995 through 2000. The word is well-earned if you owned stocks or ran a Fortune 500 company. But at less lofty levels, the boom is a bit harder to discern. The median U.S. household—the one in the very middle of the income distribution, with half the households above it and half below—was only just a hair better off in 1998 than it was in 1989. In fact, the great economic achievement of the mid-1990s was recovering from the income losses of the early 1990s. Income growth at the middle was fairly robust late in the decade, but the recession undid a good bit of that work, bringing median incomes in 2001 to a level just 6% above that of 1989. Poorer households—those in the bottom 20% of the income distribution—still didn't recover to 1989's level until 1997, and as of 2001, they were less than 5% higher than twelve years earlier. The economy was growing pretty nicely—GDP per capita was up 23% between 1989 and 2001. Growth wasn't trickling down much.

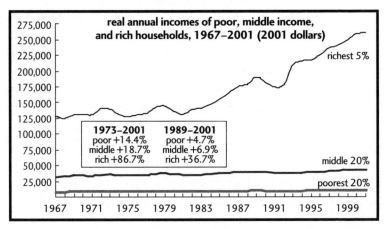

So where'd all the growth go? More than half (54%) the growth in household income between 1989 and 2001 went to the richest 20% of the population, with half of that going to the richest 5%. (Though these Census Bureau figures don't show it, other sources show that those gains mainly went to the top 1%; more on this in a bit.) Inequality of family incomes in 2001, as measured by the Gini index, was at its highest ever since the Census Bureau started publishing annual figures in 1947; ditto that for the broader category of households (which includes singles and nonfamily arrangements). Incomes, as we saw on the long-term chart on page 84, haven't been this polarized in seventy years.

The Census Bureau's annual income and poverty reports are the major source for such data in the U.S., but they have their deficiencies. They're based on the Current Population Survey (CPS), a canvass of 50,000 households (done jointly with the Bureau of Labor Statistics), whose main purpose is compiling the monthly employment and unemployment figures.[4] Every March, a special edition of the CPS asks some income questions. The process is nowhere near as rigorous as it could be, nor as other government surveys are; while incomes in the middle of the distribution comport pretty well with data from other sources, people at both extremes of the income distribution underreport their income—the poor frequently work off the books, and the rich don't like to talk about their investment income. Capital gains are excluded from income by the CPS's definition; this is important at the upper end. (Noncash benefits like Food Stamps and rent subsidies are also excluded, something that conservatives used to get exercised about in earlier decades; adding these to income would reduce inequality slightly, but not as much as adding capital gains would increase it.) Additionally, the homeless are missed entirely, and the rich generally consider answering survey questions beneath them. And, a final problem is that in order to protect the anonymity of survey respondents, all incomes above a certain amount (currently $1 million) are "topcoded," meaning that amounts above $1 million are treated as if they were a flat $1 million. While that doesn't impair the broad analysis of distribution, it does obscure what's happening in the upper reaches, which is where so much of the action has been over the last few decades.

One way around this limitation is to combine CPS data with tax data from the IRS, something the Congressional Budget Office (CBO) does periodically. An examination of the CBO data by the Center on Budget and Policy Priorities (Shapiro and Greenstein 1999) summarized in the following table shows that while the top fifth of the income distribution has done very nicely, the top 1% has done best of all.[5] The percentage changes

changes in income, 1977–1999					
	real income growth 1977-99	share of total income			income in 1999
		1977	1999	change	
poorest 20%	-9%	5.7%	4.2%	-1.5%	$ 8,800
second 20%	+1	11.5	9.7	-1.8	20,000
middle 20%	+8	16.4	14.7	-1.7	31,400
fourth 20%	+14	22.8	21.3	-1.5	45,100
top 20%	+43	44.2	50.4	+6.2	102,300
top 1%	+115	7.3	12.9	+5.6	515,600
Income is after federal taxes. *Source: Shapiro and Greenstein (1999)*					

in shares may seem small, but if the middle quintile had claimed the same share of income in 1999 that it did twenty-two years earlier, its average income would have been $3,500 higher; the poorest fifth, $3,300 higher (which is a lot when your income is $8,800). At the other end of the scale, the top 1%'s average income would have been $225,900 lower. Or looked at another way, had the *growth* in the top 1%'s share been distributed among the bottom 20%, their incomes would have been more than doubled, from a paltry $8,800 to a respectable $20,000.

Race and sex

This is to emphasize bad news a bit too much. There's no doubt that the tight labor markets of the late 1990s did a lot to bring up the incomes of poor and working-class Americans—a welcome reversal after more than twenty years of decline.

So far we've been looking mainly at the entire population, but it's important to look at how race and sex figure. As the first chart on page 91 shows, black households have been doing a bit of catch-up with whites. This is the combined result of broad income gains for black households since the early 1980s—at all income levels, except the poorest—and stagnant-to-declining incomes for the bottom 80% of the white population. Since 1993, even the poorest fifth of black households have enjoyed stronger income gains than whites. The gap remains huge, with average black incomes just 64% of non-Hispanic whites in 2001, but there's no de-

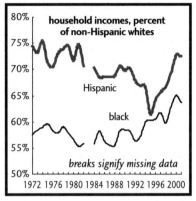

nying progress over the past decade. (It remains to be seen whether this progress will survive the attack on affirmative action.) For "Hispanic" households—a Census Bureau name and classification that many people object to, since it lumps together a highly diverse population into a single category—the news is mixed, with a bounce in recent years only partly compensating for a long earlier slide. That slide is the result of recent immigrants, many of them quite poor, bringing down the "Hispanic" average.

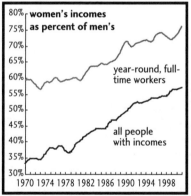

News on the gender gap is even more dramatic. Average incomes for all women were 57% of men's in 2001, a vast canyon for sure, but a lot better than 1980's 39%. Part of the reason for this gap is that fewer women work than men, and of those who do work, fewer work year-round full-time. For women who work outside the home, their incomes were 66% of men's in 2001, up from 47% in 1980 and 38% in 1970; for those who work a full schedule, their incomes were 76% of men's, up from the 60%

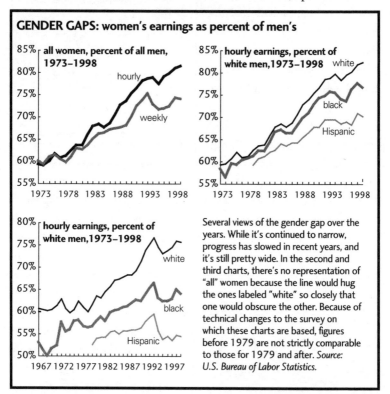

GENDER GAPS: women's earnings as percent of men's

Several views of the gender gap over the years. While it's continued to narrow, progress has slowed in recent years, and it's still pretty wide. In the second and third charts, there's no representation of "all" women because the line would hug the ones labeled "white" so closely that one would obscure the other. Because of technical changes to the survey on which these charts are based, figures before 1979 are not strictly comparable to those for 1979 and after. *Source: U.S. Bureau of Labor Statistics.*

average that prevailed through most of the 1970s. As with the black–white gap, this narrowing is the joint product of sometimes stagnant, sometime eroding male incomes and rising female ones; men's real incomes in 1998 were just 1% above 1989 levels, while women's were 14% above.

The gender gap has been narrowing for several reasons. Men's earnings, especially of those at the bottom of the educational and pay scales, have been slipping. Deindustrialization destroyed a lot of high-paying male jobs, and what is delicately called "deunionization" has lowered the pay of others. And, more pleasingly, women's earnings have been rising across the spectrum, both because they entered high-paying and largely

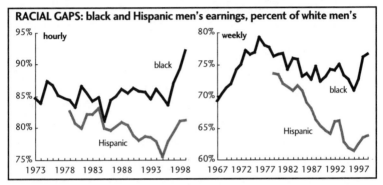

RACIAL GAPS: black and Hispanic men's earnings, percent of white men's

male occupations, and because they've been closing the gender gap within occupations. Until recently, women had been entering the labor force at progressively higher wage rates relative to men. Women aged 20–24 earned 76% as much as men the same age in 1979, and 96% in 1993; those between 25 and 34 went from 67% to 83%—but by 1999, both numbers had slipped a bit. It may be that weakened affirmative action programs and the male bias of the higher paying new jobs are responsible, or it may be that the predominant maleness of higher-paying jobs in high tech are the culprits, but we don't know for sure yet.

Putting race and sex together, we discover that white men, though still the best paid demographic group on average, have been slipping over the last two decades; white women have been gaining; some black men have been entering high-wage work, while others have been slipping into low-wage work, chronic unemployment, and prison (though the tight labor markets of the late 1990s helped narrow the racial/ethnic gap in male earnings rather sharply); some black women have been trickling into high-wage employment, though most remain concentrated in low-wage sectors; and Latino men and women have been entering the workforce in large numbers, though mostly at the poorly-paid end, with minimal penetration of higher-wage sectors (Williams 1999).

Why race and gender gaps?[6]

According to classic economic theory—most notably that enunciated by Gary Becker—discrimination is "irrational" under capitalism and it should be competed away. That is, if firms paid white men more than nonwhite nonmen for the same work, then those indulging their prejudices would make less money than those who'd transcended prejudice—and since no sane capitalist would ever forego a profit opportunity, over time discrimination should disappear. And if it doesn't? Either the "prejudice" is rational—that is, white guys are more productive than their Others, and so deserve their wage premium—or the economy is insufficiently competitive, in which case deregulation is called for.

In actual historical experience, rather than in the fantasy lives of Chicago-school economists, prejudices have been overcome only through organized political action, like the civil rights and feminist movements, with the assistance of government antidiscrimination and affirmative-action programs.

There are many reasons the gaps persist. Broadly, they can be divided into what happens before individuals reach the job market (family and neighborhood background, education) and what happens once they get there (channeling into certain raced and gendered occupations—occupational crowding—and pay discrimination after the slots are filled).

Let's look first at gender gaps. While women have moved into executive and professional occupations, below the elite level, many jobs remain highly gendered. Truck drivers, mechanics, and electricians remain overwhelmingly male (97% and higher); kindergarten and pre-K teachers, secretaries, and child-care workers, overwhelmingly female (also 97% and higher). These persistent segregations matter because in general, female-dominated industries pay less. In 1998, occupations that were over 90% male had a median wage almost 10% above average; those over 90% female, almost 25% below. More rigorously, one study (Dorman and Hagstrom 1997) found that a 30% increase in the female share translated into a 10% decline in average pay—and this is in addition to what discrimination individual workers would face. Another study (Bayard et al. 1999) estimates that a quarter to a half of the gap comes from occupational gender segregation, with yet another (Groshen 1991) coming up with even higher numbers. A widely cited study by David Macpherson and Barry Hirsch (1995) found the female share to make a rather small contribution to the overall pay gap, but their results depend heavily on imputing "unmeasured skills and preferences"—a fancy way of saying that women work in low-wage occupations because they like to. The reasoning goes: women with family responsibilities may prefer jobs with flexible schedules; jobs with flexible schedules may pay less; therefore, lower pay is an expression of preferences! QED. Let's not ask why jobs with flexible schedules pay less, or women have a disproportionate share of family responsibilities. It seems safe to conclude from all this that occupational segregation accounts for part of the gender gap, but not all.

Teaching offers an interesting case study. Women account for 38% of all college and university teachers; the field's average pay is 74% above the national average.[7] But below that elite level—where 87% of teachers teach—74% are women, and pay is 25% above average. Within that field, the highest-paid are secondary school teachers, just 56% of them women; the lowest-paid—20% below the national average—are kindergarten and pre-K teachers, 98% of them female. Elementary and special-ed teachers, a bit over 80% of whom are women, earn above average, but not as much above as secondary school teachers. The higher the level, the more men, and the better the pay.

One reason for these gradations may be that "caring" professions pay less than noncaring ones, all else being equal. Doctors require far more formal training than financiers, but earn less; the American economy values someone who tends to a sick balance sheet more highly than one who tends to a sick human. Within medicine, fields like family practice and psychiatry, which involve more than casual levels of personal contact, pay less well than those like brain surgery that don't. Day-care workers (99% women) are paid less than parking lot attendants. The underlying reason seems to be that "caring" jobs are seen as feminine, and that they involve the kinds of tasks that women do at home without pay (and often without any notice or gratitude)—with presumed emotional rewards reducing any claim for material reward (Cato 2000).

Having children is bad economic news for most women. The rationale is that time taken off to care for them results in slower accumulation of skills, which allegedly justifies lower pay over the long term. There's not much empirical evidence that women's productivity suffers from a maternity leave, and most new mothers return to work fairly quickly, but there's no doubt the hit to pay is real. Kimberly Bayard and colleagues (1999) found that the birth of a child translated into a 2% decline in earnings and slower earnings growth over the following decade. Other researchers have found that women with kids earn 10–15% less than otherwise similarly situated women without kids, and the gap seems to have been widening in recent years.[8] The opposite is true for men; fathers earn more than childless men (Waldfogel 1998). Waldfogel also offers evidence that women in countries offering maternity leave—and working for U.S. employers that offer maternity leave—enjoy a far smaller motherhood penalty than those without such a benefit. If women are permitted to return to their old jobs after giving birth, instead of quitting and then looking elsewhere when they're ready to work again, they take a much smaller hit to their earnings.

Even after accounting for occupational sorting and breaks in work experience, women suffer discrimination. Economists explain wages based on several inputs, like education, work experience, occupation, and industry. So if women who seem the equal of men, or blacks of whites, on these variables are nonetheless paid less, then discrimination is the likely reason. The invaluable team of Francine Blau and Lawrence Kahn (2000) found that even after correcting for all the relevant variables, women were paid about 12% less than men.

Such a technique misses discrimination's earlier or less measurable effects: discrimination affects access to education, for example, and people who experience early discrimination may shrink back in discouragement, not bothering to fight for a better job. Controlling for occupation obscures the fact that a large part of the pay gap comes from the channeling of women into lower-paying occupations. In other words, these sorts of studies control for things that shouldn't, in the final analysis, be controlled for. But they do prove that even when women do everything "right," they're still discriminated against.

Of course, economists who want to deny the persistence or severity of discrimination will trot out the excuse that "unobserved" differences are at work—the white guys *are* more productive dodge. Or, as Gary Becker (1985) surmised, women's devotion to housework lowers the effort they put into market work, and therefore (justifiably) lowers their pay.

There are some other interesting approaches to testing the reality of discrimination without getting into the complexities of statistical wage modeling. A study of graduates of the University of Michigan law school (cited in Blau and Kahn 2000) found that the gender gap in pay was tiny in the years just after graduation, but widened to 40% fifteen years after graduation. Some of that can be explained by women's preferences for shorter hours, or time taken off for motherhood (though these "preferences" are themselves shaped by social conventions dictating women's special domestic responsibilities). But even controlling for family status, grades, region, hours worked, and all other relevant demographic variables, men still enjoyed a 13% pay advantage. Other studies of gender—and racial—discrimination come up with results in that neighborhood: even after all relevant variables are accounted for, women (and blacks) suffer a pay hit of 10–15% relative to men (and whites). And, again, the "relevant variables," like education and work experience, are themselves shaped by discrimination.

Blau and Kahn also review several experimental studies of gender discrimination, which have been replicated with racial discrimination too. One researcher sent out pseudo-applicants for waiting jobs at high-end Philadelphia restaurants. Women were 40 percentage points less likely to get an interview, and 50 points less likely to get the job. Another study showed that when orchestras started putting applicants behind screens, women were far more likely to get the job than in the days when they were visible to their juries.

You can say much the same about racial discrimination: discrimination affects blacks and Hispanics before they enter the job market and after. Mainstream apologists solemnly offer "education" as the cure, as if that cure weren't already being tried. Since the end of slavery, black American have been persistently narrowing their education deficit relative to whites, but incomes have failed to keep up with this narrowing. A point made by the economist Patrick Mason (1998a; 1998b)—whose website <garnet.acns.fsu.edu/~pmason/research.html> is a rich source of research on discrimination—is that black educational performance is actually much higher than many people might expect. The best predictor of educational attainment is the attainment of parents, and by that measure, African Americans outperform similarly situated whites.[9] In other words, while black educational attainment is a bit less than white on average, the gap for the previous generation was significantly wider—something you could say going all the way back to the 1860s. This extra effort is exactly the kind of thing economists mean when they talk about "unobserved productive attributes," but it doesn't seem to translate into an appropriately large paycheck.

African Americans, then, have persistently swum upstream, white folk-wisdom to the contrary. Yet the economic payoff has been quite elusive, to put it mildly. Comparing otherwise similarly situated blacks and whites—similar, that is, in terms of education, work experience, occupation, and other relevant demographic variables other than race—blacks are still paid about 10% less than they "should" be, according to the predictions of standard economic models. One can safely conclude that that difference is pure discrimination.

It's not just "race" that is the cause of discrimination, it's skin shade as well. A study of dark- and light-skinned black men from the same neighborhood of Los Angeles—meaning that such variables as schools and living environment are controlled for—showed that the lighter-skinned were 52% more likely to be employed than their darker neighbors; other studies have shown that lighter skin means higher pay and otherwise "superior life chances." Similar results obtain with Latinos (Darity and Mason 1998).[10]

Finally, job-applicant experiments exploring racial discrimination have come up with results similar to those cited for gender. In one study (cited in Darity and Mason 1998), black and Hispanic applicants were three times as likely to be rejected as whites, even though applicants were trained to give similar responses in interviews, and were outfitted with indistinguishable résumés.

Apparently irrationality is a bit harder to wipe out than a free-market economist might think.

It's also worth noting two forms of discrimination that get a lot less attention than the racial and sexual kind—discrimination against gays and lesbians, and against people with disabilities.

A staple of homophobic discourse since at least Roman times has been that same-sexers are a privileged group, exemplars of an upper-class decadence. Today you hear this from the Christian right and even some fundamentalist Maoist sects. The privilege argument is used to discredit antidiscrimination campaigns: why grant this "well-off" segment of the population any "special rights" above what they already have? The work of M.V. Lee Badgett (1995; 1998) reveals this to be unfounded nonsense. She's found that gay men earn about 4–7% less than the average straight man. Lesbians seem to suffer the ordinary discrimination against women, but no additional economic injury for their sexual preferences—but certainly no special privilege in their salaries either.

As Marta Russell (1999) argues, our very notions of "disability" are intimately connected to one's ability to do market work. And for people with disabilities, the labor market isn't a friendly place. Unpublished studies by John McNeil of the Census Bureau show that 82% of people without disabilities between the ages of 21 and 64 are likely to have a job; for those with mild disabilities, the rate is 77%; for those with significant disabilities, the rate drops to 26%. Discrimination cases brought under the

Americans with Disabilities Act (ADA)—which businesspeople and their intellectuals hate with an intense and ugly passion—are resolved in favor of employers 92% of the time; of other comparable fields of law, only prisoners'-rights cases fare that badly. People with disabilities have poverty rates half again as high as the national average, and they're almost three times as likely to live in very low income households—a figure that the ADA appears to have had no effect on (Russell 2000).

Structural considerations

Aside from specific forms of discrimination, the general structure of wages and other incomes of a national economy should also be considered. For example, the U.S. is notorious for its large low-wage sector: this seems like a structural feature of our "dynamic" (or "chaotic" if you prefer), unregulated, and minimally unionized labor market. Discrimination assures that women and people other than whites are more likely to be slotted into low-wage jobs, but discrimination probably didn't create this feature in the first place. This wage structure is particularly noticeable in international comparisons of the gender gap: U.S. women are better educated and have more work experience relative to men than in most other First World countries, but the gender gap is as high as it is (see chart on page 102 for international comparisons) because of the highly polarized national wage structure, one characterized by low pay in the sectors that many women are slotted into, like retailing, and a large gap between the highly and modestly educated regardless of gender (Blau 1996; Blau and Kahn 2000).

New Economy to the rescue?

What did the New Economy do for the classic discriminations? Reinforced them, apparently. According to a study by Clinton's Council of Economic

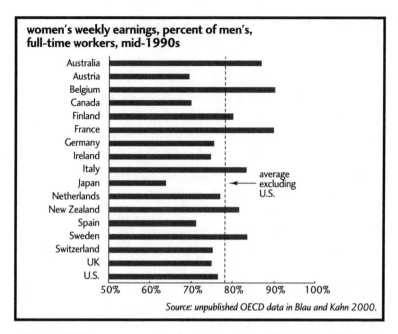

women's weekly earnings, percent of men's,
full-time workers, mid-1990s

Australia
Austria
Belgium
Canada
Finland
France
Germany
Ireland
Italy
Japan   ← average
Netherlands   excluding
New Zealand   U.S.
Spain
Sweden
Switzerland
UK
U.S.

50%   60%   70%   80%   90%   100%

Source: unpublished OECD data in Blau and Kahn 2000.

Advisors (2000), women are grossly underrepresented in the "core" infotech occupations, and those that are there are seriously underpaid. Before reviewing the numbers, however, a little perspective is in order. The CEA's list of core IT jobs included electrical and electronic engineers, computer systems analysts and scientists, operations and systems researchers and analysts, computer programmers, and computer operators. In 1998, these accounted for 2.0% of employment, and according to BLS projections, they'll account for 2.9% in 2008—roughly what "retail salespersons" account for, though they're a lot less fun to talk about.[11]

But the IT 5 were fast growing and generally high paying—with the exception of computer operators, who were at or slightly below the average. And it's little surprise that more than half of all computer operators are women, the highest female share of the five. The occupation with the lowest share of women, electrical engineers, is unsurprisingly the highest paying. In fact, the relation between the female share and pay is almost a perfect inverse correlation (r = −0.90). And the most rapidly growing occupations—computer scientists, computer programmers, and electrical engineers—are the three least female of the five. In other words, the evolving structure of IT employment is likely to widen the gender gap. And there's nothing on the horizon that seems likely to change that: women were 28% of undergraduate computer- and information-science majors in 1997, down from 37% in 1985, and the share of women getting master's degrees in those fields remains flat at 28% (Wood 2000).

Overall, weekly earnings of women in IT are 23% less than men's, and hourly earnings, 22% less. As is often the case, some of the gap can be explained by conventional measures. Controlling for educational attainment, age, and race reduces the gap to 17%. Controlling for occupation brings it down to 12%. Of course, these controls always beg a lot of questions—like why race should be brought in to explain gender gaps, when racial gaps themselves are products of discrimination; why the pay gap between young and old has widened so much over the last few decades; and why women are so often clustered in low-paying occupations and so frequently overlooked at promotion time.[12] So the effect of pure sex discrimination on pay is probably larger than 12%.

Regional outlook

It's worth a look at two regions that were microcosms of the "New Economy," insofar as there was such a thing: New York City and the Silicon Valley. While it doesn't have the high-tech concentration of the Silicon Valley (on which more in a moment), New York's economy is dominated by industries considered paradigmatic of the new order, like information and finance. Old-line manufacturing left a generation ago, making the city a laboratory of the postindustrial future.

And what did we find in this laboratory? One of the most unequal distributions of income of any jurisdiction in the First World. In 1997, New York City residents with taxable incomes over $1 million—0.3% of the population—claimed 20% of all income, while the 40% of city residents with incomes under $20,000 claimed 9% of income. Between 1987 and 1997, the millionaires' share more than doubled, at the expense of those in the middle ranks. The income share of the under-$20,000 set stayed flat, though their numbers increased substantially. At the same time, the ranks of those with middling incomes—those earning $20,000 to $125,000 (in 1997 dollars)—shrank, from 63% to 56% of the total (Jacobs 2000). What all these numbers mean is that the city, already highly polarized, polarized more intensely during the 1990s.[13] Meanwhile, poverty rose during the 1990s boom. Even the well-educated weren't immune; 24% of families with children headed by someone with some college were poor in the late 1990s, almost twice the level of ten years earlier. Of course, households with less education were much worse off, but, perversely, they represented a shrinking share of New York's many poor (Community Service Society 2000).[14] Unpublished estimates by economist Heather Boushey (personal communication) show a truly disastrous performance for low-wage workers, with the real hourly wage of the poorest-paid half falling by almost 20%, and the share of the workforce making less than $10.73 an hour (in 1999 dollars) rising from 30% in the late 1980s to 42% in the late 1990s. Only the best-paid tenth of workers got a real raise over the 1990s, and that a mere 2%. The real winners were the top 1–2%, who don't show up in such surveys. The main reason for such polarization is the extreme structure of the labor market, with highly-paid elite workers serviced by a very low-wage army of busboys and nannies, and not much in between.

In the Silicon Valley, an extremely well-paid and independent labor force coexists with one barely getting by. Productivity is among the highest of any region in the U.S., but the fruits of that productivity aren't widely shared, being claimed mostly by senior execs and financiers. Hourly wages for three-quarters of the Valley's workforce declined in real terms between 1989 and 1996; five of ten of the fastest-growing occupations paid less than $10 an hour (and some below $6). In electronics, in 1991 top execs paid themselves 42 times the average worker in 1991—and 220 times as much in 1996. Social indicators are often alarming, with vast numbers of workers without health insurance and pregnant women without prenatal care, precarious job security, rising high school dropout rates, and ground water laced with toxins. Almost one in five jobs don't meet Santa Clara County's definition of "self-sufficiency" for a single person, and more than half don't provide sufficiency for a family of four. Social-service workers say that requests for housing assistance quadrupled during the second half of the 1990s, and it's common to hear of three working-class families sharing a single house (Benner 1998; Ginsky 1999; Rojas 2000). And the recession has brought rampant unemployment, but not much relief from the stratospheric cost of living.

It goes without saying that the lower rungs in both New York and the Silicon Valley are occupied disproportionately by members of racial and ethnic minorities—though there are relatively large numbers of Asians in higher-end technical and financial occupations too.

Poverty

New Economy talk was mainly about riches—riches for all. So far, we've seen that it's meant mainly riches for some. What's been happening to people at the bottom end of the U.S. wealth distribution?

Over the long term, the composition of the group known as "the poor" has changed dramatically. Fifty years ago, poor people were likely to be Southern and rural; cities were still home to the industrial working class. Now, the population living below the poverty line is disproportionately urban, and living in families headed by single women (Levy 1998, chap. 2)—though poverty now, like the rest of America, has recently been moving out of the cities and into the suburbs.

The U.S. didn't get an official poverty line until 1965, as part of the target practice for the Johnson administration's War on Poverty, but the concept has a long history.[15] The broad project of studying the household budgets of the poor and working class goes back at least to the 1870s, a project motivated in large part by fear of unrest from below. In the U.S., immigrants were bringing radical ideas with them, which fermented dangerously in urban slums; unions were being organized and strikes being conducted—with the nationwide riots following the railway strike of 1877 having a particularly great impact. It was hoped that the collection of statistics might lead to the amelioration of the condition of the poor—and calm the unrest—but there's no simple relation between information-gathering and policy (Fisher 1997a). The U.S. has wonderfully detailed statistics of all kinds on the distribution of income, yet it also has the cheesiest welfare state and largest low-wage labor market in the First World.

Though the interest of the upper classes in the welfare of the lower classes was motivated largely by self-preservation, much of the actual research has been done by advocates for the poor, ranging from paternalistic liberals to revolutionary socialists. A disproportionate number of them have been women—something that continues to be the case—and much of the work has been done not by economists, most of whom are interested in things far more elevated than the welfare of the toiling masses, but by sociologists, social workers, union researchers, and government statisticians.

Though most poverty researchers have had meliorative intentions, not all have. In his excellent review of the history of the U.S. poverty line, George Fisher (ibid.) reviews the work of one Wilbur Atwater, who theorized that U.S. workers were too profligate in their food-buying habits, and that more careful provisioning would relieve employers of the need to pay higher wages. Atwater was particularly scandalized by the purchase of fresh fruits and vegetables, which he considered extravagant and of little nutritional value. He has been proven wrong—and not only about the nutritional value of fresh produce: studies have shown that the poor get more nutrients per dollar (or pound sterling) of food purchased than do more affluent shoppers.

Initially, "poverty" was defined not as material deprivation, but dependence on charity; around the turn of the last century, however, the definition shifted toward the lack of income. Around the same time there was a shift in the prevailing theories of the causes of poverty, from individual moral failings of the poor to structural economic and social reasons.[16] Curiously, poverty theory and practice over the last twenty years has revived nineteenth-century thinking, as conservative theorists like Charles Murray revived moral explanations; the liberal version of this shift was to emphasize not the tendency of the U.S. economy to produce lots of crummy jobs, but alleged skills deficiencies among the indigent. Also, with the end of welfare—thanks in large part to a Democratic president, Bill Clinton, and not just right-wing troglodytes like Murray—interest has shifted to getting the poor off the welfare rolls; even though most of those who lose their public assistance remain quite poor (Boushey 1999), no one in a position of intellectual or political authority really cares. As with many things, the New Economy seems to means return to the standards of a century ago.

Most pre–World War II efforts to devise a poverty line were based on assembling a basic market basket of goods and services necessary to keep body, if not soul, together, with minimal food budgets playing a prominent role. They varied considerably in generosity, ranging from the bare minimum necessary to sustain life to something approaching a reasonable degree of comfort—but many researchers strategically opted toward the minimal, so as not to appear to the better sorts as excessively generous. After World War II, however, most poverty lines were simply dollar figures plucked more or less out of the air.

The most momentous of these efforts turned out to be those of Mollie Orshansky, a researcher with the Social Security Administration, who published an article in the July 1963 of the *Social Security Bulletin* describing a set of proposed poverty thresholds for families with children. Orshansky didn't intend to devise a formal poverty line; she was merely trying to assess the relative opportunities for families of varying sizes.

Her basic technique was simple. The Department of Agriculture published a set of food budgets at varying levels of extravagance. The two that Orshansky used were called the "economy" and "low-cost" budgets, the economy version being extremely minimal, intended by its designers as a temporary emergency standard for families on hard times; it allowed just under 25 cents per meal in 1964 dollars, which would amount to about $1.38 today. The low-cost plan was only slightly more generous, allowing $1.78 per meal in today's dollars. Clearly, it would require extreme discipline and ingenuity to survive on that kind of budget.[17] Since the Ag Department also had research—dating from 1955—showing that the average family spent one-third of its income on food, a poverty line might be conceived of as three times the minimal food budget.

Orshansky followed up her 1963 paper with another published in 1965. Preprints of that paper were circulating around Washington in late

1964, just as the Johnson administration was looking for figures to set a poverty line. Of course, they used the lower of her estimates—the one based on the painfully stringent "economy" plan—and multiplied that level by three. They ignored more recent surveys showing that the share of income the average household devoted to food had declined from one-third to a quarter, which suggested that the multiplier should be four, not three, and which would translate into a significantly higher poverty line. The original low Orshansky numbers were adopted in 1965, and, aside from minor modifications, have just been adjusted for inflation ever since. The poverty line in 2003 is designed to represent the same purchasing power as it did on the day it was adopted in 1965.

In the jargon of the trade, the U.S. poverty line is an "absolute" one, based on a purchasing power fixed at a point in time and adjusted only for inflation over the years. The alternative is a "relative" measure, one defined as a percentage of average incomes that grows along with incomes.

A relative measure has several advantages. First, price indexes are notoriously devilish to work with; the recent controversy over the alleged overstatement of inflation by the consumer price index brought some of these difficulties into plain view. How do you adjust for improvements in quality? If the price of an item goes up, but its quality improves, did it really get more expensive? If the price of apples goes up, and that of pears goes down, what does that do to the price of fruit? The problems multiply over the long term: there were no VCRs or Palm Pilots in 1965; what does their development mean to the changed cost of living thirty-five years later? A relative measure avoids all these problems.

And second, relative measures comport much more closely with the way people perceive themselves. As no less revered an authority than Adam Smith (1976, bk. V, chap. 2, pt. 2, art. 4) defined it in 1776, poverty was characterized by the want of "necessaries," which he in turn defined as "not only the commodities which are indispensably necessary for the support of life, but whatever the custom of the country renders it indecent for creditable people, even of the lowest order, to be without."[18] People perceive themselves and others as poor or nonpoor by comparing them to their neighbors, not to some number invented by statisticians forty years ago and adjusted by another set of statisticians every year.

It's common among academic researchers to draw the poverty line at half the national median income. This habit is confirmed by results from the Gallup poll, which periodically asks people what their subjective impressions of a poverty line are; the results come pretty close to the half-the-median standard (which is about where Orshansky's original line fell).[19] In 1998, the poverty line for a family of three was $13,003 and $16,660 for a family of four. That year, half the median income for a family of three was $24,466 and $28,030 for a family of four—88% and 68% above the official poverty lines.[20] Even the modest assumption that the poverty line should be half again as high as it is would suggest a poverty rate of 22% in 1998, rather than the official 12.7% figure; on the less modest assumption that it should be 75% higher, the poverty rate would be 26%.[21]

Shown on the next page is a graph of the official poverty rate compared with a relative rate based on a poverty line drawn at 50% of the median, from unpublished data provided by John McNeil of the Census Bureau. (The graph stops in 1998 because McNeil retired, and no one has picked up the task.) It shows a steady uptrend into the early 1980s, and a gentle rise since, with a poverty rate of 22.3% in 1998—three quarters again as high as the official rate of 12.7%. Note that the relative rate shows less cyclical variation than the absolute one, since all incomes tend to fall in recessions and rise (though not always briskly) in expansions. Its stubborn flatness during the "boom" years of the 1990s suggests that no more bounty has been trickling down lately than it did in the previous two decades—the 1980s, now memorialized as an age of greed, and the 1970s, now memorialized as an age of stagflation and bad fashion.

The amount of money it would take to bring all officially poor households up to the poverty line is amazingly small: 0.5% of GDP, or just over 3% of the income of the richest fifth of households. It would take a bit more money to bring the poor up to a civilized standard, but not that much. Doubling the incomes of the poorest 20% of households— from an average of $10,136 (in 2001) to $20,272, which is still less than half the median—by taxing the richest 20% would require the affluent fifth to sacrifice less than 7% of their income, bringing it down from an average of $145,970 to a mere $135,834. That would reduce their share of the national

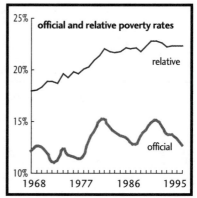

pie to late-1980s levels, hardly a period when the upper orders were suffering. But clearly it's much more important that the affluent be able to buy Hummers than to accomplish this bleeding-heart goal.

Who's poor?

Having reviewed the limits of the official U.S. poverty stats, it's now safe to look at what they say. Perhaps the most striking thing about the chart on page 112 is the flatness of most of its lines; the poverty rate in 2001, 11.7%, is exactly equal to 1979's rate, and is above 1973's all-time low of 11.1%—even though per capita GDP is up over 70% over the last three decades. And, remember, this is an absolute line, meaning that decades of economic growth have been essentially irrelevant to the officially poor.

There is a bit of good news in the chart—the continued decline in the black poverty rate, which reached an all-time low of 22.5% in 2000 (which is still scandalously high). The Hispanic poverty rate has been rising irregularly with the influx of new immigrants, who are generally a lot poorer than their predecessors.

While the poverty rate for people living in families is a bit lower than the overall rate, that for individuals living alone is almost 20%, and that for female-headed families is almost 28%, or almost twice the national average. The basic reason for this, all moralizing about husbandlessness to the contrary, is women's low pay and the minimal nature of the U.S. wel-

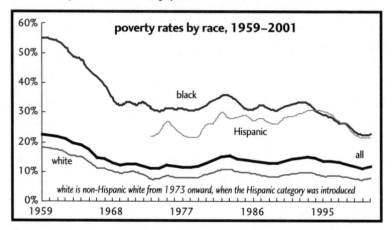

fare state (made even more minimal with the end of welfare). If women and men were paid equally, the poverty rate for single working women would fall by half, as would the overall poverty rate (Barko 2000; see also <www.aflcio.org/women/exec99.htm>).

A good deal of official poverty can be explained by the unemployment or underemployment—but not all. A report by the Conference Board (Barrington 2000), a business-sponsored research group, showed that even among the elite of the workforce—year-round, full-time workers—poverty rates have been meandering trendlessly for the last twenty-five years, rising a bit in bad times, falling a bit in good ones. But despite the "boom," the full-time workers' poverty rate actually rose between 1997 and 1998 to levels seen only in the recessions of the early 1980s and early 1990s. By contrast, the full-time worker poverty rate fell steadily between the early 1960s and early 1970s. But since then, "long-term economic growth has had little impact on poverty among full-time workers."[22] The poverty rate among such workers is admittedly low—only around 3%—but these are the best-positioned workers in the labor force, and the poverty line is a pretty undemanding benchmark. As the report's subtitle said, "America's Full-Time Working Poor Reap Limited Gains in the New Economy."

Inclusion of "the New Economy" isn't just PR spin; as the report points out, "an increase in the relative share of low-skill employment is one characteristic of this 'New Economy…,'" though "low-pay" is more relevant to the analysis than "low-skill." That's not what most New Economy rhetoric emphasized, of course, but the bubble's sales force never deployed much of rigorous evidence.

Apologists were quick to point out that the Conference Board's report didn't include the beneficial effects of the Earned Income Tax Credit (EITC), which has boosted the incomes of the working poor dramatically: in 1998, almost 20 million returns claimed the EITC, and $32 billion was paid to those who filed them (Herman 2000). That works out to an average of $1,600 per return, which is a lot better than nothing, but which amounts to just $4.38 a day. But while the official measure, on which the Conference Board relies, doesn't include the EITC (or Food Stamps), it also doesn't account for taxes or child-care expenditures. Since those deductions would outweigh the additions from the benefits, a poverty rate that more accurately measured resources available to people would be a couple of points higher than the official rate. And, though the EITC has improved the lives of millions, it really is a public subsidy to low-wage employers, and part of a political strategy to differentiate between the deserving (working) and undeserving (not working for pay) poor.

Mobility

A standard right-wing reaction to tales of poverty and inequality in the U.S. is to appeal to the allegedly stunning upward-mobility characteristic of American life (and it's always upward mobility in the standard version, never downward). Actually this isn't the case at all. And, as we'll see at the end of this chapter, U.S. mobility stats are little different from those prevailing in countries with far more egalitarian income distributions.

Mobility is often asserted as a virtue, as if the word is inseparable from its occasional modifier, "upward." But mobility works in both directions; someone who loses a $45,000-a-year job at an auto plant and ends up bagging groceries at the 7-Eleven is experiencing mobility, too. "Instability" and "volatility" are less-flattering synonyms that deserve wider currency.

The right's sacred text on mobility is W. Michael Cox and Richard Alm's essay "By Our Own Bootstraps," published in the Federal Reserve Bank of Dallas's 1995 annual report and incorporated wholesale into their terrible book, *Myths of Rich and Poor* (Cox and Alm 1996; 1999). While the class position of Fed research may not be to everyone's liking, it's usually rigorous and informative. Cox and Alm's stuff isn't. Their study was designed to make a point, and it stacked all the numbers accordingly.

Mobility studies are very sensitive to definitions, time scales, and data quality. Honest researchers slice the data several ways to see how robust the findings are; not Cox and Alm. They used all the sensitivities to their own advantage. They were out to prove that America is "the land of opportunity," the incomplete sentence that serves as their opening line. "Opportunity pervades our folklore," and folklore pervades their economics. They say that of the bottom quintile (fifth) of income earners in 1975, just 5% were still there in 1991; 60% were in the top two quintiles

They stacked their results in several ways. Because they made individuals, not households, the focus of their analysis—which they say is standard practice, though it isn't—subjects as young as sixteen qualified. So the lower ranks were swelled by teenagers who contributed vastly to mobility just by growing up. To compare incomes over time, they used changes in real (inflation-adjusted) incomes over time, rather than comparing them to prevailing averages of each moment—that is, they measured changes in absolute rather than relative incomes. While absolute changes matter some, most people judge their status and well-being against the rest of society, not against an ancient base fixed by a statistician. Peter Gottschalk's (1996) reworking of the numbers massively deflates their claims. Cox and Alm found that just 2% of those in 1975's bottom quintile remained there in 1991; by Gottschalk's calculation, 36% did. And instead of 39% ending up in the richest quintile, just 20% did. With relative measures—which Cox and Alm didn't use, of course—43% of 1975's bottom quintile would have remained there in 1991, and just 11% would have hit the top.

One reason that most studies of income and poverty are based on snapshots is that they're so much easier to do. The government's main monthly statistical effort, the Current Population Survey (CPS), polls its participating 60,000 households for the better part of a year, making it possible to track the same people over a short period of time, but by the next year, it's a new set of faces. If you want to trace what happens to representative real individuals over time, the CPS is useless.

Most long-term studies rely on the University of Michigan's Panel Study of Income Dynamics (PSID), which started tracking 5,000 families in 1968. As those families gave birth to new ones, they've been added to the study, but about half the originals have disappeared over the years (though specialists assure us that that doesn't matter). A serious drawback of the PSID is that it asks its most detailed work-and-income questions about the "head" of the household—the male of a married couple. He's asked to report on other members of the family, but the detail is poorer and the numbers probably less reliable than self-reported ones. As a result, most studies based on the PSID focus on men.

Mobility can be thought of as having long- and short-term aspects, or "permanent" and "transitory" components, as economists prefer to say. Additional schooling, experience, or a lucky or unlucky choice of occupation contribute to permanent mobility; job loss or an unusually good raise contribute to transitory mobility. In an influential 1994 study, Peter Gottschalk and Robert Moffitt took the measure of the two kinds of movement by looking at white men in the PSID. (They said their attention to white men was justified by their "stable labor market patterns" and their status as "the group most frequently examined in past work," as if those weren't two good reasons to broaden the inquiry.)

They found that two-thirds of the increase in wage inequality from the early 1970s through the late 1980s was caused by changes in permanent earnings, and about one-third from increasing transitory fluctuations. Most hit by transitory income shocks were workers without a high school diploma. So, not only did less-educated workers see their wages fall relative to those of more educated workers—they became a lot more likely to have a bad year. But the increase in instability affected white male workers in all age, education, and income categories. And both the volatility of weekly wages and the number of weeks worked per year increased. It's a constant of this field that income inequality has increased no matter how you slice it; as Lawrence Katz put it in a comment on the Gottschalk/

Moffitt paper, "Inequality has increased between skill groups and within them, between sectors and within them, between establishments and within them, and along both permanent and transitory dimensions."

What explains the increase in volatility? Deunionization, for one; union workers show more income stability than do nonunion ones. Not industry shifts, like that from manufacturing to services, though; almost all the increase in short-term instability was the result of changes within industries, not across them. Short-term volatility also increased for people who changed their jobs, either voluntarily or involuntarily; things were nearly stable for those who kept their jobs. Though other studies show little or no long-term trend toward greater job turnover (contrary to everyone's impression), it does seem that those who do lose their jobs have had a progressively rougher time of it.

What about upward mobility itself? Over the long term, found Peter Gottschalk and Sheldon Danziger, about 46% of male earners in the low-est quintile in 1968 had moved out of it by 1991—28% of whites and 54% of "nonwhites." That's not to say that they didn't enjoy increases in real income over the period; most did. But relative positions are pretty sticky. Greg Duncan, Johanne Boisjoly, and Timothy Smeeding (1995), also using the PSID, found that young workers who turned twenty-one sometime in the 1980s earned less to start and enjoyed smaller raises than those of the 1970s. This was true "of workers at all skill levels and from all types of parental background." Among workers who came of age in the 1980s, just 42% were able to earn a "middle-class income" (defined as twice the official poverty line for a family of three), and just 18% made it into the "heart of the middle class" (three times poverty). If you were black, came from a poor family, your mother was a high school dropout, and/or you didn't go to college, you did especially badly. Even among couples in which both work, and in male-female pairs in which the woman earned as much as

the man, the authors point out, those without a college degree (about 70%
of the workforce) would be "hard pressed to even reach middle class." Despite the late-90s clichés about stock trading, entrepreneurial Gen Xers,
most haven't been doing all that well, money-wise.

<table>
income mobility of families, 1969–1994					
		1994 quintile			
		poorest	2nd	middle	4th	richest
1969 quintile	poorest	41.0	24.9	16.2	12.1	5.8
	2nd	22.4	24.7	23.9	16.1	13.0
	middle	16.9	21.0	23.5	22.8	15.9
	4th	11.3	18.5	19.7	24.2	26.3
	richest	9.5	10.6	16.6	24.5	38.8
</table>

Table reads as follows: of the families in the poorest quintile of the income
distribution in 1969, 41.0% were still there in 1994, 24.9% had moved to the
second quintile, 16.2% to the third, etc. *Source: Economic Policy Institute, from
calculations by Peter Gottschalk <www.epinet.org/datazone/incmobil.html>.*

Long-term mobility is illustrated in the table above. Most income moves
are to nearby quintiles; long moves are rare. Ceilings seem stickier than
floors; people are more likely to stay in the top quintile than the bottom.

Wealth

Wealth is a lot more intensely concentrated than income, though it gets
less prominent attention from government statisticians. (Voyeuristic attention from the tabloids is another story.) Though the Census Bureau
does look at assets as part of its Survey of Income and Program Participation (SIPP), the best look at wealth comes from the triennial Survey of
Consumer Finances (SCF), sponsored by the Federal Reserve. The SCF is
based on extensive interviews with more than 4,000 households.[23] Aside

from the rigor of the interview—which involves reviewing financial records rather than the simple unaided Q&A process in Census income surveys—the SCF is unique in that it oversamples rich people, who are generally missed by most conventional surveys.

Wealth inequality matters a lot, maybe more than income inequality. Wealth insulates its lucky holders from personal economic crises, like unemployment and sickness. It offers the opportunity to go to school, start a business, or make big purchases without going into debt. It confers a degree of social prestige and political power. And it can be passed on across the generations. By contrast, income is a lot more ephemeral; you can have a good year, followed by a bad year. But wealth, if it's not recklessly invested, is usually there through thick and thin.

From the top

Arthur Kennickell (2000, 2003), who heads the SCF program, regularly urges people to look at the *Forbes* 400 for a picture of the top of the U.S. wealth heap; the SCF excludes that elite by design, along with "a relatively small number of very famous people." Not that this set would let surveyors into their posh houses for a look at their brokerage statements; *Forbes* reporters have to do educated guesswork to put their list together. It's amazing how little we really know about the people who own the world.

The *Forbes* gang has been doing very well lately. Between 1989 and 2002, the average wealth—assets less debts—among that posh group rose 133%. And, as the table on the next page shows, the higher you go up in the rankings, the better the performance: the wealth of the 400's poorest member rose a mere 44% over those thirteen years, while that of the richest was up 496%. The 400 as a group controlled over 2% of total personal wealth in 2002, up from 1.6% in 1989 and just 0.8% in 1982, just as the great millennial bull market was about to take off.

wealth of the *Forbes* 400, 1989–2002

rank	wealth, millions of 2001 dollars				percent change			
	1989	1995	2000	2002	1989–95	1995–2000	2000–2002	1989–2002
1	7,106	17,002	64,318	42,361	+139	+278	−34	+496
10	3,417	4,940	17,356	11,723	+45	+251	−32	+243
50	1,736	2,068	4,798	3,152	+19	+132	−34	+82
100	957	1,034	2,654	1,773	+8	+157	−33	+85
200	615	689	1,531	1,084	+12	+122	−29	+76
300	478	500	1,000	763	+5	+100	−24	+60
400	376	391	740	542	+4	+89	−27	+44
mean	921	1,025	3,057	2,148	+11	+198	−30	+133

Source: Kennickell 2003.

Things went pretty well for the three million Americans just below the *Forbes* 400—the richest 1%, though their best days may be behind them, as the graph below shows. In 2001, the richest 1% of the population controlled 38% of all wealth (excluding the principal residence)—a slightly smaller share than 1995's 42% of the wealth, which was their highest share since 1929's 48%, just before the great stock market crash. Concentration

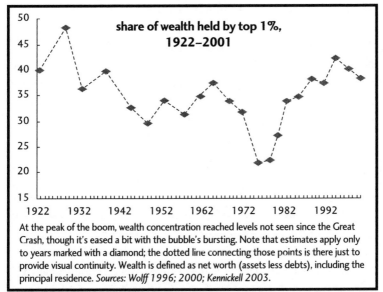

At the peak of the boom, wealth concentration reached levels not seen since the Great Crash, though it's eased a bit with the bubble's bursting. Note that estimates apply only to years marked with a diamond; the dotted line connecting those points is there just to provide visual continuity. Wealth is defined as net worth (assets less debts), including the principal residence. *Sources: Wolff 1996; 2000; Kennickell 2003.*

fell during the depression, as fortunes were wiped out, and plumbed great depths in the 1970s, contributing no doubt to the conservative counterrevolution. That counterrevolution got the wealth share rising from the early 1980s into the mid-1990s. But looked at over the very long term, it's striking that the top 1%'s share has oscillated around the 35% level for quite a long time. Even in the early ninetenth century, the richest 1% of New Yorkers controlled about 40% of the city's wealth (Wachtell 2003).

Enough about the upper crusts; what do things look like below? In a few words, the richest tenth of the population has a bit over three-quarters of all the wealth in this society, and the bottom half has almost none—but it has lots of debt. The bottom fifth owes more than it owns (meaning its net worth is negative).

Most middle-income people have most of their wealth in their houses. That allows them some security, and even an economic payoff sometimes, but as a form of wealth, it's limited. Yes, you can borrow against accumulated home equity, but you can't liquidate that equity very easily without moving onto the sidewalk. You can't draw down your residential wealth to start a business or pay college tuition bills. For that reason, most analysts of income and wealth distribution strip away the primary residence from the list of assets and the mortgage on that residence from the list of debts. So the figures I'm quoting refer to this concept, nonresidential wealth.

And that is very, very concentrated.[24] Many people know that income is highly concentrated in the U.S., but the wealth distribution numbers are far more skewed. The bottom half of the population claimed about 20% of all income in 2001—but only 2% of nonresidential wealth. The richest 5% of the population claimed about 23% of income, a bit more than the entire bottom half. But it owned almost two-thirds—65%—of the wealth. The richest 1% of the population—average wealth almost $12 million—took in about 15% of all income but held 38% of the wealth.

It's hard to see much democracy in the distribution of stock ownership. The bottom half of the population held 1.4% of total stock in 2001, with an average portfolio of just over $3,000. And since only a minority of bottom-half households own any stock, that average is deceptively high. The richest 10% own three-quarters of all stock—and that's figured by sorting people by their net worth, not their stockholdings. Many rich people, especially older ones, may be more interested in preserving capital or generating current

share of assets and debts by wealth grouping, 2001

	bottom 50%	next 40%	next 5%	next 4%	top 1%	top 10%
percentiles:	*0–50*	*50–90*	*90–95*	*95–99*	*99–100*	*90–100*
net worth	2.8%	27.4	12.1	25.0	32.7	69.9
assets	5.6	29.9	11.7	23.4	29.5	64.6
financial	2.5	25.4	14.1	26.6	31.5	72.1
liquid	6.0	32.7	13.3	21.9	26.2	61.3
CDs	4.3	53.5	17.3	18.7	6.2	42.3
savings bonds	4.1	45.4	10.0	21.8	18.5	50.4
bonds (direct)	0.2	4.0	8.8	22.6	64.4	95.8
stocks (direct)	0.5	11.4	9.9	25.3	52.9	88.1
mutual funds	0.9	20.5	17.9	32.6	28.1	78.6
retirement accounts	3.3	36.4	17.6	29.1	13.6	60.3
life insurance	7.2	46.5	15.6	18.0	12.7	46.2
annuities, trusts, etc.	0.3	13.0	12.1	28.2	46.4	86.6
miscellaneous assets	4.1	17.1	5.3	33.1	40.4	78.7
nonfinancial	7.8	33.1	10.0	21.1	28.0	59.1
vehicles	27.9	48.3	9.5	9.3	5.1	23.8
principal residence	12.3	50.6	12.2	16.0	9.0	37.1
other resisdence	1.9	26.8	11.7	30.5	29.1	71.3
nonresidential real estate	0.6	14.4	9.1	35.2	40.8	85.0
business	0.4	9.9	6.6	24.9	58.3	89.8
other	4.6	17.7	6.8	25.7	45.3	77.7
debts	25.9	47.9	8.6	11.6	5.9	26.1
principal residence	23.5	51.7	9.1	11.1	4.7	24.9
other residence	4.2	40.2	10.4	28.1	17.0	55.6
installment	48.0	37.5	5.7	5.2	3.6	14.5
lines of credit	13.8	23.5	5.0	28.5	29.2	62.8
credit cards	49.8	41.6	3.2	4.9	0.6	8.6
other	15.9	18.7	10.9	21.7	32.8	65.5
equity (direct + indirect)	1.4%	21.7	14.4	29.0	33.5	76.9
average	*$3,049*	*57,730*	*307,981*	*764,116*	*3,458,455*	
income	22.9%	38.1	9.2	15.3	14.5	39.0
average	*$31,868*	*128,377*	*263,767*	*976,727*	*[fix]*	
nonresidential net worth	1.8%	21.5	11.7	26.7	38.2	76.7
average	*$11,254*	*170,148*	*745,547*	*2,095,791*	*11,708,455*	

Share of assets and debts held by sections of the U.S. population ranked by net worth. Table reads as follows: The bottom 50% of the population holds 2.8% of net worth—5.6% of assets, and 25.9% of debts. Average dollar amounts for each wealth group are shown for the bottom rows; the bottom half of the population holds 1.4% of all stock hold directly and indirectly (as through mutual funds), with holdings averaging $3,049 (and since not all members of the category own stock, and large holdings can distort the average, this overstates the prevalence of stockholdings). *Source: Kennickell 2003.*

income than in maximizing the growth in their wealth, so they may hold bonds instead. If you sort households by their stockholdings (excluding pension), you find that the richest 1% of stockholders own over half the stock held by individuals; the bottom 80%, under 2%.[25] Adding pension accounts makes these figures only slightly less lopsided (see table below for details).

In his analysis of the 1998 SCF, Edward Wolff (2000) provided a fascinating estimate of how long households in each quintile of the wealth distribution could live on their savings; the figures for 1998 are shown in the table on the next page. Though the richest households could coast for more than two years, most households could sustain their current standard of living for no more than a month or two. The bottom quintile's projected financial lifespan was 0 for every survey since 1983; figures for the next two quintiles are below 1983 and 1989 levels; those for the richest quintile are by far the highest on record (a record that goes back to 1983).

Wolff's figures cover middle-aged households; Oliver and Shapiro (1995, p. 87) show that two-thirds of younger households—those "headed" by someone thirty-five or younger—were unable to sustain a poverty-level standard for three months, compared to 45% for households headed by someone aged thirty-six to forty-nine; 38% of white, 72%

distribution of stock ownership, 1998		
	without pensions	with pensions
top 0.5%	41.4 %	37.0%
next 0.5%	11.8	10.7
next 4%	27.7	27.2
next 5%	10.3	11.3
next 10%	7.2	9.8
bottom 80%	1.7	4.1
top 1%	53.2	47.7
top 10%	91.2	86.2
Source: Poterba 2000.		

of Hispanic, and 79% of black households who couldn't sustain a poverty standard for three months.

All these numbers point to a fundamental conclusion: despite myths of rampant wealth, most people don't have money to burn. By the old-fashioned definition of working class—people who couldn't make ends meet without a paycheck—the overwhelming majority of the U.S. population belongs, despite rumors of that class's social death.

Racial angle

Unfortunately, the major published reports on the SCF (Kennickell et al. 2000; Aizcorbe et al 2003) divide the population only into "white non-Hispanic" and "nonwhite or Hispanic" (and there's no gendered reporting at all). But there too, the wealth figures are stunningly more lopsided than income figures. In 2001, the average "white" household had an income 76% higher than that of the "nonwhite or Hispanic" household in 1998—but had a

on the edge
number of months financial reserves, 1998

quintile	current consumption	125% of poverty line
richest	25.2	81.5
fourth	8.2	18.4
middle	2.2	3.4
second	0.1	0.1
poorest	0.0	0.0

First column shows average number of months households headed by someone aged 25 to 54 in each wealth quintile could sustain their current level of consumption by drawing down their savings; second, how long a standard equal to 125% of the official poverty line could be sustained. *Source: Wolff (2000), based on the 1998 Survey of Consumer Finances.*

net worth (including residence) over seven times as high. Both numbers are significantly higher than they were in 1992—broad racial gaps have widened.

Wolff (2000) provides a lot more detail. For example, black incomes were 54% of white incomes in 1998—but black net worth (including residential) was 12%, and nonresidential net worth, just 3% of white. For Hispanics, incomes were 62% of white; net worth, 4%, and nonresidential net worth was 0%. Just under 15% of white households had zero or negative net worth, compared with 27% of black and 36% of Hispanic. Even at similar levels of income, black households were significantly less wealthy than white ones;

black households in the $25,000–49,999 income bracket had net worths equal to 46% of white averages; those in the $75,000+ category had 29% of white. Similarly with stock ownership: 54% of white households had some but just 30% of black ones did. And average black stockholdings were just 20% of whites'. The democratization of ownership has a way to go yet.

Wealth is an important part of the economics of race in America: it "sediments" privilege and deprivation (Oliver and Shapiro 1995, p. 5). Though blacks in general have much lower incomes than do whites, there's a vast racial wealth gap between households with otherwise similar demographic characteristics (like education and income). The reasons aren't hard to fathom: the first African Americans weren't merely forbidden to accumulate property, they *were* property, but even after emancipation, discriminatory laws and practices prevented blacks from accumulating wealth and passing it on to their children. So even middle-class blacks don't have the benefit of spare change in the bank to take advantage of a business opportunity or to survive a bout of sickness or unemployment. This has long been compounded by continued discrimination in mortgage and housing markets—which persists statistically even after income and other demographic factors are accounted for—denying many black Americans access to that major component of middle-class wealth, the owner-occupied house.

Optional effects

During the boom it was argued that wealth inequality had been reduced by the allegedly large number of workers receiving stock options from their employers. Now, of course, most of the options are worthless, except for those senior executives lucky enough to have their packages repriced. Back in 2000, though, the National Center for Employee Ownership estimated that between 7 and 10 million nonmanagerial workers received stock options in early 2000, up from just 1 million a year earlier. Managers, an earlier NCEO (1998) study conceded, still receive the lion's share of available options, and the later release fails to mention that even 10 million represents less than 10% of total employment—and frequently served as a phantasmic substitute for real money.

A San Francisco Fed study of the impact of IPOs on the California economy (Mattey 2000) estimated that some 134,000 employees enjoyed options on stock issued between 1997 and 1999, with an unrealized value of $68 billion (now, of course, largely melted away)—an average of $500,000 per lucky worker. That sounds like a lot, but the author failed to offer any perspective. Option-granted workers represented just under 1% of total employment in California, and their unrealized wealth equaled just 7% of the state's personal income. Big news for the optioned work-ers, for sure, and big news for the Northern California real-estate markets they inflated, but not something that changed the fundamentals of the U.S. economic hierarchy.

And finally, the Financial Markets Center examined fifty representative firms in the *Fortune* 500, and found that 21% of options were awarded to the top five executives. Nonmanagerial employees got little or none (Morrissey 2000).

The wider world

This survey so far has, provincially, looked only at the U.S., but it's time for a look at the world beyond New Economy headquarters. There are several ways to look at income distribution on the global level. The easiest is to compare average national and regional incomes over time. The advantages of this are that the figures are easily available and relatively up to date. The disadvantages are several. Average incomes—which usually mean GNP or

GDP divided by population—tell you nothing about distribution; Brazil and Poland are at roughly equal per capita income levels, but Poland's poor get three times the share of national income that Brazil's claim, and its rich a lot less.[26] Estimates of global income distribution that uses people, rather than nations, as the unit of analysis, are preferable, but are extremely difficult to produce. Thankfully, World Bank economist Branko Milanovic has made a first attempt, about which more in a bit.

Big picture

According to economic theory, the income gaps between rich and poor countries should narrow over time, as laggards "catch up" with leaders. Proponents of such theories assume that technology is the driving force behind economic development; as technology diffuses throughout the world, the advantage enjoyed by the pioneers should fade.

Reality has consistently failed to conform to this pleasing theory. Nearby are several charts showing long-term estimates of global income gaps for the major regions of the world, as well as for several important countries. All "developing" regions are farther behind the U.S. than they were in the nineteenth century. For most—East Asia being a prominent exception—the last two decades have been a time of backsliding, not progress. Eastern Europe, a region dominated by Russia, did a bit of catching up between 1929 and 1973 (that is, during the "socialist" period, now universally derided as a failure), progress that's since been turned into considerable regress. Japan made stunning progress between 1950 and the late 1980s but has since hit a wall. You could say much the same about South Korea. Britain fell behind the U.S. in the late nineteenth century and has stayed there; the rest of Western Europe did some catching up in the first thirty-five or forty years after World War II, but that rise has since flattened out. China's been making rapid progress, but it still has a long way to go.

This isn't too surprising to anyone who thinks power matters a lot in economic development. Technology doesn't "diffuse" like squid ink in ocean water. Leaders guard their technological secrets jealously, and the U.S. has been pushing for even tighter intellectual-property restrictions in global trade talks since the Reagan years. Poorer countries, most of them with heavy debt burdens, can't afford to invest heavily in education; they're lucky to get people through high school. For all capitalism's admitted dynamism, the global economic hierarchy has remained remarkably stable for more than a century.

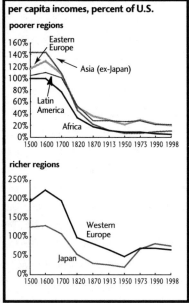

Global shares

Let's move beyond the geographical abstractions of nations and regions and look at the world's people. At the most extreme level, 1.3 billion people, or almost one-quarter of the world's population, lived on less than $1 a day in 1993, 3 billion, nearly half the world's people, on less than $2 a day (World Bank 1999). As a share of the world's population, those figures are barely changed from the World Bank's first poverty exercise in 1985. About a quarter of East Asians and Latin Americans live on $1 a day or less, and about 40% of South Asians and Africans. There was a slight lessening of absolute poverty in East and South Asia between the mid-1980s and mid-1990s, and a slight worsening in Latin America and Africa, but overall, global poverty figures seem immune to overall economic growth. Every region mentioned had positive economic growth figures for the 1980s and 1990s, but poverty rates hardly budged.

The World Bank poverty numbers have been severely criticized on several counts (Reddy and Pogge 2003). They use an arbitrary poverty line, divorced from any cultural or social context. Many of the surveys they rely on are far from exhaustive, and they rely on currency conversions that may understate the real cost of living. These points are well taken, and the World Bank estimates no doubt understate the case, but even their numbers are huge.

It's easy for those of us who live in rich countries to forget that most people don't live like we do. Thanks to Branko Milanovic, we can put some firm numbers on the observation. Milanovic has made a pioneering effort to combine scores of national household surveys to come up with the first estimate of income distribution from the point of view of individual residents of the earth. His numbers are stunning.

Of course, Milanovic couldn't get household survey data—that is, income estimates based on asking people questions about their incomes, as opposed to aggregates like national GDP accounts—for every country. But he did get data covering 86% of the world's population in 1988, and 91% in 1993.

There are always serious problems in comparing national statistics: coverage, definition, and reliability all vary. Unlike the Luxembourg Income Study (of which more in a bit), which makes an effort to massage national data into an internationally comparable form, Milanovic had to take what was on offer. Price levels also vary around the world—and within countries, too; an income of $20,000 would mean very different things in Manhattan and rural Mississippi, as would $20,000 converted at market exchange rates into Russian rubles.

Milanovic uses purchasing power parity (PPP) exchange rates, which attempt to equalize buying power across borders, ignoring the distortions frequently introduced by financial market fashions.[27] PPP rates typically boost the incomes of poor regions compared to market rates, since prices are generally lower in poorer countries than in rich ones (the same effect is responsible for the differences in buying power between Manhattan and rural Mississippi). For example, at market rates of exchange, average African incomes were $673 a year in 1993, but $1,757 at PPP exchange rates. But estimating PPP exchange rates is a rather wobbly science, involving considerable estimation—and they take no account of regional differences in purchasing power. Life in Rio is more expensive than life in rural Brazil, but one PPP rate has to stand for the whole national population. Those caveats firmly in mind, let's move on to Milanovic's findings.

National inequality measures are no preparation for Milanovic's global figures. The global Gini index was .659 in 1993 using PPP exchange rates. At market exchange rates, the global Gini was .801—the highest Gini ever reported for any population anywhere. But Ginis are rather abstract;

more pungent ways of expressing global inequality are in the graph above and in the box on page 132. The facts in the box speak for themselves, but as the chart shows, 90% of the world lives on incomes under $10,000; 80%, under $4,500; 50% under $1,044; and 20% under $430.

The five-year interval between Milanovic's observations is pretty short, but it does show a fairly substantial polarization of world incomes between 1988 and 1993. Though he doesn't provide any guesses for the longer term, this fits well with a trend towards global polarization that goes back at least into the early nineteenth century (as shown in the previous section).

---

global facts

- The richest 1% of people in the world receive as much as the bottom 57%, or in other words, less than 50 million of the richest people receive as much as the 2.7 billion poorest.
- Someone with an income equal to US$25,000 is richer than 98% of the world population.
- World median income was $1,044 in 1993.
- The poorest tenth of Americans have average incomes higher than two-thirds of the world.
- The richest tenth of Americans—about 25 million people—have aggregate incomes equal to the poorest 43% of people in the world, almost 2 billion people.
- The ratio between the average income of the world's top 5% and world's bottom 5% increased from 78 to 1 in 1988 to 114 to 1 in 1993.

Source: Milanovic 1999.

But that brings us back to the national level, which ignores all the within-country differences in income distribution. Recently two French economists, François Bourguignon and Christian Morrisson, have made a heroic attempt to measure "the distribution of income among world citizens" from 1820 to 1990. It involves lots of guesswork, imputations, and extrapolations—lots more than in Milanovic's work. So these conclusions should be taken with a boulder-sized grain of salt. But here they are: "world income inequalities have truly exploded since the early nineteenth century," mainly because of massively divergent national performances. They also find a slowing of polarization trends since 1950 compared to the previous 130 years, with China's rapid growth of the last twenty years playing an important role—but no reversal.[28]

It must always be emphasized that there's no simple relationship between money income and material welfare, much less human happiness. As a country "develops," peasants are frequently thrown off the land and stream towards cities looking for work. While on the land, their incomes might have been zero or close to it, but they could feed and house themselves outside the cash economy. In a city, their money incomes might be higher, but they have to pay for necessities that previously they'd produced for themselves. But that sort of analysis is beyond the scope of a single chapter in a little book like this.

Income and poverty in the First World

How does U.S. income distribution compare with that in other rich industrialized countries? Fortunately, a complicated statistical patch job isn't required to answer that question, thanks to the Luxembourg Income Study (LIS). The LIS is both a collaborative research project among scholars of income and poverty around the world and an internationally comparable database they've developed. In the pre-LIS days, it was hard to compare income distributions across borders, since every country did things in its own statistical fashion. Since the mid-1980s, though, the LIS database has changed that, and LIS-associated researchers have produced a formidable literature. (Most of the rich industrial countries are included with the notable absence of Japan.)

First, a few big-picture items. As the next chart shows, the U.S. excels at extremes: after Russia, it has the largest share of poor and well-to-do (all defined relatively), and the smallest share of middle-income population

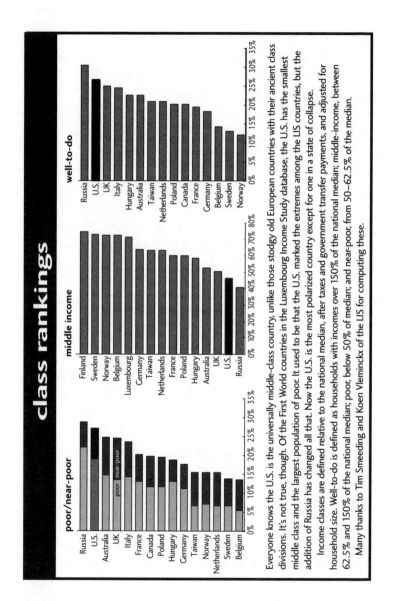

class rankings

poor/near-poor

Russia
U.S.
Australia
UK
Italy
France
Canada
Poland
Hungary
Germany
Taiwan
Norway
Netherlands
Sweden
Belgium

0%　5%　10%　15%　20%　25%　30%　35%

poor / near-poor

middle income

Finland
Sweden
Norway
Belgium
Luxembourg
Germany
Taiwan
Netherlands
France
Poland
Hungary
Australia
UK
U.S.
Russia

0%　10%　20%　30%　40%　50%　60%　70%　80%

well-to-do

Russia
U.S.
UK
Italy
Hungary
Australia
Taiwan
Netherlands
Poland
Canada
France
Germany
Belgium
Sweden
Norway

0%　5%　10%　15%　20%　25%　30%　35%

Everyone knows the U.S. is the universally middle-class country, unlike those stodgy old European countries with their ancient class divisions. It's not true, though. Of the First World countries in the Luxembourg Income Study database, the U.S. has the smallest middle class and the largest population of poor. It used to be that the U.S. marked the extremes among the LIS countries, but the addition of Russia has changed all that. Now the U.S. is the most polarized country except for one in a state of collapse.

Income classes are defined relative to the national median, after taxes and government transfer payments, and adjusted for household size. Well-to-do is defined as households with incomes over 150% of the national median; middle-income, between 62.5% and 150% of the national median; poor, below 50% of median; and near-poor, from 50–62.5% of the median.

Many thanks to Tim Smeeding and Koen Vleminckx of the LIS for computing these.

in the LIS universe. A fact like this should revise the U.S.'s self-image of being universally middle-class—but it's those despised social democracies that come closest to that status. Clearly it takes an active state-sponsored redistributionist mechanism to counter capitalism's natural tendencies toward polarization.

These are based on relative income measures, which is the practice of most LIS researchers. But how does the U.S. fare in terms of absolute measures? While we have a very high relative poverty rate, since average incomes in the U.S. are higher than in many European countries, maybe our poor are still better off than theirs.

Yes, in some cases, but surprisingly few. Shown on this page is an estimate of poverty rates using the equivalent of the U.S. poverty line in national currencies, not relative measures. Note that even though

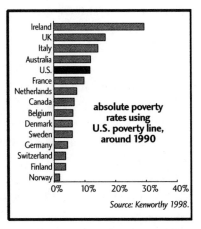

absolute poverty rates using U.S. poverty line, around 1990

Source: Kenworthy 1998.

the U.S. has the highest average income of all countries shown, most have a smaller share of their populations below the U.S. poverty level than does the U.S. itself. The only exceptions are poorer countries like Ireland and Italy and other liberal countries like the UK and Australia (about which more in a bit).

Absolute measures are also important in evaluating a classic right-wing critique of welfare-state measures: if generosity results in lower growth than in stingier countries, the stingier countries might do better over the long term at raising the absolute incomes of their poor. But, as Lane Kenworthy (1998) shows, that's not the case. While the recent sluggishness in European economies is frequently blamed on their generous welfare states, there's no evidence for such an effect over the long term (from 1960 to 1990). Using several measures—government transfers as a share of GDP, and qualitative and quantitative measures of "decommodification," such as pensions, sickness pay, and unemployment benefits—Kenworthy found that generosity was no hindrance to growth, and that generous welfare states succeeded not only in reducing relative poverty rates over the study's thirty-year timespan, but in reducing absolute levels as well.

Mobility

As with any domestic critique of U.S. income distribution, international comparisons are often met with appeals to our supposedly greater mobility, in contrast with the stodgy Old World. But assumptions to the contrary, the U.S. isn't unusually mobile. This, and the smallness of our middle class, should lead to a substantial revision of several national myths, but it probably won't.

Several recent studies by the Organisation for Economic Cooperation and Development (OECD) give the best international perspective on mobility. A study of the early 1990s by OECD staff economists (Antolín et al. 2000) of Canada, Germany, the UK, and the U.S. found that Britain's poverty performance during the early 1990s was the worst of the four, with 38% of the population experiencing at least one spell of poverty (defined as an income less than half the national median) over a six-year period, compared with 28% for Canada, 26% for the U.S., and 20% for Germany. But both the U.S. and British poor were more likely to stay poor for a long period of time: almost half of all people who were poor for one year stayed poor for five or more years, compared with 30% in Canada and 36% in Germany. And, despite claims of great upward mobility in the U.S., 46% of the poor rose out of poverty in a given year, compared with 45% in the UK, 53% in Germany, and 56% in Canada. And of those who did exit poverty, 19% of Americans were likely to make a round trip back under the poverty line, compared with 16% in Germany, 10% in the UK, and 7% in Canada. As the authors conclude, "Canada and Germany stand out as having particularly high exit rates from poverty and lower re-entry probabilities…while the opposite is the case of the United Kingdom and the United States."

Of the countries for which OECD staff economists have mobility data, the U.S. comes in roughly second, after Denmark, but the differences aren't very big, and the "picture is…one of considerable similarity." And U.S. low-wage workers—who are, remember, in very plentiful supply—have the weakest upward trajectory of all. Of all low-wage U.S. workers in 1986, 39% were unemployed five years later, 34% were still low wage, and 27% were working at a better-than-low-wage job. In most other countries, twice as many workers were able to rise out of low-wagehood (Organisation for Economic Cooperation and Development 1996; 1997).

Some might look at the chart on page 138 or read these upward mobility figures and declare that the prevalence of low-wage employment in the U.S. could be a blessing in disguise—in Europe, these unfortunates would be unemployed. But, says the OECD (no friend of worker-coddling, it should be said), there's "little solid evidence" that low wages have done anything to put the more "vulnerable" members of the labor force—women and youth—to work.

Those were relative income comparisons—what about absolute mobility? Here, too, the U.S. record is bad. U.S. workers of both sexes at almost every wage level fared worse than their peers elsewhere in the OECD between the mid-1980s and mid-1990s. Looking not at averages, but at individual workers, the U.S. also stands out when it comes to those experiencing large pay cuts. This is mobility of a sort, for sure.

What about mobility across generations? It's lower in the U.S. than in Sweden, according to one study of fathers and sons (Aaberge 1996). A quarter of male baby-boomers born to poor fathers in Sweden remained poor, compared to 40% for Americans. Just a quarter (25%) of Swedish men born to well-off fathers stayed in the upper-income class, compared with 40% of Americans. Sweden, then, was a more fluid society, at least by income, than the U.S., and with a larger middle class to boot.

Causes

Why does the U.S. have such a polarized income structure? The answers are simple: the largest low-wage labor force in the First World (see chart to the right) and the weakest welfare state. The wage issue is straightforward; it's an empirical fact that the gaps between the well-paid and poorly paid are wider in the U.S. than just about anywhere else. The welfare state issue is more controversial.

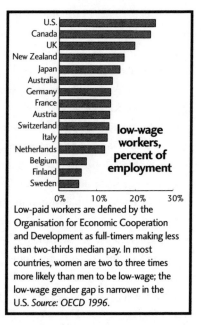

low-wage workers, percent of employment

Low-paid workers are defined by the Organisation for Economic Cooperation and Development as full-timers making less than two-thirds median pay. In most countries, women are two to three times more likely than men to be low-wage; the low-wage gender gap is narrower in the U.S. *Source: OECD 1996.*

Since the great backlash began twenty to twenty-five years ago, right-wingers have been arguing that redistributionist measures either have done nothing to reduce poverty or have made things worse, by encouraging laziness and dependency. That argument made itself into the mainstream; it was the theory behind Clinton's call to end welfare and behind the end-of-welfare legislation that he eventually signed. There are modern, high-tech versions of this theory, but it was neatly expressed by the ever-quotable Alexis de Tocqueville, who warned almost two centuries ago that "Any permanent, regular administrative system whose aim will be to provide for the needs of the poor will breed more miseries than it can cure." Or as the inimitable Charles Murray put it, "We tried to provide more for the poor and produced more poor instead."

Clever theory, but it isn't true. All the LIS studies showed that government policies can take from the rich and give to the poor, thereby flattening the income distribution and reducing poverty. In fact, differences among countries in the distribution of market incomes are generally smaller than after their tax and transfer systems kick in. In most countries, the redistributional work is mainly done through spending on benefits; in most countries, taxation runs from mildly regressive to mildly progressive. Interestingly, taxation is most progressive in some of the countries with the chintziest welfare states. In the U.S., the tax system does about two-thirds the work of redistribution (which isn't much, since the U.S. doesn't do much redistribution). A flat tax or national sales tax would completely turn this upside down, making the government into an agent of upward redistribution.

A very useful way of thinking about how states redistribute incomes was first proposed by Gosta Esping-Andersen in 1990. Listed in descending order of their interference with market incomes, these are: the social democratic (the Scandinavian countries), the corporatist (including most continental European countries, with Germany as the ideal type), and the liberal (the predominantly English-speaking countries, with the U.S. at the extreme; liberal is used in the European sense of minimal interference with the market). Since the liberal countries interfere least with market incomes, they have the highest poverty rates and most inegalitarian income distributions; the social democratic countries occupy the other extreme; and the corporatist states fall in between. Also, roughly speaking, the liberal countries saw the largest rise in poverty rates between 1980 and 1990, the social democratic ones saw the least, and the corporatist ones came down in the middle. Of course, such typologies always do a bit of violence to actual details—Canada's welfare state is a lot more generous than its southern neighbor's, for example—but they're still clarifying in thinking about the politics of welfare.

The corporatist model was heavily influenced by Catholic social teaching. It's organized around the idea of communities or organized interest groups—like economic sectors or occupational categories. Societies are still conceived of in class- and interest-group terms, but with cooperation replacing conflict as their relationship style, and with the socialist dream of universality dismissed. Union representatives on the boards of German companies are an example of corporatist organization. Corporatist welfare states offer benefits mainly to workers through employers; those not working are given short shrift. Liberal regimes have the stingiest welfare states, with the U.S. the stingiest of all. Benefit checks are typically small and of the "safety net" sort. By contrast, the social democratic states offer extensive income support, social and health services, and free educational systems—universally, without regard to income. The effect is to "decommodify" economic life, to weaken the dependence of people's material welfare on market incomes alone.

Esping-Andersen's model was criticized for its inattentiveness to gender relations and family policy, but the oversight can be remedied. In liberal states, child support or family policy are pretty much what the market delivers. The corporatist states offer more support, but typically through a husband's employment contract, and paid to him; they assume a two-parent, male provider/female housewife family. Day care is offered, but stingily. "Home-mother ideology" is a powerful force. The Scandinavian countries offer much more support to mothers who want to work—particularly an extensive day-care system. Child poverty rates follow a familiar pattern, with the social democratic countries around 5%, the corporatist around 10%, and the liberal around 20% (with the U.S. at 27%). In liberal and corporatist countries, families with children are more likely to be poor than the average, but in the social democratic countries, there's little difference. Similar things can be said about single-parent households (80–90% of which are headed by women in all countries studied), with poverty rates around 5% in the social democratic countries, 20% in the corporatist, and 40–60% in the liberal (led of course by the U.S.). And women's participation in the paid labor force follows an interesting pattern—for married women, approaching 80% in the social democratic countries (where support is heavy), 40% in the corporatist (where policy discourages it), and 60% in the liberal (where there's lots of economic pressure but little support).

The structure of aid matters a lot—not just for poverty reduction, but for politics too. Conservatives—including a lot of Clintonish Democrats, as well as World Bank economists—argue that aid should be carefully "targeted" on the poor, like a smart bomb. In fact, some (no doubt well-fed) theorists have argued that the less targeted a system is the worse it is for the poor. As reasonable as it all might sound on first hearing, the reality isn't so pleasant. Countries with targeted (or "means-tested") systems have higher poverty rates than those with broader systems.

There are sound political reasons for this. Walter Korpi and Joakim Palme (1998) argue that targeted systems weaken popular support for redistributionist politics, setting working- and middle-class taxpayers against presumed poor beneficiaries. (They use an electoral model of power, which assumes that people get the government they want; it could easily be translated into more blooded class-struggle language.) In countries with broad or universal systems, working- and middle-class taxpayers appreciate their benefits, even if some public money is paid to affluent beneficiaries who don't deserve it. Generous benefits paid to middle- and upper-income citizens also reduce the need for private insurance policies. Americans who cherish low taxes and small government forget that they pay a lot for private insurance, health care, and tuition.

All together, this makes for broader and deeper support of public spending than in liberal, individualistic systems. Because of that firm popular foundation, the aid budget is big enough to bring the poor out of monetary poverty and to insure most people against the worst risks of economic life. In countries with targeted systems, popular support is so weak that the welfare budget is too small even for its target, and it does a terrible job of taking the sting out of poverty or unemployment. Corporatist systems, by organizing programs around different sectors—Germany makes distinctions between blue- and white-collar workers—fracture support, though given wider coverage, probably not as much as in liberal countries. Curiously, tax rebellions have occurred most in liberal countries with their lower tax rates; despite the higher rates paid by taxpayers in countries with more universal systems, benefits remain broadly popular. Proof of that can be seen in the difficulties Western European governments have had in hacking away at their welfare states, despite the urging of American economists and editorialists—and Euro-elites' use of the budgetary strictures demanded by the Maastricht unification treaty as a kind of external force demanding austerity.

So, it is no accident that Social Security privatizers argue for means-testing the system, or for lowering the tax threshold on affluent pensioners. While a more timorous approach than overnight privatization, such maneuvers would weaken political support for the public pension system, and would lead, almost inevitably, to Social Security's transformation into a stingy, intrusive welfare system.

There's no great mystery to making the poor less miserable and the middle more secure. You start with unions, add vigorous antidiscrimination programs, and finish with a civilized welfare state. Not very fashionable in the year 2003, for sure, but if nineteenth-century notions of social policy and economic organization can be rebranded as "new," then anything's possible, with the right organization.

4 Globalization

I still have faith that globalization will make us better off, but it's no more than faith.
—free-trade economist Robert Z. Lawrence[1]

"Globalization" has been on so many lips over the last few years that it's easy to forget how recently it entered daily speech. Shown on page 146 is a graph of the word's appearances in the *New York Times* and *Washington Post* since 1980. While not as instant a star as the phrase "New Economy" (graphed on page 4), its trajectory is remarkably similar, flatlining its way through the 1980s and early 1990s, then showing a near-vertical ascent in the late 1990s—though "globalization" saw its point of inflection around 1995, three years before the New Economy, and it's shown more staying power.

"Globalization," both in elite and common speech, is a pretty spongy concept. Like many deeply ideological words, it's rarely defined explicitly; everyone is expected to know what it means. Elites mean something like the internationalization of economic, political, and cultural life, as if these haven't long been internationalized. Nonelites, including quite a few antiglobalization activists, seem to mean everything bad that's happened over the last decade or two. That's hardly an exaggeration; writing in *The American Prospect,* Mark Greif (2001) reported on a focus group, held for corporate clients worried about the antiglobalization backlash. Thirty

ordinary Americans were gathered together in a hotel in the rather unglamorous locale of Secaucus, New Jersey, by a Jungian market researcher
with the Pynchonesque name G. Clothaire Rapaille, and asked what globalization meant to them. After a slow start, the answers started coming:
"Nothing's personal." "No more privacy." "It's all machines." "The world
is getting too small. There's no
more mystery anymore…." Pressed
for more detail, respondents com-
plained about speedup, the "fight
for the dollar," atomization, alienation, powerlessness, growing gaps
between haves and have-nots and
workers and bosses, the deterioration in health care. An impressive
array of complaints, but it's not
clear how "globalization" is their
cause. They sound more like ven-

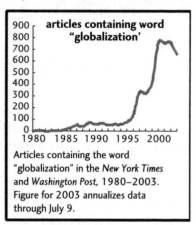

Articles containing the word
"globalization" in the *New York Times*
and *Washington Post*, 1980–2003.
Figure for 2003 annualizes data
through July 9.

erable complaints about capitalism in general—surprising in their breadth
and intensity in these supposedly conservative times—and not particularly
its internationalizing aspects. The shrinkage of space and the acceleration
of time, which seem like particularly modern or even postmodern concerns, actually entered Western thought in the sixteenth century (Douglas 1997). But that's the problem with the word—it serves as a kind of
wastebasket taxon, a term biologists use to describe a catch-all category, a
repository for critters you don't really know how to classify.

Let's look at a couple more attempts from the experts. The French
international relations analyst Dominique Moïsi (2001) defined globalization as "complexity, interaction and simultunaneity," a phrase that could
also describe a crowd of tipsy customers chatting flirtatiously at a bar.

The British sociologist Bob Jessop (2001), for another example, avers that "'globalization'" (quotes in the original) "is best used to denote a multicentric, multiscalar, multitemporal, multiform, and multicausal process"—one of scales "no longer...in a neat hierarchy but as co-existing and interpenetrating in a tangled and confused manner," one that is "multicausal because it results from the complex, contingent interaction of many different causal processes...the complex, emergent product of many different forces operating on many scales." Isn't that clarifying?

Jessop further avers that the globalized economy is the "fast economy," and that the fast economy requires fast policy, which "privileges the executive over the legislature and the judiciary, finance over industrial capital, consumption over long-term investment." But consideration of how the U.S. Congress denied President Clinton fast-track trade negotiating authority, how the U.S. Supreme Court chose the winner of the 2000 election, how multinational corporations (largely industrial, not financial, entities) and their long-term investments play a starring role in "globalization," you have to wonder exactly what Jessop is looking at.

Closely related to the confused attempts to define globalization are the sentimental evocations of "place" that often serve as globalization's opposite. Not surprisingly, given his propensity for important-sounding but empty turns of phrase, Manuel Castells (1996, p. 423) declares that **"A place is a locale whose form, function and meaning are self-contained within the boundaries of physical contiguity"** (boldface in original). As an example of place, he cited the Belleville neighborhood of Paris. In 1962, as a political exile from Spain, Castells was given shelter there by an exiled Spanish construction worker and anarchist union leader. Exile, anarchism, and organized labor are hardly meanings self-contained within Belleville, and no doubt a ruralist would find the urban neighborhood itself hopelessly fallen from nonalienated grace.

Whatever place is, we're told that it matters less in these globalized days. But is it true? So-called industrial districts still matter a great deal, from Silicon Valley to the Silicon Alley to Bangalore. In fact, greater regional inequalities in attracting desirable "knowledge" work suggests that "location has actually become *more* rather than less important" (Huws 1999).

Claims

Let's take a closer look at some common claims about globalization (which, all bad definitions aside, seems to be about the increased internationalization of economic, political, and cultural life). It's described as an innovation, when it's not; it's described as a weakening of the state, though it's been led by states and multistate institutions like the IMF; it's been indicted as the major reason for downward pressure on U.S. living standards, even though most of us work in services, which are largely exempt from international competition; and it's been greeted as an evil in itself, as if there were no virtue to cosmopolitanism.

First, the novelty of "globalization." One of my problems with this term is that it often serves as a euphemizing and imprecise substitute for "imperialism." From the first, capitalism has been an international and internationalizing system. After the breakup of the Roman Empire, Italian bankers devised complex foreign-exchange instruments to evade Church prohibitions on interest. Those bankers' cross-border capital flows moved in tandem with trade flows. And, with 1492 began the slaughter of the First Americans and with it the plunder of the hemisphere. That act of primitive accumulation, along with the enslavement of Africans and the colonization of Asia, made Europe's takeoff possible. John Maynard Keynes (1973, vol. 7, p. 139) argued in his *Treatise on Money* that:

the booty brought back by Drake in the *Golden Hind* may fairly be considered the fountain and origin of British foreign investment. Elizabeth paid off out of the proceeds the whole of her foreign debt and invested a part of the balance (about £42,000) in the Levant Company; largely out of the profits of the Levant Company there was formed the East India Company, the profits of which during the seventeenth and eighteenth centuries were the main foundation of England's foreign connections; and so on.

He was probably exaggerating a bit, and characteristically emphasizing the financial angle while ignoring the exploitation of people and the land, but the fundamental point is solid.

For a less literary take on the matter, we can turn to this testimony from Anne O. Krueger, second-in-command at the IMF, who put it concisely in a January 2002 speech (given in Melbourne, thus the Australian content):

The phrase "emerging market" only came into common use in the 1980s, but capital flows into developing countries of course have a much longer history. Stock markets were operating in Turkey by 1866, India by 1875, and Brazil by 1877. Widespread sovereign borrowing—in the sense that we think of it now—got under way in the late 18th century, when the spread of constitutional forms of government led to more stable nation states that recognized continuing liabilities to lenders....

International flows of investment capital were particularly robust in the late nineteenth and early twentieth centuries, against a backdrop of free trade and exchange rates fixed under the gold standard. Indeed, flows to developing countries were larger in relation to the world economy during this first "golden age" of financial globalization than they are today. Here in Australia, capital flows financed half of all domestic investment in the late 1880s. Capital was cheaper abroad. In 1884, banks in Sydney had to pay 5.5 percent to attract 12-month term deposits, whereas the New South Wales government was able to sell bonds to overseas investors in London paying just 4 percent.

James Petras (1999) wrote: "From the 15th to the nineteenth century Latin America's external trade and investment had greater significance than in the twentieth century. Similarly, one-third of English capital formation in the seventeenth century was based on the international slave trade." It wasn't until the nineteenth century, Petras argues, that internal national markets began to develop. Still, capitalism was relentlessly global until World War I; the effort to restore the old order in the 1920s failed miserably in 1929. Capitalism's retreat to national economies and trading blocs was a sign of crisis. Petras argues that the global turn began in the 1970s, but that seems too late. At war's end, one of capital's main policy tasks was to restructure the international monetary system (under U.S. supervision), and Washington laid great emphasis on getting the world trading system going again, with the Marshall Plan, pressure on U.S. businesses to invest abroad, and a global military buildup all pushing liquidity onto world markets. A post-Depression, postwar return to economic health required that the global mechanisms be restored.

It's probably more fruitful to think of the present period as a return to a pre–World War I style of capitalism rather than something unprecedented, and to rethink the Golden Age of the 1950s and 1960s not as some sort of norm from which the last twenty-five years have been some perverse exception, but the exception itself.

Another thing that must be thought about more clearly is the role of the state. While there's no question that the state's positive role has been either sharply reduced or under sharp attack, the rollback of state power has been highly selective. In the U.S., we've more than quadrupled the prison population since 1980, a cruel boom that was accompanied by increased snooping and behavioral prescriptions, public and private. Elsewhere, the neoliberal project has been imposed by states, whether we're talking about the Maastricht process of European union, or structural adjustment in the so-called Third World—states acting in the interests of private capital, of course, but that's the way states have been acting for centuries. And, over the last twenty years, we've seen an almost entirely new role for the state, preventing financial accidents from turning into massive deflationary collapses—bailouts that insulate creditors from risk while assuring that costs of adjustment are largely paid by the poor and weak.

So what about pressure on living standards? We First Worlders have to be very careful here, since the initial European rise to wealth depended largely on the colonies, and while we can argue about the exact contribution of neocolonialism to the maintenance of First World privilege, it's certainly greater than zero. It's embarrassing to hear Ralph Nader and his associated fair-trade campaigners describe NAFTA and the World Trade Organization as threats to U.S. sovereignty, echoing the rhetoric of Pat Buchanan. Washington has abused the sovereignty of scores of nations over the decades, while refusing to observe decisions of global bodies like the World Court.

The U.S. objects to other countries raising barriers against its goods, capital, and political preferences, but it's never shy about asserting its own national autonomy. For example, the FBI asked regulators to hold off on approving Deutsche Telekom's takeover of VoiceStream, the cellular telephone provider, while it could determine whether the deal would complicate its ability to tap phone calls. While the Bureau's concerns didn't block the deal, it is a measure of how seriously federal agencies—often joined by members of Congress—take the matter of preserving U.S. security prerogatives in a supposedly borderless world. The U.S., of course, expresses no qualms when American telephone companies take over foreign companies; quite the contrary, opening up foreign telecoms markets is one of the most fervent passions of U.S. trade negotiators—mainly for commercial reasons, but the National Security Agency probably isn't displeased either.

And even while it lectures other countries on the need to open their markets, the U.S. has never been shy about erecting trade barriers to protect domestic industries. In the 1980s, the Reagan administration talked free trade and yet persuaded Japan to impose "voluntary" export restraints on cars and computer chips. And in 2002, the Bush administration imposed heavy duties on imports of foreign steel. The U.S. has too much sovereignty for the rest of the world's good.

None of this is intended to deny that plant relocations to Mexico and outsourcing contracts in China have put a sharp squeeze on U.S. manufacturing employment and earnings, or that the threat of those things has greatly reduced the bargaining power of U.S. workers. But how much has this contributed to downward mobility and increasing stress? The econometricians say that trade explains, at most, about 20–25% of the decline in the U.S. real hourly wage during the 1970s and 1980s. While not insignificant, that still leaves 75–80% to be explained, and the main culprits there are mainly of domestic origin. And why, if globalization were so decisively immiserating, did the real hourly wage rise after 1995, even as NAFTA took effect and trade penetration increased?

An important reason that trade doesn't explain more of our unhappy economic history since the early 1970s is that 80% of us work in services—and a quarter of those in government—which is largely exempt from international competition. What did "globalization" have to do with Teddy Kennedy and Jimmy Carter pushing transport deregulation, or with Reagan's firing the air traffic controllers, or with Clinton's signing the welfare bill? What does "globalization" have to do with tuition increases at public universities or attacks on affirmative action? While lots of people blame the corporate downsizings of the 1990s on the globalization and its demonic traveling companion, technology, the more powerful influences (as we'll see in chapter 5) were Wall Street portfolio managers, who were demanding higher profits.

Blaming foreign competition for the exploitation of labor is, as Marc Linder (2000, p. xiii) puts it, a "venerable" tactic; in the 1840s, British employers defended forced overtime as "necessary to compete with the lightly-taxed foreigner." A steel industry functionary testifying against a bill to regulate the hours of work cited global competition as a strike against it; it would put U.S. producers at a "disadvantage" relative to producers in other lands, "beyond the paternal control of the Congress of the United States." Aside from the slightly antique language, you'd be hard pressed to know that the argument was made in 1898, not 1998.

Are globalized economies more unequal than nonglobalized ones? The consulting firm AT Kearney has been computing a yearly globalization index for *Foreign Policy* magazine.[2] It's not a perfect measure, which isn't surprising, because no one really has a good definition of what globalization is. This particular index is a composite of the trade share of GDP, the relative convergence of domestic and world prices, cross-border income and capital movements, tourism, international telephone traffic, and Internet connectivity. If you chart the relation of the index to country rankings for inequality, the results are not what a typical antiglobalization activist would expect. The relation is noisy, but if anything, more globalized countries are *less* unequal than less globalized ones.

A problem with the index is that quite a few of its components correlate positively with income, so you get a clustering of poor countries at the bottom and rich ones at the top of the globalization league charts. But you could also make some striking comparisons among countries at roughly equal levels of income. Western European social democracies are

more globalized than the U.S. but less unequal—as is Canada, to a lesser
degree. South Korea is much more globalized than Brazil but less unequal;
so is Mexico. The point is not that promoting globalization would promote equality, but that the foregrounding of globalization as the cause of

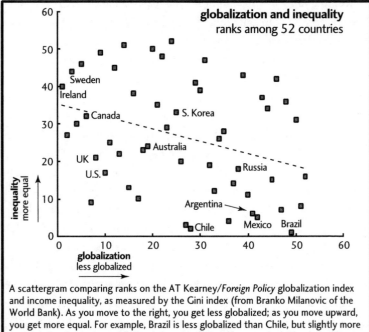

A scattergram comparing ranks on the AT Kearney/*Foreign Policy* globalization index
and income inequality, as measured by the Gini index (from Branko Milanovic of the
World Bank). As you move to the right, you get less globalized; as you move upward,
you get more equal. For example, Brazil is less globalized than Chile, but slightly more
unequal; Sweden is more globalized than the U.S. and less unequal. The dotted line is
a regression trend line (r^2=0.11). See text for discussion.

inequality isn't as simple a case to make as people think. Income distribution depends more on domestic institutions like unions and welfare states
than on any measure of internationalization.

Of course, this is hardly a rigorous exercise, and it compares levels
at one moment in time. Has "globalization" contributed to inequality?

While it's an article of faith among activists that it has—and among the orthodox the feeling is just the opposite—it's actually quite difficult to prove the case either way. China's rapid growth over the last twenty years has contributed a lot to narrowing the economic gap between nations—but inequality within China has increased. World Bank economist Branko Milanovic (1999) argues that inequality has increased, while IMF alum Xavier Sala-i-Martin (2001, 2002) argues the opposite. But it all depends on how you define and measure.[3] And those and similar efforts focus mainly on recent history—but over the long term, global income gaps have widened considerably. According to Angus Maddison (2001), African and U.S. incomes were roughly equal in 1600 (whatever that means exactly), but with industrialization, they started diverging in earnest. U.S. incomes were three times Africa's in 1820, five times in 1870, ten times in 1913, and twenty times in 1998.[4] You could perform similar exercises for other parts of the world, though the African case is extreme. When was the moment of "globalization"?

Boiling this down into a soundbite: capitalism has always produced poverty alongside wealth, and capitalism has from the first been an international and internationalizing system—so it makes little sense to try to isolate the "global" aspect as the major culprit in the production of inequality.

The MNC

Those who identify globalization as the major force behind the production of inequality frequently point to an alleged "race to the bottom," driven by multinational corporations (MNCs) who constantly ransack the globe searching for low costs and high returns. This too isn't as easy a case to prove as one might think.

U.S. multinational corporations
foreign investments and returns

| | investments | | | return | | |
| | \$b/% of total | | change | | | change |
	1982	2002	1982–2002	1982	2002	1982–2002
all	\$207.8	\$1,521.0	+632.1%	12.0%	8.1%	–3.8%
rich countries and						
Asian NICs	**76.5%**	**76.7%**	**+0.2%**	**9.6%**	**8.4%**	**–1.3%**
Canada	20.9	10.0	–10.9	6.7	7.3	+0.6
rich Europe	44.4	51.2	+6.8	10.4	7.4	–2.9
EU 15 only	*36.7*	*46.0*	*+9.4*	*9.2*	*7.0*	*–2.2*
Germany	7.4	4.3	–3.2	6.4	4.6	–1.8
Netherlands	3.3	9.6	+6.3	15.9	9.9	–6.0
Switzerland	6.2	4.6	–1.6	11.1	11.2	+0.1
United Kingdom	13.3	16.8	+3.5	11.2	4.4	–6.8
rich Asia	7.8	7.0	–0.8	7.9	9.1	+1.2
Australia	4.4	2.4	–2.0	7.0	7.1	+0.2
Japan	3.1	4.3	+1.2	9.4	10.4	+1.0
Asian NICs	3.4	8.4	+5.0	22.4	14.6	–7.9
Hong Kong	1.4	2.4	+1.0	22.4	13.9	–8.5
S Korea	0.3	0.8	+0.5	10.0	9.3	–0.7
Singapore	0.8	4.0	+3.2	27.5	16.4	–11.1
Taiwan	0.3	0.7	+0.4	23.2	10.8	–12.4
rest of world	**23.5**	**23.3**	**–0.2**	**19.5**	**7.4**	**–12.0**
poor Europe	0.1	1.2	+1.1	2.6	8.3	+5.7
Latin America/						
Caribbean	13.6	17.9	+4.4	16.2	6.2	–10.0
Argentina	1.4	0.7	–0.6	8.1	–7.6	–15.7
Brazil	4.5	2.1	–2.4	10.0	2.4	–7.6
Chile	0.1	0.8	+0.6	–21.2	6.0	+27.3
Mexico	2.4	3.8	+1.4	–1.0	7.8	+8.8
Bermuda	5.5	4.5	–1.0	12.1	6.9	–5.2
poor Asia	2.5	2.3	–0.1	35.6	12.2	–23.4
China	0.0	0.7	+0.7	–6.1	14.1	+20.2
Indonesia	1.1	0.5	–0.6	75.6	12.8	–62.8
Africa	3.1	1.0	–2.1	12.1	12.9	+0.8
Middle East	1.7	0.9	–0.8	35.7	13.2	–22.5

The first two columns show the value of investments held by U.S. multinational corporations in the regions and countries shown; the first is for 1982, second, 1999. For ìall,î the number shown represents the value of those investment holdings in billions of dollars (not adjusted for inflation); for all subsequent rows, the number is the percentage share of total investments held in the region or country named at the beginning of the row. The third column shows the percentage point change in that share from 1982 to 2002. The fourth and fifth columns show the rate of return on those investments—that is, profits before tax divided by the value of the investments in the region or country. The sixth column shows the percentage-point change in that rate of return between 1982 and 2002. *Source: computed from data published by the U.S. Bureau of Economic Analysis.*

Despite popular images of multinationals scouring the world for maximum return, going abroad seems to lower, rather than raise, profits (Click and Harrison 2000). Firms operating internationally show a lower return on assets and a lower stock market value relative to assets than do otherwise similar domestic firms. Companies that export from their home base, however, show superior performance. In this analysis, multinationalization looks like a poor substitute for old-fashioned exports. Reasons are unclear, but it may be that managers of MNCs are more interested in empire-building than in profit maximization. Even if this conclusion is overstated, there's little evidence that going worldwide is the profit-swelling strategy that both antiglobalizers and business ideologues assume.

On the facing page is a table showing the location and profitability of foreign investments by U.S. multinationals. A couple of points stand out from the colorless mass of numbers. First, such investments are overwhelmingly located in rich countries. Over half is accounted for by Western Europe; Canada weighs in with another 10%, and the richer countries of Asia (Japan, Australia, and New Zealand) with 8%. So, over two-thirds of the total stock of U.S. foreign direct investment is in countries with incomes roughly comparable to ours. Throw in the four classic Asian Tigers and you've got over three-quarters of the total. Other regions account for a lot less than people might think; the poorer countries of Europe (mainly in the east) are home to under 1% of U.S. foreign investment, and China, even less. Mexico, which occupies a large space in both globalizers' and antiglobalizers' imagination, accounts for just 3% of the total stock, not much of an increase from 1980. That's not to say that Mexico isn't important in certain industries (like autos and electronics), or that it isn't an important club that employers use to scare workers—but the relocation of production to Mexico isn't quite the driving force of economic evolution that it's sometimes thought to be.

Another surprising feature of the table is that the poorer countries aren't the profit gushers one might expect. Yes, Mexico's number is high, but Switzerland's is higher, and Latin America's overall figure is below Canada and Western Europe's. Note too that while the profit picture in Mexico turned around between 1980 and 1999, it didn't elsewhere in the region. Latin America's two decades of stagnation-cum-depression have been hard on firms trying to sell into domestic markets like Brazil's.

Recent work by Wendy Carlin, Andrew Glyn, and John Van Reenen (2001) confirm the so-called Kaldor paradox, Nicholas Kaldor's (1978) finding that countries with the fastest improvement in export performance were also those with the fastest increase in costs. Carlin and her colleagues offer a simple chart comparing the change in market share and the change in labor costs (adjusted for productivity and exchange-rate changes, measured for each country relative to all the others) for fourteen rich OECD countries from 1970 to 1992.[5] Finland, Italy, Germany, and Japan all gained in export share while labor costs increased. The U.S., the Netherlands, Canada, Sweden, Australia, and Belgium lost market share even though their wages lagged behind those of their competitors. France and Denmark were pretty much unchanged, and Britain and Norway saw higher labor costs and lower market share. These results are a complex product of wage, productivity, and currency changes, so it's hard to generalize about them, but it seems that the picture of a globally imposed regime of savage cost minimization may be a bit overdone.

So too images of a revolutionary "global assembly line," with multinationals integrating production and assembly performed in far-flung sites around the world. The output of U.S. multinationals—output defined as value added, that is, sales less the costs of inputs—has changed little over the last two decades: the output of U.S. MNCs worldwide was 9% of world product in 1982, 7% in 1989, and 8% in 1999. In other words, the trend is flat, not vertical. And second, the output of U.S. MNCs is overwhelmingly domestic; 76% of their output in 1999 was within these borders, almost exactly the same share as in 1982 and 1989. Over the same seventeen-year period, old-fashioned exports have actually grown faster than production by U.S. multinationals abroad. Output by foreign branches of U.S. multi-nationals accounted for less than 2% of world product in 1999, a share that has changed little over the last two decades. Their operations in Mexico accounted for 0.1% of world product. These are not large numbers.

That's not to say that production isn't being internationalized in some areas. But it's concentrated mainly in a few industries—autos, electronics, textiles. And that what multinationalization has occurred is much more selective than global. Auto production, for example, is increasingly inte-grated among the three NAFTA countries, neighbors with long borders and long ties (ties that all too often have consisted of the U.S. telling Canada and Mexico what to do). In this case, "regionalization" is a better description than "globalization."

Critics

OK, enough stick-bending for now. Even if multinationalization isn't the pure evil it's sometimes made out to be, neither is it the road to peace and universal prosperity. Surely there are things being traded now that wouldn't be traded in a more rational, humane world. The social gains to, say, Nike's producing shoes in Indonesia is claimed mainly by Phil Knight and the shareholders of Nike. Indonesian resources and labor would be much better devoted to feeding, clothing, schooling, and housing Indone-sians than making $150 basketball shoes while being paid pennies an hour. (Apologists argue that multinationals pay higher-than-prevailing wages, which may well be true, but in economic terms—the gap between wage and product and the resulting profit windfall—the level of exploitation is extraordinarily high.) It's a tremendous waste of natural resources to ship Air Jordans halfway around the world. Export-oriented development has offered very little in the way of real economic and social development for the poor countries who've been offered no other outlet.

But does that mean trade itself is bad? At a debate at Seattle's Town Hall during WTO week 1999, then–Undersecretary of Commerce for International Affairs David Aaron asked Ralph Nader how a consumer advocate could support restricting trade, since that would restrict choice and drive up prices. Nader had a hard time coming up with a good answer, sputtering and saying at one point that restricting trade would promote national self-sufficiency. Why national self-sufficiency is such a worthy goal he didn't say, but it seems like a retentive and unfriendly goal. Nader footnoted his expression of that strange desire with the revelation that he also supports restricting pornography imports; he didn't say why this was a good idea either.

Of course Nader is a special case, a man who seems proud of his (locally produced) hair shirt. But he's not alone in his preference for localism and self-sufficiency; there's a whole strand of the antiglobalization movement that shares his way of thought. Even professed internationalists evoke the beauties of the local. In a May 2003 talk at New York's Brecht Forum, the Italian activist Luca Casarini evoked the beauty of a world without borders, only to wax communitarian moments later.[6]

The localist way of thought deserves scrutiny. It's perhaps most prominently represented by the International Forum on Globalization (IFG), which has appointed itself the intellectual leader of what is unsatisfactorily called the antiglobalization movement (or so it's called in the U.S.—in bolder parts of the world it's sometimes called anticapitalist, but Americans don't have much of a political vocabulary for that sort of thing).

Founded in San Francisco in January 1994, the IFG entered the public stage in a big way at a conference in New York in November 1995, the first in a promised series of antiglobalization roadshows—a promise they've since delivered on. At the time, the IFG was identified as "a project of El Bosque"—and El Bosque was a project of Doug Tompkins, who made his fortune from Esprit, a clothing manufacturer and retailer he cofounded with his former wife Susie Tompkins. No ordinary garmento, Tompkins preferred the title "image director" to his official one of president and CEO.

Tompkins established the Foundation for Deep Ecology (FDE) in 1991. The FDE defines "deep ecology" as "a new movement among westerners that rejects the prevailing anthropocentric (human centered) paradigm of technological society, in favor of a biocentric ethic and practice." Nature exists not as a life-support system for humans, but has its own "intrinsic value." Whatever this means in theory, in practice it's often quite antihuman. Tompkins' favorite theoretician, Dave Foreman, one of the founders of Earth First!, dates The Fall at the development of agriculture about 10,000 years ago, and welcomed an Ethiopian famine as nature's method of population control. A columnist pen-named Miss Ann Thropy wrote in EF!'s magazine during the days when Foreman controlled it that AIDS, too, did valuable Malthusian work. Deep Ecologists, according to Kirkpatrick Sale, think that the human population of the earth, now approaching 6 billion, should be less than 1 billion, with some bids in as low as 100 million. The FDE's latest mission statement says: "The flourishing of human life and cultures is compatible with a substantial decrease of the human population. The flourishing of nonhuman life requires such a decrease" <www.deepecology.org/deepplatform.html>. Any volunteers?

Tompkins funded the Wildlands Project, guided by Dave Foreman, which aims to depopulate huge swaths of North America and return them to wilderness—so that "grizzlies in Chihuahua have an unbroken connection to grizzlies in Alaska," with "pre-Columbian populations of plants and animals." Unexplored is the need, said to be recognized privately by Project members, to reduce the human population by two-thirds for this "rewilding" to work. The FDE also funds the scary Negative Population Growth and Carrying Capacity Network, which has no compunctions about promoting the agenda of reducing the human population.

Tompkins' stated principles didn't stop the FDE's 1995 portfolio from holding stocks or bonds of Allstate, which insures cars; Citicorp, and three foreign banks, which fund the globalization the conference bemoaned; Fannie Mae, which greases suburbanization; Grupo Televisa, the Mexican TV network, a nice irony given their localist rhetoric and program director Jerry Mander's hatred of TV; HCA-Hospital Corp. of America; Telefonos de Mexico, which Wall Street viewed as a way of playing the expected NAFTA "boom"; and Wal-Mart, enemy of small-town shopkeepers everywhere.

Those stockholdings reflect the hypercapitalist way Tompkins first made his money, selling stylish garb made in California and Third World sweatshops. In 1972, Esprit shut a factory in San Francisco's Chinatown after the workers organized a union; the NLRB rebuked Doug Tompkins' "paternalism" for seeing the union as an expression of "ingratitude." Esprit took ten years to pay off the back wages the government ordered them to pay (Udesky 1994).

The IFG's kickoff conference's opening plenary, held in New York's Riverside Church, assembled a long night's worth of speakers—Maude Barlow (of the Council of Canadians), John Cavanagh (Institute for Policy Studies), Barbara Dudley (Greenpeace), David Korten (author), Ralph Nader (who needs no parenthetical ID), Carl Pope (Sierra Club), and Vandana Shiva (Third World Network). The MC was adman Jerry

Mander, who believes that TV, which he hates, will soon implode of its own contradictions. Mander was on the board of El Bosque and is the globalization program director for Tompkins' Foundation for Deep Ecology (FDE), whose funding was acknowledged, along with that of the Goldsmith Foundation. Almost all the featured speakers came from organizations that have gotten grants from the FDE.[7]

Korten's book *When Corporations Rule the World* was a crucial document that embodied and influenced a lot of the (anti)globalization movements' analysis of the world. In his prologue, Korten says he was born "into a conservative, white upper-middle-class family," which ran a retail business in a small Washington timber town—and the unexamined consciousness of a small-town worthy permeates the entire book. He went to Stanford, got an MBA and a PhD; and taught at the Harvard Business School, which he left for the Ford Foundation and then the U.S. Agency for International Development (AID). Korten shares these details "to establish the depth of [his] conservative roots"—a theme that recurs in his hymns to Adam Smith. While with AID, Korten had an epiphany—AID was too big, too bureaucratic, and too centralized, stifling local autonomy and initiative. He left AID for the NGO world, where people were "asking basic questions about the nature and process of development."

Korten exhibits an American distaste of big government, apparently without noticing that the U.S. has one of the most decentralized systems of governance on earth, with an array of states, localities, and special-purpose districts overlapping and competing for responsibility. This decentralization has accomplished not local "empowerment" (a word that deserves a long vacation) but fragmentation, duplication, and bidding wars for corporate investment—not to mention Jim Crow laws, the racist charms of the states'-rights movement, and, more recently, objections to federal environmental regulation in the name of local autonomy.

It's common in quasi-radical thinking to imagine a Golden Age with a better set of rulers, now displaced by vile usurpers. And Korten is no exception. In the old days, he declares, "rich and poor alike...shared a sense of national and community interest." So "the problem is not business or the market per se but a badly corrupted global economic system that is gyrating far beyond human control. The dynamics of this system have become so powerful and perverse that it is becoming increasingly difficult for corporate managers to manage in the public interest, no matter how strong their moral values and commitment."

When was this Golden Age? The 1960s, when GE was filling the Hudson River with PCBs? The 1930s maybe, when Chase was banking with Nazis? Or the 1890s, perhaps—when Carnegie's Pinkertons were shooting strikers? If not then, was it in the 1850s, when British industrialists kidnapped children to work in their factories, and when the locally owned bakeries of London worked their staffs up to twenty hours a day to produce bread fortified with, in the words of a contemporary, "a certain quantity of human perspiration mixed with the discharge of abscesses, cobwebs, dead cockroaches and putrid German yeast, not to mention alum, sand and other agreeable mineral ingredients" (Marx 1977, p. 359)?

Golden Age myths belong to literature, not nonfictions, but even there they vanish on close inspection. As Raymond Williams tells it in *The Country and the City,* F. R. Leavis' circle in the 1930s lamented the loss of the "organic community" of the turn of the century; just before that century turn, Hardy wrote of the lost England of the 1830s; the 1830s had Cobbett writing of the paradise of the 1770s...on back to Piers Plowman. In the Golden Age mode, says Williams, a feudal order is idealized as more "natural"; sure enough, in one of the small sessions at the IFG's 1995 conference, one of the panelists described the Middle Ages as a time of "real community." But, for "the uncountable thousands who grew crops and reared beasts only to be looted and burned and led away with tied wrists, this economy, even at peace, was an order of exploitation of a most thoroughgoing kind: a property in men as well as land; a reduction of most men to working animals, tied by forced tribute, forced labour, or 'bought and sold like beasts....'" (Williams 1973, chap. 4). Against this, a community-undermining capitalism can feel almost like a breath of fresh air. *Almost.*

Antiglobalizers are frequently antidevelopmentalists as well, and like Nader, sport a closet full of hair shirts, not just for themselves but for everyone in sight. So they typically complain about how big business stokes the desire for things to keep the flywheel of consumption turning. Korten reliably holds up Nike as an example of "the distortions of an economic system that shifts reward away from those who produce real value to those whose primary function is to create marketing illusions to convince consumers to buy products they do not need at inflated prices." But capitalism has always been a system that shifts rewards away from the real producers of value; the mill girls of nineteenth-century Lowell were rewarded little better than the women who toil for Nike in Indonesia and Vietnam. And the illusion-spinners are not the prime reward-getters—senior managers and stockholders are.

But critics of the moralizing Kortenesque sort usually prefer to talk about consumption rather than the ownership and organization of production. Yes, Nike's shoemakers are hideously exploited—but is there really anything fundamentally wrong with the desire to wear stylish shoes?

In a rant like Korten's, the list of woes barely admits any progress—the lengthening of lives, the reduction in infant and maternal mortality, the far-from-complete liberation of women (accomplished in part by the availability of factory jobs, which offer them a way out of rural patriarchy), the spread of literacy—in the First and Third Worlds over the long sweep of things. Of course there's a chasm between what is and what could be, but what could be depends a lot on what is. It's evil that Merck will steal plants from indigenous people and then patent them, and be protected for doing so under international trade law, but the plants wouldn't do much good if it weren't for some large, complex organization to develop and process them. Socialize Merck, don't dissolve it.

In developing his prototype for utopia, Korten points to a group of countries that Alan Durning of the Worldwatch Institute called "sustainers" ($700–7,500 per-capita income), vs. the "overconsumers" ($7,500+) and "excluded" (under $700). These correspond roughly to what the World Bank calls, respectively, middle-, high-, and low-income countries. To Korten and Durning, the countries of the middle group (which includes Indonesia, Mexico, and Russia) offer the model of a sustainable life.

At the time Korten's book was published, those middle-income countries had, on average, life expectancies nine years shorter than the high-income (77 vs. 68); a female illiteracy rate of 30%, compared with less than 5%; an infant mortality rate of 39 per 1,000 live births, vs. 7. They include the victims of the structural adjustment programs that antidevelopmentalists rightly criticize; it's strange to see them as models. It's especially strange that a Malthusian should, since the population growth rate of the sustainers is three times that of the rich countries.

Korten, who even mentioned Malthus by name, gingerly endorses the goal of bringing the world's population down to 1–2 billion from the present 6 billion, though without saying how. Malthus, at least, was honest enough to advocate the promotion of death: "Instead of recommending cleanliness to the poor, we should encourage contrary habits." Korten probably isn't a partisan of mortality-promotion, but advocating the disappearance of billions of people without saying how invites terrible speculations.

The demon of Korten's book—like that of many populist screeds, left and right—is the "corporation." To Korten, corporations betray Adam Smith's ideal of competitive markets, by reaching for monopoly and smothering "local enterprise." He seems unaware of Karl Polanyi's claim that free markets impose an unbearable discipline on participants, resulting in deflation in the economic realm and atomization in the social. And he seems equally unaware of economic history. Despite myths of free competition among small producers, early capitalist Britain was plagued by local monopolies; a town often had a single baker, a single brewer, rather than an array of vendors in benign competition. It wasn't until the development of national markets that real competitive markets developed.

Early capitalism wasn't as local and personal as myth has it; from its beginning it was deeply international. In the U.S., early nineteenth century merchants imported British industrial goods and exported cotton, acting as financiers at every stage. Their financial arrangements, in Alfred Chandler's (1977, p. 23) words, were a "long chain of credit stretching from the banks of the Mississippi to Lombard Street" in London. Rarely did merchants know the consumers and producers they brought together, a commerce accomplished through a "long chain of middlemen, transporters, and financiers who moved the goods through the economy." Moving a good and its payment from one place to another required a long chain of credits; every player was on the hook to someone else. When the chain was broken, the disruption quickly spread—one reason for the severity of nineteenth-century financial panics. For all the complaint about modern instability, the nineteenth century was far more volatile, with panics leading to depressions every decade or so. This was the Smithian market—anonymous, atomized, and unstable.

Market apologists always ignore the costs of market transactions—comparison shopping takes time, and there's always the risk that you may get burned in any deal—which can be reduced when things are done within the walls of a single firm rather than through outside markets. While many crimes, from price-fixing to murder, aided the creation of the modern giant firm, there are great advantages to be gained from planning production on a larger-than-local scale.

Korten and the antiglobalizers are right that economic growth doesn't necessarily make people happier, and can even make them miserable; that institutions like the World Bank have made the rich richer while making the nonrich poorer; that conventional ideas of free trade are wonderful for managers and stockholders, but can be hell on workers and nature; and that a turn away from the accumulation of things and toward more humane pursuits would be highly welcome.

But to turn from that to a dream of local self-sufficiency is suffocating and reactionary. On this, Korten is outdone by some of his IFG comrades. Kirkpatrick Sale wants to smash computers and live like the Amish, who have the damnedest time keeping their young from leaving the anti-modernist fold (though Sale does use the phone—which causes him physical and mental anguish—and electricity). Sale's objections to technology are extraordinary; he complains that the invention of printing doomed the forests of Europe, and that the mass literacy that printing spawned doomed oral traditions, which were the glue that held "community" together (Kelly 1995). Who needs literacy, really, wonders Sale, when what we're reading is of little "merit"? Civilization, says Sale, is a "catastrophe," and he longs for its "collapse." This is snobbery, elitism, and despair masquerading as radical critique.

The ecofeminist Vandana Shiva views technology as a male disruption of the sacred woman-nature dyad, and she advocates a "subsistence" economic model. Shiva, it should be noted, is more popular in the West than in India. As sociologist Swasti Mitter wrote (1994), the Bangladeshi women workers she's studied in both their native country and London want jobs, training, and good wages, and do not want to return to their villages.

Shiva opened her talk at the conference by noting that one of the "positive externalities" of globalization was that she'd made so many good friends around the world. Korten's acknowledgments describe his book as "the product of an international collaboration" involving colleagues from around the world. If "globalization" can produce such desirable things as friends and books (even bad books), perhaps it's wrong to name it as your main enemy.

It's ironic that people should rack up the frequent-flier miles while touting the virtues of localism—writing books and running institutes while telling the masses that they should stay home and tend to their lentils. This recalls T.S. Eliot's remark that "on the whole it would appear to be for the best that the great majority of human beings should go on living in the place in which they were born." At least Eliot, who was born in St. Louis but moved to London at age twenty-six, was an avowed royalist and snob.

Nationalist nostalgias

Among antiglobo activists, there's a strange nostalgia for the nation-state, as if it's one of the innocent structures that the forces of globalization are undermining. It's always good to remember, as the autonomist journal *Wildcat* (1999) anonymously wrote, that "Imperialism was not always carried out by nations. India and Indonesia were founded by companies."

At least two aspects of the nostalgia for nation are worth picking apart. First, in the narrow economic sense, fond memories of the pre-1980 protectionist regimes are often evoked. Like many nostalgias, the historical record doesn't justify the sentiment. It's worth remembering that even the most protected developmental state is shaped by external forces; the height of the tariff walls and the vigor of the state intervention themselves are testimony to that. But they seem to flourish in particular historical enclaves, like the Latin American import-substitution model from the 1930s through the debt crisis of the early 1980s, and run into trouble when their moment passes. By the late 1960s, for example, growth slowed in Latin America as import-substitution industrialization reached its limits. Domestic firms were inefficient, and average incomes were too low to sustain much of a home consumer market (Hoogvelt 1997, chaps. 3, 11). Labor agitation was met with repression. As Hoogvelt (ibid., p. 49) writes, "Politically, the easiest option for the national bourgeoisie was to suppress internal revolt by blaming the continuation of imperialist forms of domination of their countries, while masking their own complicity in this domination."

On the left, dependency theory gave this position some ideological cover, and today's debates are often filled with similar sentiments. Among NGOs and intellectuals working on development issues, there is talk of apartheid South Africa and Smith's Rhodesia as models of a possible autarkic delinking from the world economy, and admiration for Mahathir's capital controls in Malaysia during the 1997–98 Asian financial crisis. It's often overlooked that Mahathir is a repressive bigot, and that the Southern African examples were part of strategies to sustain horrible societies. Any "progressive" alliance with national capitalism in the name of resistance to international capitalism can get very smelly.

In the U.S., the Citizens Trade Campaign has taken support from the troglodytic textile tycoon Roger Milliken.[8] That's bad enough, but Naderite trade rhetoric about how the World Trade Organization threatens U.S. sovereignty is pretty bad too; the world has suffered from too much U.S. sovereignty and could do with a little less. Nader himself isn't very interested in those sorts of questions, though; in the early 1980s, he objected when Tim Shorrock, then editor of the Nader-founded *Multinational Monitor,* wanted to run stories linking the CIA to the interests of U.S. corporations abroad—and finally fired him for running a story without Ralph's approval on Bechtel's alleged bribery of South Korean officials to get construction contracts. So much for editorial independence.

Such unseemly alliances operate in the world of culture as well. Let's take as a proof text a little book called *The No-Nonsense Guide to Globalization,* by one Wayne Ellwood. The book doesn't live up to its title, since it contains a lot of nonsense about globalization. Perhaps most nonsensical of all is this passage:

> Whether you walk the streets of New York or Nairobi, Beijing or Buenos Aires, globalization has introduced a level of commercial culture which is eerily homogenous. The glittering, air-conditioned shopping malls are interchangeable; the fast food restaurants sell the same high carbohydrate foods with minor concessions to local tastes. Young people drink the same soft drinks, smoke the same cigarettes, wear identical branded clothing and shoes, play the same computer games, watch the same Hollywood films and listen to the same Western pop music.
>
> Welcome to the world of the multinational corporation, a cultural and economic *tsunami* (tidal wave) that is roaring across the globe and replacing the spectacular diversity of human society with a Westernized version of the good life…. In the words of the sociologist Helena Norberg-Hodge, there is 'a global monoculture which is now able to disrupt traditional cultures with a shocking speed and finality and which surpasses anything the world has witnessed before.'

Really? Let's read this text closely. According to the World Bank, Kenya's average income is about 3% of the U.S.'s, China's about 11%, and Argentina's about 32%. I doubt there are as many air-conditioned shopping malls in China as in the U.S., or that many Kenyan kids are playing video games. But even within New York City, there isn't anything like a monoculture; Queens, one of the five boroughs that make up New York City, is one of the most ethnically and culturally diverse jurisdictions in the world, with Chinese, Indians, Central Americans, and third-generation descendants of Italian migrants living side by side. Some residents of Queens listen to Mozart, others to Eminem, and still others to Indian and Chinese music that most readers of *The No-Nonsense Guide* have never heard of. And that's within one quarter of New York City, which famously bears little resemblance to the rest of the United States.

The world still looks and feels pretty different as you travel or otherwise make your way about it. Bangalore is not likely to become indistinguishable from Palo Alto. And there are lively new cultures being made as people move about—as in the just-cited case of Queens, and also along the Mexico–U.S. *frontera*. What should bother us is that these migrants move under conditions of often extreme exploitation—trying to escape it at home, only to find a fresh version of it in their new world—not that the integrity of cultures is threatened.

A lot of antiglobalization discourse is all too close to what Etienne Balibar and others have called neoracism. Balibar (in Balibar and Wallerstein 1991, pp. 21–2) argues that a "differentialist racism" has arisen. This new racism, appropriating an earlier tradition of anthropology that was once the staple of a "humanist and cosmopolitan anti-racism" that argued against colonial notions of a hierarchy of cultures and instead that all cultures were equally complex, now argues "that the 'mixing of cultures' and the suppression of 'cultural distances' would correspond to the intellectual death of humanity and would perhaps even endanger the control mechanisms that ensure its biological survival." The "spontaneous" reaction of cultures—usually identified as nations—is to fight off the intrusion in the name of preserving traditions and identity. And, as Balibar further argues, the definition and production of a "nation" always seems to come with some form of racism, some disparaged Other that the nation is defined against.[9]

The sweet green version of this is illustrated by David Korten (1999), who argues that like organisms, "[h]uman economies similarly require permeable—but managed—borders at each level of organization from the household and community to the region and nation that allow them to maintain the integrity, coherence, and resource efficiency of their internal processes and to protect themselves from predators." There's a lot of mischief in "permeable"—Pat Buchanan is perfectly happy to let in Northern Europeans—but leave that aside for now. Threats come from the outside—a border-jumping "capitalism" that has ruined the localist "market economy" of Smith's day. You'd never know from Korten's description of the eighteenth century that Britain was building an empire and trading in slaves: "Smith wrote about place-based economies comprised of small, locally owned enterprises that function within a community-supported ethical culture to engage people in producing for the needs of the community and its members.... The relationship of capitalism to a market economy is that of a cancer to a healthy body." The political history of cancer metaphors isn't always a pretty one.

Why should purity be so jealously guarded? Norberg-Hodge, the sociologist so worried about the spreading monoculture, is Norwegian. Norway is a rather homogenous place compared to the U.S.—but just how is the preservation of that homogeneity a furtherance of diversity? Diversity happens when people meet, not when they're defending against foreign carcinogens.

It's tempting to read a lot of the fears of globalization—alleged threats to the primally innocent community, to sororial solidarity—as a set of fantasies about a threatening Other, one that threatens the innocent world before The Fall. It makes a great deal of sense for right-wingers, eager to protect the primal space of community or nation from contamination, who would include human beings like immigrants among the external contaminants, to subscribe to this view of the global threat. But for leftists, heirs at least in part to an internationalist, cosmopolitan tradition, to embrace this is creepy and troubling. But it's not entirely without precedent; it must be conceded that Hayek had a point when he identified the nationalism implicit in socialism and social democracy, which have aimed at using the nationally constructed state as the agency of planning and redistribution—although Hayek was indifferent to the hierarchies and compulsions created by nationless capital.

While indicting the nationalist fantasies of antiglobalizers, we shouldn't forget the fantastic component of capitalist "globalization"—a millennial hunger to encompass the globe, to prowl freely without the slightest impediment of law or custom. This is the territory of what Joel Kovel has described as the capitalist ego, voracious and implacable in its desire to appropriate and incorporate. Its temper was captured by an old Merrill Lynch TV ad from the 1980s, with their trademark bull strutting to a jingle about a world that knows no boundaries: the bull needs no invitation, enjoying self-proclaimed *droit de seigneur.*

A global ruling class (in formation)?

Much of this chapter has been devoted to arguing that "globalization" isn't as new as is often thought. I'll admit that I sometimes get carried away with making that point, and I come dangerously close to arguing that 2003 is essentially 1913 plus fiber optics. It's not, of course. So what is genuinely new about the present situation?

One thing is the evolution of a global elite. But almost as soon as I concede that, I feel compelled to qualify it: it's only embryonic, or fetal, beyond the quickening maybe but not ready to be born. But let's look at some signs of its development.

Writers like William Robinson and Jerry Harris (2000) take a fairly extreme position—though one you frequently hear in both left and popular discourse. To them, the sharp increase in cross-border investment over the last few decades has created a transnational capitalist class (TCC), comprising the people who run transnational corporations (TNCs). The innovation of the TNC is the transnationalization of production; while finance has long been global, and trade has long been important, what makes this a new era is the global organization of production itself—the creation of the proverbial global assembly line. And with this new corporate form, the TCC has transcended the nation-state, which no longer seems of much importance.

But it's not through the TNC alone that the TCC is doing its business. There are also legal arrangements like NAFTA, and organizations like the IMF and WTO, which are the cells of an embryonic transnational state. Robinson and Harris single out the World Economic Forum (WEF), a group founded in 1971 by Klaus Schwab, a Swiss professor of business, policy entrepreneur, and social climber. At first it was quiet and mostly European, but it grew over time, and by the 1990s had evolved into a gathering of a global business, government, and media elite—most famous for its annual meetings in Davos (though the 2002 edition was held in New York). It's undoubtedly one of the ways by which that world elite has constituted itself, learning to think, feel, and act in common.

Robinson also co-wrote an essay in *Science & Society* with Roger Burbach sporting the ambitious title "The Fin de Siecle Debate: Globalization as an Epochal Shift." This was 1999, and millennial feeling was thick in the air. To Burbach and Robinson, the present is capitalism's fourth era. First was mercantilism and the early stages of European colonization—primitive accumulation. Then came the era of industrial capitalism, with the development of the big bourgeoisie and the nation-state. Then came corporate or monopoly capitalism—the emergence of the joint-stock company as the dominant form. And now we have globalized capitalism, born in the early 1970s. Epochs aren't what they used to be; unlike humans, they seem to have shortening lifespans. They date their first epoch, Marx's "rosy dawn of the era of capitalist production," from 1492 to 1789, 357 years. The second, the day of the industrial capitalist, from 1789 to 1900, 111 years. The third, the corporate era, lived about seventy years from 1900 to the early 1970s. And now the global era, in its early thirties. Among all the things that have speeded up these days, epoch-making is among the speediest.

Periodizations done during the thick of events are prey to the human habit of overvaluing new information at the expense of older news, and of getting carried away with conclusions too heroic for their underlying evidence. Writers like Robinson and Harris cite the growth in cross-border investment—so-called direct investment, which is what multinationals do when they take over foreign companies or set up new plants abroad, and portfolio investment, which is what investors do when they buy stocks or bonds traded in countries outside their own. And those numbers have shot upward. But what exactly do they mean?

With portfolio investment, a lot of those flows are wads of hot money scouring the world for a quick euro or ringitt. They inject and withdraw liquidity from national economies, sometimes with lightning speed, creating alternating booms and busts. But by definition, a lot of this money doesn't stick around long enough to become part of the scene; shareholders don't get involved with corporate management, they just move on.

With direct investment, though, the story is a bit different; those firms often do become part of the local scene, affecting both economic and political life. As we saw earlier in this chapter, we should be a bit cautious in drawing conclusions about the breadth and depth of these developments. But despite the partial integration of production across national boundaries, how much integration in the political sphere has there been? U.S. ruling circles have barely been penetrated by new Canadian or Mexican members. Or take another example of regionalization, the fifty-year project of European economic integration. Despite long economic and political ties, despite years of attempts to erase national borders within Europe (though Europe's external borders are considerably less porous to African migrants), and despite the birth of a common currency, European politics remains heavily national. And while the Euro-elite is becoming more integrated, they still quarrel constantly over policy and appointments. So even that project of integration, which has everything going for it, has a long way to go. And again, it's fairer to call it regional, involving as it does only half the European continent, rather than truly global.

Back to the World Economic Forum. In the 1990s, the meetings were reportedly much giddier affairs, when the U.S. economy was booming, the new economy was still new, and the creature that Thomas Friedman of the *New York Times* calls Davos Man seemed young and healthy. For the last few years, the WEF was convening against a backdrop of very bad news—Enron, Argentina, recession, terrorism, and protests outside directed against them and all they stand for. Reporting on the 2002 New York meeting, the *Washington Post* noted with apparent surprise, "The titles of workshops read like headlines in The Nation: 'Understanding Global Anger,' 'Bridging the Digital Divide' and 'The Politics of Apology.'"

That's not all there was; other session titles could have come out of *The Economist* or *Foreign Affairs*. Still, the men and few women of Davos are feeling considerably less triumphant these days. The stars of the 2002 worryfest were the unlikely duo of Bono, the lead singer of U2, and Bill

Gates, the world's richest human. Bono—who identified himself on the opening day of the conference as a "spoiled-rotten rock star" who loves cake, champagne and the world's poor—hammered at the need for debt relief. And Gates worked at the consciences of attendees with remarks like: "It's a healthy thing there are demonstrators in the streets. We need a discussion about whether the rich world is giving back what it should in the developing world. I think there is a legitimate question whether we are." No one was rude enough to point out that Gates's personal fortune alone could retire the debts of about ten African countries.

Gates's appreciation of the demonstrators points to what was doubtless the best thing about the 2002 Forum: the 12,000 of them who marched through the streets of Manhattan on February 2 proved that the so-called antiglobalization movement—which is a global movement if there ever was one—was not put out of business by September 11. It's alive and well—so alive and well that it set much of the WEF's agenda.[10] And it's also been setting at least the rhetorical agenda of the World Bank and the IMF, who now have to hold routine meetings under heavy guard (to protect them from orange-haired twenty-year-olds), and who have to affect a great concern for poverty reduction. So is there a global ruling class (in formation)? Yes, but the formation is very slow and very full of contradictions, and its members today are feeling a bit besieged. And the Bush administration's unilateralism is badly straining its solidarity.

Opposition

James Petras (1999) has argued that the proponents of "globalization"—big capital, state functionaries, and capital's intellectuals—have rich international links, but that the "exploited adversaries" are fragmented within and between countries, with weak ties. That appears less and less true.

Even the IFG, for all its promotion of localism, has "international" in its name, and it features people from all over the world at its teach-ins. Even indigenous rights movements, which could be thought of as paradigmatically local, often have roots quite distant in space and time from their sites of struggle. The Philippines Rural Reconstruction Movement, for example, goes back to the early twentieth century. Its intellectual origins are in efforts to provide basic education for Chinese migrant laborers in Europe during World War I. Those efforts, along with Tolstoyan social ideas, helped inspire the Japanese New Village Movement, which in turn helped inspire village development schemes in China, which in yet another turn found their way to the Philippines. (Curiously, many of these ideas were picked up by the U.S. authorities to help fight the Marxist virus in Asia and Latin America.) Other indigenous movements, like those of the Ainu in Japan, were strongly influenced by the U.S. civil rights movement, the worldwide student movements of the 1960s, and indigenous rights campaigns in the Americas and Antipodes (Morris-Suzuki 2000). So even the apparently "local" is often part of a global web, though not always explicitly so.

But other popular movements are becoming quite explicitly global and even high-tech, in contrast to the Luddite localism of Korten, Sale, and Mander. A coming-out party for this aspect of the movement was the worldwide mobilization against the Multilateral Agreement on Investment (MAI)—a movement that so exercised David Henderson, former chief economist of the OECD, that he wrote a polemical booklet denouncing it that was simultaneously published by several elite thinktanks around the world (Henderson 1999). The MAI, which would have been a bill of rights for multinational capital to do just as it pleased with little popular redress, was being negotiated in effective secrecy. A draft of the agreement was posted on the web in 1997, and within days, there was a worldwide mobilization against the treaty. Henderson was outraged that this short-circuited the normal channels of representative government—those normal channels being notable for their lack of popular representation. Though there were considerable points of disagreement among the major negotiating powers, the street protests helped derail the negotiations. There followed Seattle, Quebec, and Genoa—mobilizations that brought international trade and finance into the open as live political issues and not the exclusive province of capital-friendly experts, global mobilizations that would have been impossible without the Internet and cell phones.

A lot of that mobilization hasn't been carefully or explicitly theorized. Many activists still talk locally, even as they're acting and thinking globally. One encouraging sign that that's changing is the popular success of Michael Hardt and Antonio Negri's *Empire*. There's a lot wrong with the book, but it's an excellent starting place for understanding the present and finding the way to a better future.

One positive aspect of the book and its influence is its optimism, thanks to its roots in autonomist Marxism, an approach which emphasizes the creative and revolutionary power of workers on their own, apart from state and party. Next to typical left pessimism, autonomists can seem dreamily optimistic, seeing struggle and victory where others see apathy and defeat (which seem to have been in plentiful supply over the last couple of decades). Where most people see capital as acting and labor as reacting, autonomists see capital as the reactive side of the relation.

But aside from its emotional refreshments, *Empire* is an ambitious attempt to theorize the economic and political world today. Though clearly in a Marxist tradition, it's hardly orthodox. Though it pays appropriate homage to Lenin's famous pamphlet on imperialism, there's little that's Leninist about its analysis or—especially—its politics.

For our purposes, the book's relevance is its emphasis on the dispersed nature of power today, a decentered structure Hardt and Negri call "Empire." Take the ownership and governance of giant corporations. Early firms were generally owned by a single capitalist or a small network of partners. By the end of the nineteenth century, the likes of Morgan and Carnegie were assembling groups of small firms into giant combinations like U.S. Steel. By the early twentieth century, it was easy to conclude, as Lenin (and Rudolf Hilferding, in his classic *Finance Capital*) did, that industry was coming under the ownership of a handful of big banks, arranged in cartels often protected by price-fixing and high tariffs. Things didn't turn out that way. Now, giant firms are owned by thousands, even millions, of shareholders, and it's hard to point to a controlling force other than "the markets." And individual workplaces don't really count for much these days; the entire world is now an integrated workplace, a giant "social factory."

Global political power is also dispersed. Unlike nineteenth-century imperialism, when Nation X owned Colony Y, today's hierarchy is hard to specify. There are few cases of outright ownership, and the boundaries between the First and Third Worlds are getting blurrier—literally, in the case of the U.S.–Mexico border, but also in the sense of the movements of large numbers of migrants from South to North, and the proliferation of skyscrapers and McDonald's in the South. Yes, the Bush administration has been cracking down on immigration since 9/11, but people continue to arrive.

Cartels and classic imperialism turned out to be blocks to capitalist development. Cartels inhibited competition, capitalism's disciplinarian, as well as technological innovation, jointly leading to inefficiency and stagnation; tariffs, currency regimes, and other instruments of colonial preferences blocked trade and capital flows, inhibiting the development of a single world market; and frequent imperial wars promoted physical and financial ruin that were obstacles to the accumulation of capital. By contrast, the age of Empire is one of deregulation and the promotion of trade and capital flows—all designed to encourage competition and technological innovation.

Empire evolved over the last several decades, as capital's response to the great rebellions of the 1960s and 1970s. In the rich countries, a variety of rebellions flared, from traditional labor movements to new feminist, ethnic, ecological, and gay movements. In the so-called Third World, there were numerous wars of national liberation, combined with an increased assertiveness by the poorer countries demanding higher commodity prices and a global redistribution of power and income—a movement that peaked with an oil embargo and the U.S. defeat in Vietnam. It looked like domestic and international hierarchies of power were under serious threat.

But the masters rose to the challenge. Hardt and Negri are light on the details, but the history is a familiar one: the creation of a deep global recession in the early 1980s, which scared the hell out of First World labor and threw the Third World into the debt crisis; an acceleration of technical change, which produced the familiar cybergadgetry of today; the dispersion of production into smaller, more flexible units often far from population centers and one another; cutbacks in the more benign aspects of the state, like social spending, and an increase in the punitive ones, like jails; the casualization of employment, along with speedup and givebacks; and the propagation of a whole new ideology, which repositioned the Keynesian social democratic state as obsolete and stifling, and the new world of hypercapitalism as a realm of freedom and adventure.

So what's to be done about Empire? A lot of thinkers and activists would love to recover a lost world of nation-states or self-sufficient localities. Hardt and Negri (p. 43) will have none of this:

> [W]e insist on asserting that the construction of Empire is a step forward in order
> to do away with any nostalgia for the power structures that preceded it and refuse
> any political strategy that involves returning to that old arrangement, such as trying
> to resurrect the nation-state to protect against global capital. We claim that Empire
> is better in the same way that Marx insists that capitalism is better than the forms
> of society and modes of production that came before it. Marx's view is grounded
> on a healthy and lucid disgust for the parochial and rigid hierarchies that preceded
> capitalist society as well as on a recognition that the potential for liberation is
> increased in the new situation.

This isn't a popular view. But their critique of the nation-state deserves serious attention. For example, though there are undoubtedly progressive aspects to classic national liberation struggles—those directed against colonial powers—it's a recurrent fact of history that once established, nation-states thrive on creating new hierarchies, and by excluding, to some degree or other, those not deemed members of the tribe. Any progressive political movement today should be looking beyond hierarchy and exclusion toward a society that's egalitarian and truly universal.

In our normal work lives, we're all linked—often invisibly—with a vast network of people, from across the office or factory to the other side of the world. Standard globalization narratives, mainstream or critical, often efface this fact, seeing capital, rather than the billions who produce the goods and services that the world lives on, as the dominant creative force. That cooperative labor deserves to be acknowledged in itself, as the creative force that it is, but also as a source of great potential power. *Empire* uses a lyric from Ani DiFranco as one of its epigraphs: "Every tool is a weapon if you hold it right." They could have also used a line from Patti Smith: "We created it. Let's take it over."

Unfortunately, *Empire* sometimes reads like a cascade of assertions with little or no evidence. Its heavy reliance on metaphors and religious imagery makes it seem at times like a theological fantasy, more a dream-work than an exercise in political economy. The prose is often heavygoing (though next to Negri's earlier works, it's an easy read), and there are long detours into the history of political theory whose relevance to the book's overall argument isn't clear. There's virtually no analysis of the institutions of Empire—the World Bank and the IMF are invoked now and then, but their actual working and associated ideologies are barely noticed. Ditto agents of opposition like unions, political formations, or NGOs. Actual cross-border campaigns, whether for debt relief, immigration amnesty, or getting cheap AIDS drugs to Africa, are barely mentioned, if at all.

Hardt and Negri's program, like much of their analysis, is a bit thin on details. They call for absolute freedom of movement and a "global citizenship," which are lovely idea but right now seem achievable only in the imagination. And they also call for "a social wage and guaranteed income for all," though they don't disclose how this would be organized in a world beyond the nation-state. Who'd write the checks? Would there even be money?

Hardt and Negri are often uncritical and credulous in the face of orthodox propaganda about globalization and immateriality. They exaggerate the decline of the nation-state—NATO and the IMF are, after all, made up of national governments—and they ignore evidence that production networks aren't as seamlessly global as the business press would have us believe. They sometimes play down the preeminent role of the U.S.; they say that today's Empire has no Rome, but Washington, Wall Street, and Hollywood are pretty good approximations; NATO, for example, is meant to bind Europe to the U.S. in a subsidiary role, and any talk of independent European initiatives makes Washington very nervous. They assert that immaterial labor—service work, basically—now prevails over the old-fashioned material kind, but they don't cite any statistics: you'd never know that far more Americans are truck drivers than are computer professionals. Nor would you have much of an inkling that three billion of us, half the earth's population, live in the rural Third World, where the major occupation remains tilling the soil.

These are not minor flaws, but making these complaints almost feels like quibbling. Even though the book isn't really a *Capital* for our times, it's provocative in every sense of the word. The authors' emphasis on the dispersed nature of power today, the rich potential of the social networks uniting people worldwide, and the refusal of all nostalgias is fresh and often profound.

And aside from the provocation to think freshly, the value of *Empire* is also in its spirit—not gloomy or resigned, as is so much left writing these days, but full of optimism and a fresh urging to see the possibilities inhering, often invisibly, in the present. Their revolutionary isn't "anything like the sad, ascetic agent of the Third International whose soul was deeply permeated by Soviet state reason"—a passage reminiscent of Foucault's injunction, "Do not think that one has to be sad in order to be militant, even though the thing one is fighting is abominable."

Supporting that optimism is the utterly wonderful growth in activism over the last five years—what's often called the antiglobalization movement, a name its detractors are fond of. That's interesting, since it suggests that opinion-shapers see opposition to the global as going down badly with popular audiences. Movement activists and intellectuals now often take pride in the movement's internationalism, calling it a global justice movement. But IFG ideology is hardly dead. According to Walden Bello, many attendees at the 2003 World Social Forum in Porto Alegre rejected industrialization as a development strategy, choosing the preservation of rural life instead. (Of course, most attendees flew in from distant cities.)

But you hear less of that and more about erasing borders. Even better would be to hear no more of globalization. Using the word makes it harder to talk sharply about things like the intensified rule of money, the dismantling of social protections, and the exercise of imperial power. "Globalization" has had a busy decade; it needs a long rest.

5 Finance

I believe in the market/I believe in me.
—Brown & Co. ad on CNBC

It took about fifteen years for the bull market to make it big in pop culture. Yes, the 1980s had Oliver Stone's *Wall Street*, but we were well into the 1990s before you could walk into a bar and watch CNBC where you once would have seen ESPN. There'd never been anything like it. Despite tales of speculating shoeshine men in the 1920s, only about a million Americans played the market. Depending on definitions, figures for the late 1990s were as much as one hundred times as high, Now it's mostly recalled with nostalgia or a "What were we thinking?" slap on the forehead. Why did it happen, and what did it leave us?

Most people think that, aside from its gambling function, the stock market somehow provides nourishing finance to real corporations so they can invest and expand. The IPO wave of the late 1990s would seem to confirm that on both counts. But while the case for gambling is solid, that for the provision of finance isn't. Over the long haul, firms are overwhelmingly self-financing—that is, most of their investment expenditures are funded through profits (about 90%, on long-term averages), and surprisingly little by external sources, like banks and financial markets. And it's especially true of the stock market, which has historically provided only a sliver of investment funds. This is true not only of the U.S., but for virtually every economy known to economics.

And then there are periods like the late 1990s, during which the stock market serves as a conduit for shoveling huge amounts of cash into speculative ventures, most of which have evaporated. Instead of condemning it all as an extravagant waste, we could adopt the spirit of Keynes, who loved the giddiness and even the cultural richness of booms. Most material progress during the nineteenth century, he claimed, came during the boom periods that so distressed the puritans of finance. And, "by far the greater proportion of the world's greatest writers and artists have flourished in the atmosphere of buoyancy, exhilaration and the freedom from economic cares felt by the governing class, which is engendered by profit inflations" (Keynes 1973, vol. VI, pp. 137, 246). Evidently the cultural elasticity of profit isn't what it used to be. Shakespeare died rich, said Keynes, the beneficiary of one of the great bull markets of all time, the greatest the world had seen before the American 1920s. The American 1980s and 1990s were a massive bull move; we got "Friends."

But booms aren't forever, and they're no advertisement for the efficiency of our capital markets. Much, maybe most, of what was financed in the 1990s didn't deserve the money. It had its social benefits. The IPO gusher brought oxygen bars to San Francisco's Mission and bistros to Manhattan's Avenue B. Semioticians fresh out of Brown could get jobs at Razorfish paid mainly in options. *Wired* spawned an empire—books, TV, Suck.com—on its anticipated stock flotation. Despite having Goldman Sachs as its banker, the IPO failed—*twice*. The peripheral divisions were shut, and the magazine was sold off to Condé Nast, one of the New York–based dead-tree behemoths that *Wired* used to mock.

But let's set these morbid thoughts aside for a moment and recall the mania, one of the greatest of any place or time. The usual birthdate given for the Internet boom is the 1995 IPO of Netscape (which later suffered the indignity of being bought by AOL). But the mania entered its climax phase with the 1998 offering of TheGlobe.com, a web "community" with tiny revenues, big losses, and a very short operating history. Offered at $9 a share, the stock instantly popped to $97. Less than two years later, in July 2000, the stock was trading at less than half its offering price, with the company losing more than $2 for every $1 it took in in revenue; management told the *Wall Street Journal* that it was "committed to achieving profitability," an aspiration that would never be realized. In February 2003, it traded at 0.075. But who could have imagined this in 1998? Inspired by TheGlobe.com's performance, bankers were hot to foist anything on the public, and the public was hot to buy.

There's not much point in recalling the madness in detail, and it would distract from the serious business at hand. But it's impossible to resist the temptation to savor some memories, like the guy in the 2001 ad that ran on CNBC who was watching videotapes of the network's coverage of the bull market. CNBC was central to stoking the madness. The 1980s had FNN, which was amateurish and obscure, and was eventually absorbed by the better-financed GE subsidiary in 1991. Not only did CNBC deliver fresh stock prices and the latest news on Mary Meeker, it also created financial TV's first sex symbol, Maria Bartiromo, "the Money Honey," as the *New York Post*'s Page Six dubbed her.

Pre-Maria, the typical female talking head on financial TV was attractive but not overtly sexy. Typically blond, WASPy, and sporting pearls, she evoked old money. Not Bartiromo, with her Italian name, generous mouth, Brooklyn accent, and often unpearled toughness. And she was sharper and more knowledgeable than the Fairfield County types who preceded her. (CNBC reportedly tried to coach the Brooklyn out of her accent, with her enthusiastic cooperation but incomplete success.) In classic late-1990s style, New York Stock Exchange CEO Richard Grasso observed that Bartiromo was "a brand"—a brand that stood for "helping the 'average' investor crash the remnants of Wall Street's old boys' club," as brand consultant Ruth Patkin (2000) put it. She personified the democratization of wealth and turned on the boys all at once. Joey Ramone even wrote a song about her:

> What's happening on Wall Street?
> What's happening at the Stock Exchange?
> I want to know
> What's happening on Squawk Box?
> What's happening with my stocks?
> I want to know
>
> I watch you on the TV every single day
> Those eyes make everything okay
> I watch her every day
>
> I watch her every night
> She's really outta sight
>
> Maria Bartiromo (3x)

But TV is old technology; the Internet was the new big thing. Not only did fantasies about the future webbing of the world feed the optimism of the bull market, the web also provided a means to tell tales and trade furiously. Previously sane people quit their jobs and took up day trading, and teenagers spread investment tips via websites and chatrooms. Most web traders should have stuck to phoning their broker; the more people trade, the worse they generally do, and the web made them able to trade quickly and badly like never before (Barber and Odean 20001a, 2000b).[1] This isn't what the productivity revolution was supposed to be about.

Enough nostalgia. The early 1990s were filled with books about the 1980s boom hitting the wall, and the early 2000s about the end of the 1990s, but we haven't seen many books exploring the propensity of the U.S. economy to alternate wacky booms with protracted collisions.

A survey of that territory might start with some measure of the financialization of everything. For decades, economists dreamed of a world where everything was under constant auction, just like on the stock market, with instantaneously changing prices and rapid turnover. This was thought to maximize efficiency and wealth. And Wall Street and its colleagues around the world have gone a long way to realizing that dream.

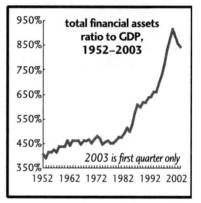

For the last twenty years or so, there's been an inexorable rise in the quantity and variety of financial assets and in the speed with which they're traded. One way of confirming that point is the nearby chart of total financial assets in the U.S. relative to GDP.[2] Figures don't go back to the boom of the 1920s, but we know that financial assets were ravaged after the 1929 crash. When the chart picks up the story in 1952, the financial scene was quite conservative, rather tightly regulated by government and custom. Memories of the Depression were fresh, and the speculative spirit was subdued. There was a pickup in exuberance in the 1960s, but nothing much. But it was only with the takeoff of the Reagan bull market in August 1982 that the creation of equity and debt and everything else really got going.

"Everything else" includes derivatives, which aren't included in the Fed's flow of funds accounting, the source of the numbers behind the chart. They're completely outside the conceptual realm of traditional accounting, which can think of debt and equity, liabilities and assets, but not more insubstantial instruments like options, futures, and inverse floaters. And unlike stocks or loans, it's hard to put a dollar volume on them, since the purported face value of the transaction—the notional principal—is usually far more than the sum of money actually at risk. The Bank for International Settlements reports the notional principal of derivatives at $151 trillion in June 2002, up a stunning 38% from eighteen months earlier. (These are worldwide statistics; it's likely that about half involve Americans.) These figures, which are many times GDP, induce more awe than understanding. But the very immeasurability of the things underscores the point about financialization: layers of claims have been piled upon layers of claims, most of them furiously traded, with some resisting definition and measurement. But if there were some way to capture their growth, the line on the chart would no doubt run off the page.

Economics and finance

What's it all mean? Mainstream economics actually has little of interest to say about the stock market specifically, or finance in general. Most economists treat finance as an afterthought, if they treat it at all. In fact, money itself, even though it's one of the central institutions in our lives, is considered largely "neutral"—a convenient substitute for barter, but with no influence of its own. The view of finance is surprisingly similar. If firms or households need some extra cash, they can borrow it and pay it back later.

High interest rates will discourage borrowing (and, in the case of corporations, investment); low rates will encourage borrowing (and investment). Sometimes firms in need of cash will sell stock to outside investors. And that's about it. There's little consideration of the relation between how firms finance themselves—the mix of debt and equity on their balance sheets, the level of debt, or the sources of the debt (banks or the bond market)—and their performance.

That indifference sometimes affects whole economies. In an interview, former World Bank chief economist Joseph Stiglitz (Henwood 2002) recalled how the IMF urged the Asian countries who faced financial crises in 1997 to raise their interest rates. That would supposedly entice capital to stick around instead of fleeing in a panic. But instead it drove their economies into a tailspin, as firms suddenly faced crushing financing burdens. It would seem that anyone who read a daily newspaper could have predicted this, but not the IMF economists, who didn't allow for bankruptcy. "They're macroeconomists, and it's not in the model," Stiglitz explained.

Within the discipline there is a subspecialty known as financial economics, but it's mainly concerned with how the markets work, not with their relation to the real world. From the 1960s until the early 1980s, the field was dominated by efficient market (EM) theory, a doctrine which percolated into the popular consciousness as the familiar "the market is always right" reflex.[3] More precisely, in its most popular form, it held that prices reflect all available information, which means that there can be no undervalued or overvalued securities. There could be no such thing as smart money, since prices instantly reflect the collective wisdom of millions of investors—an argument Alan Greenspan used in the late 1990s to dismiss worries about a bubble.

In some sense, EM theory is trivially true: of course prices reflect the collective judgments of investors, or at least their buying and selling. But what about the quality of those judgments? If markets are affected by crowd psychology, then prices could be efficiently reflecting delusions. Certainly you wouldn't need a lot of heavy math to prove this to someone who's lived through the past few years.

Cracks began appearing in the EM consensus in the early 1980s. In a classic 1981 paper, Robert Shiller—later more famous as the author of *Irrational Exuberance*—showed that stock prices were far more volatile than were dividends, typically exaggerating the up-and-down moves through the economic cycle; if the market were rationally valuing shares, prices and underlying dividends should move more or less in tandem. (Shiller used dividends, but the concept would work with profits as well.) Shiller subsequently developed theories of markets as arenas of crowd psychology, tending toward fad and overreaction. Papers published throughout the 1980s and early 1990s confirmed Shiller's results.

A series of studies, beginning in the late 1970s and continuing to today, have identified serious, even amusing, anomalies in prices (mostly of stocks, but other speculative markets as well). Returns on the stocks of small firms are generally better than on those of large firms. Stocks with low price/earnings ratios generally outperform those with high ones. Returns are better in January than in other months, but worse on Mondays than other days. Holidays bring good cheer; returns the day before them are better than on other days. Stocks do better when it's sunny in New York than when it's not—and most mysteriously, they do much better around new moons than full.

All this still presumes that investors are often irrational, but not systematically fleeced. In normal times, that's a close enough approximation of reality to explain things. But in extraordinary times, like the late 1990s, it's not even close. One quick way of making that point: according to Zacks Investment Research, of the 8,000 recommendations made by brokerage-house analysts on the stocks comprising the Standard & Poor's 500 in 2000, the year of the market peak, just twenty-nine—0.36%—were recommendations to sell (Morgenson 2001).

And it wasn't just normal American optimism at work. As is now well known, analysts were publicly recommending stocks that they privately disdained. The most striking example of this was star Merrill Lynch analyst Henry Blodget's characterization of a now-forgotten stock called 24/7 as a "piece of shit" even though the firm's public recommendation was "accumulate" (Saigol 2002). In the amazingly light $1.4-billion settlement that Wall Street reached with the authorities in April 2003, it was revealed that investment banks actually paid each other to write glowing research reports on their stocks, an impressive innovation in outsourcing.

The reasons were to move product off the shelves—the stocks that no sane, fully informed person would ever have bought—and to preserve the relationships between brokerage houses and the firms being analyzed. There are two aspects to those relationships. First, the analysts don't want to alienate the firms they cover; if executives stopped talking to them, they analysts would lose what they see as an important source of information. You'd think they'd be better off foregoing this kind of "information"—it's mostly PR spin anyway—but the analysts disagree. And second, the investment banks don't want to forego the lucrative opportunity to underwrite securities for the analyzed firms, and nothing makes executives likelier to look elsewhere than a sell recommendation. Of course, by law and cliché there's supposed to be a "Chinese wall" between investment banking and research, but it's more of an air curtain than a solid structure.

There's no better case study of both irrational exuberance and stacked decks than what happened in the telecommunications industry in the 1990s.

Synergy

It's often said that the U.S. financial system is a miracle of dynamism and innovation, contributing to the dynamism and innovation in the broad economy. This is taken as a given, a self-evident proposition needing no proof. And it may be a good thing that no proof is required, because it's sometimes hard to find. Basic science is heavily funded by the public sector and nonprofit institutions like universities (which, despite their steady transformation into the research arms of the corporate sector, are not yet run by stockholders). Most product innovation comes from large firms, not perky startups. And the role of finance during the late boom was to fund many things that shouldn't have been funded.

The dot.coms are, of course, the headline example. It's hard to imagine any definition of market rationality or efficiency that could explain the funding of Pets.com. But a much grander, and less appreciated, waste of capital occurred in telecommunications in the late 1990s. Given a license to merge or speculate almost without limit by the Telecommunications Act of 1996, the industry, blessed by Wall Street, went on one of the great sprees of all time. In the words of former investment banker Nomi Prins, from 1996 through the end of the boom:

> Wall Street raised $1.3 trillion of telecom debt and sparked a $1.7 trillion merger spree, bagging $15 billion in fees for the effort. Then, the accumulation party ended. The industry collapsed amidst a $230 billion pile of bankruptcies and fraud, wiping out $2 trillion in market value and defaulting on $110 billion of debt (half of all defaults). Telecom execs pocketed $18 billion before they cut 560,000 jobs. And in 2003, over 96% of the capacity built lies dormant.

Many chefs fed the frenzy. Perhaps the most exuberant was George Gilder, who spent the boom celebrating the "telecosm" and touting the stocks that would develop it. In his first incarnation as techno-cheerleader, during the 1980s, Gilder enthused about the miniaturization of everything. But in his 1990s reincarnation, Gilder shook his pom-poms for bandwidth—the ever-fattening, ever-lengthening pipes through which machines, and ultimately humans, could communicate with one another. His favorite bandwidth creator was Global Crossing, which became the fourth-biggest bankruptcy in American history when it filed in 2002. But during the boom, Gilder was awed by its ambitious plan to string fiber optic cable across land and ocean. He declared it his favorite stock—and put his money where his mouth was. He was stunned when it went bust—and he went bust along with it, as did many of his clients.

Like most cheerleaders, though, Gilder was standing on the sidelines during the boom. Not so the investment bankers. No one personified the moment like Jack Grubman of Salomon Smith Barney (SSB). Nominally a telecommunications analyst, he was the industry's great cheerleader and impresario during its late 1990s bubble. He'd attend company board meetings and advise CEOs on strategy—acting as "*consigliere*," in the words of an associate—then come back to his desk (under a "BUY NOW" sign) and write research reports recommending WorldCom, Qwest, and Global Crossing. He didn't actually work the investment banking side, arranging finance or selling securities, but he strongly shaped the nominally independent operation. So he strongly influenced the funding and strategy of the firms he was analyzing. "What used to be a conflict is now a synergy," he explained to *Business Week* (in a story published when the NASDAQ was 28% off its peak). Being "in the flow" helped him to help bankers "think about the industry." When the *BW* reporter wondered if being "in the flow" compromised his objectivity, Grubman would have none of it. "Objective? The other word for it is uninformed" (Elstrom 2000).

Grubman was multiply talented. On his SSB resume, he claimed a degree from MIT, when he had actually gone to Boston University; in his autobiographical narrative, he claimed he was from the same South Philadelphia neighborhood as Frankie Avalon—and even more important to the former boxer Grubman, as the fictional Rocky Balboa. But he wasn't; he was from a nearby section with lots less cachet. Grubman explained his competitiveness and indefatigability by pointing to his modest origins. "I refuse to let anyone topple me. That's why I'm so myopically focused" (ibid.). Evidently his unconscious knew the definition of "myopic" even if his conscious mind didn't.

No doubt small investors bought stock based on TV or print exposure to Grubman, but he had a dedicated following among money managers, who are paid to know better. Money managers eagerly put billions into his deals, and buyers shunned firms that didn't have his blessing. An "insatiable" demand for bandwidth (just ask George Gilder) would guarantee the success of firms like WorldCom, Qwest, Global Crossing, and Level 3, now all wreckage. And though the often-staid *BW* did raise ethical questions about Grubman's multiple roles, like everyone else at the time, they took bandwidth insatiability as axiomatic.

And what do we have to show for the binge? Miles of fiber-optic cable that will forever go unused. Reinforced and underregulated monopolies for the former Baby Bells. And six national cellular phone networks, half of them superfluous, and only one of them (as of early 2003) profitable, and that one (AT&T Wireless) only barely so. The industry as a whole has never made a profit in its twenty-year history. The U.S. cellular system is, as an anonymous *Financial Times* columnist put it, a "third-world" system (Lex 2003). But no one has the cash to upgrade the system; instead, they're cutting capital spending. Mergers are certain—good news for investment bankers, who can earn fees on the shrinkage of the sector they helped swell to absurd proportions.

Grubman wasn't Wall Street's only renaissance man—nor was telecommunications the only industry field in which the multiply talented actors performed. At Credit Suisse First Boston (CFSB), another son of South Philly, Frank Quattrone, played promoter, banker, and analyst. He operated from the Silicon Valley, far from CFSB's New York headquarters, prompting comparisons to Michael Milken's Beverly Hills operation in the 1980s, which was largely independent of Drexel Burnham Lambert's Manhattan home office. One of his synergistic innovations, which once might have been considered a conflict of interest, was that he also ran a venture-capital fund; Quattrone's shop would invest in startups, then take them public in an IPO. But not many people asked the question, obvious both in theory and in hindsight, "If this is such a great investment, why are you selling it to me?" At the peak, Quattrone made as much as $100 million a year (Pulliam and Smith 2001).

A third great synergist was Morgan Stanley's Mary Meeker, who cheered her stocks as tirelessly on the way up as the did as they were losing 90% of their value. She defended her multiple roles as banker, promoter, consultant, and analyst as not conflicting, but as a kind of "stewardship" and a "responsibility." In 1995, she helped bring Netscape public, an event that many consider the originary moment of the Internet bubble. Soon after, she wrote a 300-page report touting the forthcoming cyberboom that became the bubble's sacred text. She too drove the bank's whole tech effort, visiting startups, cultivating ties to venture capitalists, arranging underwritings and leaving the bankers just the details to handle. Annoyed at having lost the eBay IPO to Goldman Sachs, Meeker cultivated chair Meg Whitman by inviting her to dinner and bringing along a draft report—glowing, of course—on eBay. Whitman said she felt honor-bound to stick with Goldman. Meeker published her report on the day eBay began trading, and half a year later, when the firm did another offering, earlier loyalties were forgotten, and eBay forced Goldman to split the deal with Morgan Stanley. Meeker was big on all the substitutes for profits that became so fashionable in the late 1990s—"eyeballs," "hits" and "page-views." She dismissed worries about preposterous valuations by saying that we'd entered "a new valuation zone." (Elkind 2001).

Synergy was the theme of the era. Not only could one person's left hand promote the work of the right, one branch of a bank could promote the work of another. The repeal of the Glass-Steagall Act, which had separated investment and commercial banking since the 1930s, provided great opportunities for cross-promotion, reminding us exactly why the businesses were separated seventy years ago. The commercial-bank side of the business would extend loans to companies that didn't deserve them, just so the investment-banking side could underwrite the clients' stock and bond offerings, a far more lucrative endeavor than old-fashioned bank lending.

Telecommunications benefited from this banking miracle, but so did energy companies. Enron, of course, was the most famous (and it also played the telecoms game too)—but there were also Dynergy, El Paso, and Duke. The story there was that newly deregulated markets like electricity would lead to massive efficiency gains, and with those, massive profits. Neither materialized. The closest the sector came to massive profits was during the California energy crisis of 2001, which starred Enron, and depended mostly on market manipulations and political connections (Slocum 2001).

Deregulators like Enron always portray themselves as vigorous free marketeers, but there was nothing invisible about their hands. They spent millions on lobbying, and worked every level, from statehouses to the Senate. In 1992, when she was chair of the Commodity Futures Trading Commission (CFTC), Wendy Gramm exempted Enron's trading in electricity futures from oversight. Enron happened to be a big funder of her husband, Texas senator Phil Gramm (another friend of the free market who drew public paychecks almost all his working life). Six days after that ruling, Gramm left the CFTC, and five weeks later she joined Enron's board. In December 2000, Senator Gramm helped push a bill through Congress that deregulated trading in energy. Enron's electricity trading business swelled, and some of the firm's only real profits were made. Without owning a single California power plant, Enron came to control the state's market. Rolling blackouts became the norm, prices skyrocketed, and the state racked up billions in debt. Phil Gramm blamed environmentalists for the crisis. Finally, price controls were imposed and the bubble burst. Deprived of its cash cow, Enron hit the rocks a few months later.

But of course the biggest profiteers were the synergists themselves, the investment banks and venture capitalists (VCs). Underwriting fees for IPOs alone were nearly $4 billion in 1999, an all-time record, well over twice the early-1990s average—and five times the average of the late-1980s. Venture capitalists (VCs) made out like bandits. The example of eToys is inspiring: idealab, an Internet incubator that invested in startups, paid $100,000 for a stake in eToys in June 1997. A bit more than two years later, idealab sold some of its shares for $193 million. Public investors did less well; the retailer went public in May 1999 at $20 a share, hit $76 before the end of its first day of life, hit $84 five months later—and then lost 93% of its value. It should be pointed out that most individual investors didn't get in at the offering price; offerings are reserved for brokers' favorite customers, like big institutions and the occasional politician. Most small-time punters probably got in around $70 or higher. This history is further proof of the maxim that it's generally a bad idea to buy what rich, sophisticated investors are selling. Other deals were even richer for VCs; Benchmark Capital's $5 million early investment in eBay, one of the few dot.coms that managed to make a profit, sold its stake for $4.2 billion around the turn of the millennium—an 83,800% return (Ip et al. 2000).

Those were the fat years for the VCs, who raise money from institutional investors and rich individuals and invest the proceeds in lots of risky startups, hoping that a few will win big and offset the inevitably larger population of failures. They make their big money by taking the winners public, while writing off the losers. Usually it works out that way, especially in times like the late 1990s, when public investors were willing to buy almost anything. Venture funds that were formed in 1996 returned 117% of the original outlay to investors, and the companies they'd invested in were worth more than four times the amount originally raised. Sadly, funds that were formed in 1999, just before the peak, returned 17% of the original cash to investors in 2002, and the portfolio of companies was worth half as much as what outside investors had ponied up (Prasso 2003).

Industry salaries, always the highest for which the Bureau of Economic Analysis reports data, greatly expanded their premium over the average, as the chart shows. Figures are only available with some delay, so we'll see if the premium has followed the NASDAQ southward.

Finance and power

After such lurid tales, it's tempting to denounce the whole Wall Street racket as parasitical, which it can be, and utterly pointless, which it isn't. The "excesses" of the period shouldn't lead to an effort to try to recreate something more "normal."

Most financial claims involve relations of ownership and power and appropriation of other people's money. Dividends on stock are disbursements from profits, which originate in the uncompensated labor of the firm's workers and those of its outside contractors. Capital gains on stocks reflect, in large part, markups based on the growth in those profits. Interest on corporate bonds comes from the same source, and on government bonds from taxpayers. Even something as abstract and nonsensical as efficient market theory isn't pointless; it served as a nice intellectual rationale for class warfare. If the market is always right, then doing what pleases it is ideal social policy. What pleases it is maximizing profits, which means keeping wages and other costs as low as possible—and capital's costs are often others' benefits. Michael Jensen (1989), one of the leading theorists of our financial capitalism, is a furious class warrior, listing striking workers and Ralph Nader as destructive obstacles to economic progress. In a 1995 interview, he told me that GM was overstaffed by 20–25%, though he didn't say how he knew this.

Financial power is about more than monetary transfer; financial claims confer real authority on their owners. Stockholders have demanded steadily higher profits, which kept corporations downsizing and outsourcing even in the best of times. Bondholders have pressured state and local governments to trim their budgets. Bankers and bondholders (in alliance with state institutions like the IMF) have forced severe economic restructurings on debtor countries.

Driving American financialization was the great upsurge in corporate profitability from 1982 through 1997, after a long erosion from its 1966 peak, shown on the chart on the next page.[4] That's what drove the stockmarket rally, promoted the exuberant mood, and provided the cash to keep things going.

New Economists would argue that conventional measures of profitability shown here—profits divided by the value of the capital stock—undervalues intangible assets like brand names, patents, and ways of working. But to include them as capital would lower the profit rate—and since the value of such intangibles has putatively been rising, adding them to capital would reduce the great upsurge of the 1980s and 1990s. Conceptually, these intangibles seem instead like ways of increasing profit—though often at the expense of competitors.

It's not hard to figure out what caused the fifteen-year profit boom—a reversal of the forces that produced the sixteen-year bust that preceded it. The conventional story is that excessively stimulative and indulgent government policies led to a great inflation, compounded by the oil-price shocks of 1973 and 1979.

There's some truth to the standard story, but it also needs to be translated into political language. The long post–World War II boom had fed the expansion of the welfare state. The sting of unemployment was lessened, and workers became progressively less docile. Wildcat strikes were spreading, and factory workers were smoking pot on breaks and sabotaging the line. Internationally, the U.S. had lost the Vietnam war and discovered that its conscript army was an undisciplined horde that was not shy about shooting commanding officers. The Third World was in broad rebellion, demanding global wealth redistribution and a new world economic order, a point that OPEC made forcefully in 1973 and again in 1979.

Behind the economic concept of inflation was a fear among elites that they were losing control. That's not to deny the importance of accelerating prices. The inflation that peaked in 1980 didn't set any records, as the chart shows, but its predecessors (1864, 1917, and 1947) were all during or just after major wars, when the economy is worked well beyond capacity to fund the military effort. The inflation upsurge that began in the late 1950s and accelerated in the 1960s and 1970s was unique in that it was not the by-product of a major war effort and that it looked more like a sustained increase than a temporary spike. (The Cold War buildup and the Vietnam war were major expenditures, but nothing like World War II—though another way of looking at it is that permanent war mobiliza-

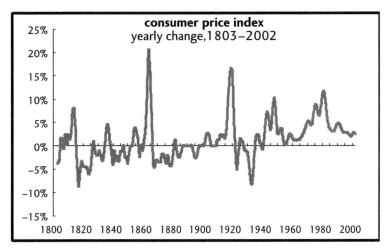

consumer price index
yearly change, 1803–2002

tion became normal behavior.) It seemed that something structural had changed. Financially, that was experienced as deteriorating portfolios for bondholders, as interest rates failed to compensate for inflation's erosion of principal; if you held on to a portfolio of long-term Treasury bonds between 1950 and 1981, you'd have lost 73% of your capital in real terms. T-bonds were nicknamed "certificates of confiscation." Stocks did better; returns on a portfolio mimicking the S&P 500 stayed positive through the

1970s, but still turned in the third worst performance of any decade since 1820 (exceeded in badness only by the 1910s and 1930s).

What had changed structurally, aside from permanent war mobilization, was the growth of the welfare state and sustained low unemployment rates. In his classic paper, Michal Kalecki (1943) explored the reasons why economic policymakers would never tolerate an unemployment rate approaching zero for long:

> Indeed, under a regime of permanent full employment, the "sack" would cease to play its role as a disciplinary measure. The social position of the boss would be undermined, and the self-assurance and class-consciousness of the working class would grow. Strikes for wage increases and improvements in conditions of work would create political tension.

That would mean the loss of "discipline in the factories" and would put "political stability" at risk—which explains a good bit of the 1970s, not only in the domestic U.S. economy, but worldwide: a loss of discipline in the whole social factory.

That indiscipline was met with the rightwing ascendancy of the late 1970s. For the first few post–World War II decades, the generosity of the state expanded worldwide, even in the U.S., where social democratic politics has a historically weak presence. Many countries protected their industries and regulated finance and other sectors, cross-border capital flows were often restricted, and currencies weren't always easily convertible into other currencies.[5] The nineteenth-century economics of light regulation, tight budgets free prices, and self-equilibrating markets—what Keynes derided during the Depression as "the Treasury view"—seemed deeply buried.

You needn't take the word of a long-dead Marxist like Kalecki for it, though; there's supporting testimony from Alan Greenspan. Several times during the late 1990s, Greenspan worried publicly that, as unemployment drifted steadily lower the "pool of available workers" was running dry.[6] The dryer it ran, the greater the risk of "wage inflation," meaning anything more than minimal increases. Productivity gains took some of the edge off this potentially dire threat, said Greenspan, and so did "a residual fear of job skill obsolescence, which has induced a preference for job security over wage gains"—the threat of the "sack," as Kalecki put it, still had its sting. Workers were nervous and acting as if the unemployment rate were higher than the 4% it reached in the boom. Still, Greenspan was a bit worried, because as he put it with characteristic wit, if the pool stayed dry, "significant increases in wages, in excess of productivity growth, [would] inevitably emerge, absent the unlikely repeal of the law of supply and demand." Which is why Greenspan & Co. raised short-term interest rates by about two points during 1999 and the first half of 2000. There was no threat of inflation—with much of the world economy flat on its back, it was one of the last things to worry about—nor were there any signs of rising worker militancy. But wages were creeping higher, and the threat of the sack was losing some of its bite. The share of respondents to the Conference Board's monthly survey declaring jobs to be "plentiful" reached an all-time high of 56% in July 2000—as the share calling them "hard to get" reached an all time low of 10%. Of course, the monetary tightening also burst the stock bubble and ended the boom, which was more than Greenspan bargained for.

Central bankers

Though elements of the U.S. elite had never accepted the New Deal—and the inclusion of unions as junior partners in governance—for decades, their political influence was largely confined to the loony right. To be a free-market conservative in the early 1970s was only a little more respectable than being a necromancer. By the end of the decade, it was another story entirely. Inflation and sagging profits meant that all the civilizing restrictions on capital had to go. Academic economists and think-tankers provided the intellectual rationale, and politicians soon picked up the line. Though many liberals today portray the transformation of economic life through deregulation and austerity as a "conservative" affair, in most parts of the world, major parties on both sides of the spectrum have done its work. In the U.S., transport deregulation was concocted in part in the senatorial office of Ted Kennedy and put into practice in the Carter years. Carter appointed Paul Volcker chair of the Federal Reserve, leading to a regime of tight money like the U.S. hadn't seen in decades. In Europe, social democratic parties were often the most aggressive marketizers.

Volcker was a crucial figure. He declared early in his reign, "the American standard of living must decline" (Rattner 1979) and made it happen. When he took office in August 1979, the federal funds rate—the interest rate banks charge each other for overnight loans, a rate entirely determined by Fed policy and the benchmark for other short-term rates—was around 11%. Volcker pushed it up to near 14% by year-end. A recession began that January (though it wasn't officially announced as one until June)—a short, sharp one that scared the Fed into cutting rates. Fed funds bottomed out at 9% in July, just as the recession was ending. And then Volcker began his major financial offensive, driving fed funds steadily upward to their peak of 19% by July 1981—the beginning of a long, deep recession that would empty factories and break unions in the U.S. and drive debtor countries to the brink of insolvency, beginning the long era of structural adjustment.

Volcker—who got reinforcements in the class war with Reagan's inauguration in January 1981—let the recession drag on. Unemployment was 6% when he took over; less than a year later it was pushing 8%. He eased off a bit in late 1981, and unemployment drifted lower. But he soon tightened again, and he pushed rates higher into 1982. In August 1981, Reagan fired the striking air traffic controllers, breaking a long taboo against replacing strikers—and organized labor did nothing to fight back. Unemployment rose to near 11%—the highest level by far since 1941. Despite the savage slump, long-term interest rates kept rising into 1982; apparently, Volcker's austerity program had not convinced the creditor class that inflation wouldn't return when the business cycle turned up.

Everything changed in August 1982. Mexico announced that it couldn't pay its foreign debts. At almost the same minute, the U.S. stock market bottomed and began the long bull run that would last for eighteen years. Volcker couldn't allow Mexico to "blow," as he said; Mexico's crisis marked the climax of his squeeze, and he had to ease. Wall Street understood that, and bought stocks, which has usually been a good idea when monetary stringency turns to ease. As they came to say on Wall Street, "bailouts are bullish."

But bailouts are bullish only when they confirm or reinforce the power of capital. Domestically, Volcker had won the war. The American standard of living had declined: between his taking office in 1979 and the recession's bottom in November 1982, the average real hourly wage fell almost 6%, the ranks of unemployed had doubled, and the consciousness of workers had filled with fear.

Volcker kept a tight rein as the economy recovered. He raised rates again in 1983 and 1984—tightenings that were reversed in 1985 and 1986. But still, real interest rates (nominal rates less inflation) remained high by historical standards. Unemployment didn't fall convincingly below 7% until late 1986, and was still 6% when he left office in August 1987.

His successor, Alan Greenspan, raised rates after taking office, but the

October 1987 stock market crash forced him to retreat and engineer the first of the panic bailouts that would become routine in the Greenspan years. But once the crash rescue had passed, Greenspan spent the second half of 1988 and the first half of 1989 tightening, provoking the long early-1990s slump. Unemployment rose and real wages continued to fall. Even though the economy was officially in recession for only a short time in 1990–91, the job market remained flat into 1992, the days of the first "jobless recovery." Wages finally bottomed out in 1995, after falling by more than 10% from the time Volcker begin his attack.

The whole period was a practical application of the principles laid out by Kalecki. In combination with everything else that was going on—benefit cutbacks by employers, outsourcing, speedup, permanent downsizing, cutbacks in regulation—the central-bank-led class war succeeded in more than doubling the profit rate for nonfinancial corporations between 1982 and 1997.

That profit upsurge is the fundamental reason for the great bull market of the 1980s and 1990s. Since stocks are claims on profits, higher profits generally mean higher stock prices. But that's not all. The profit gusher meant that corporations had more cash to distribute, which they did by buying up other corporations as well as their own stock—jolts to demand that also decreased the supply of available stock, a double-barreled boost to prices. The upward redistribution of income meant that the rich had more money to pour into stocks. And compounding the valuation mark-ups and the geyser of cash was the exuberance of the investing class, which had won victory after victory, from the crushing of labor to the neoliberal restructuring of the South to the greatest prize of all, the collapse of the USSR. Capitalism American style had conquered the world and there was no remotely plausible rival. It wasn't until the late 1990s that investor exuberance crossed from rational to irrational—about the time that profits were peaking and the American masses were plunging into the market for the first time.

But the profit surge was its own undoing. Some of the profit increase found its way back into the markets—not in the form of dividends, but mainly through takeovers and stock buybacks—because firms had no more profitable outlet for them in their underlying businesses. But profits were nice enough that firms could invest passionately too, especially in computers and telecommunications gear. Overinvestment led to falling profit rates and unused capacity, and when the financial bubble burst, so did the high-tech equipment boom. Even though such gadgets depreciate quickly, memories of the excess kept capital spending low well into 2003.

The new princes

We've been considering developments mainly at the high political level, which, among other things, is a reminder that talk of markets eclipsing the state is premature. Central banks are great class warriors. But class war was also fought in the world denominated in shares of stock.

In the U.S., the modern corporation—characterized by dispersed stockholders entrusting management to hired professionals—emerged in the last years of the nineteenth century and the first years of the twentieth. The scale of production had greatly outstripped an ownership structure dominated by individual owners and small partnerships; those closely held entities were merged or converted into public corporations whose shares traded on the open market. That transformation had its moment of irrational exuberance; the period around the turn of the century was full of talk of a New Era—one blessed by miraculous bursts of productivity with no end in sight, very similar to the millennial discourse of our New Economy moment of the late 1990s.

It *was* a new era in the sense that it meant the emergence of the corporation as the most significant private economic institution, capital's preferred organizational form. And with it came modern stock markets. Stock markets have a long history, but there weren't many companies to trade until the late nineteenth century, and they were of little economic significance. But they became central to the governance of the public corporation—which isn't to say that it's been an easy task.

Owners of shares are legally entitled to the residual profit earned by firms after they pay business expenses and interest. That leaves managers with a great deal of wiggle room: they can always shirk and swindle, and shareholders are often in a weak position from which to scrutinize them.

Sometimes the stock market does very well, and shareholders are quietly happy. Other times the market does poorly, which makes shareholders very sad. Shareholders were very happy during the 1920s, but their happiness came to a dramatic end with the crash of October 1929. Rising share prices can be a great narcotic, causing investors to overlook a lot of serious problems. Falling prices, though, force open a lot of closet doors, revealing a great supply of hidden skeletons.

An important milestone in thinking about the corporation came in 1932, with the publication of Adolph Berle and Gardiner Means's classic book, *The Modern Corporation and Private Property.* Berle and Means described a world in which shareholders had been fleeced by managers—an understandable position, after all the scandals of the 1920s. But they were powerless to respond—too dispersed and detached to do the work of reining in their hired hands. They listed several avenues of managerial abuse of disenfranchised owners: "out of professional pride," managers may "maintain labor standards above those required by competitive conditions," or "improve quality above the point" that is likely to be maximally profitable to shareholders. This held the potential for "a new form of absolutism, relegating 'owners' to the position of those who supply the means whereby the new princes may exercise their power." It's not the *rentier* who is the parasite in this model, but the managers who run production.

In his preface to the 1967 edition, Berle described the new system as one of "collective capitalism," an affair that yokes together thousands of corporations, and millions of employees, owners, and customers—too many people to be considered private enterprise in the classic sense, and since the state was now so deeply involved, no redefinition of "private" could ever be broad enough to apply. Research was no longer carried out by lone inventors, but in teams, and no longer within a single enterprise, but in cooperation with university and government researchers—not to mention with subsidies from public and nonprofit sources. To the 1967 Berle, these changes had moved us "toward a new phase fundamentally more alien to the tradition of profit even than that forecast" in the first edition of their book, published thirty-five years earlier.

That all seems pretty quaint now, but it was 1960s orthodoxy. The same year that Berle updated his classic, John Kenneth Galbraith published another, *The New Industrial State*. Galbraith's stockholders were almost vestigial, a "purely pecuniary association" divorced from management, too numerous and dispersed to have any influence. When displeased with "their" corporation, they would sell the stock rather than pick a fight with management. Stockholder rebellion among large corporations was "so rare that it can be ignored," because trouble-free profitability was the norm. Galbraith's corporation was run by a "technostructure" of suits and geeks.

Profit maximization was a thing of the 1960s past. To Galbraith, high profits would only be passed along to shareholders and would undoubtedly come only with an increase in risk. Pay was relatively modest and unconnected to the stock price. Secure mediocrity was the goal. Galbraith's corporation had become subservient to the larger society and the state, with the state providing economic stabilization and an educated workforce. Keynes's goal, the euthanasia of the *rentier,* had been largely achieved.

This nice world came apart in the 1970s. Stocks had their worst decade since the 1930s, and bonds performed miserably, failing even to keep up with inflation. As we saw earlier in the chapter, to the ruling classes, things were wildly out of whack, with American workers acting insolent and the Third World in rebellion. Subduing the Third World was left to Ronald Reagan and the *contras,* but Wall Street declared war on the workers' insolence—and in this case, corporate managers were a special kind of worker that also needed to be subdued.

To accomplish that subduing, Wall Street has tried several strategies over the last two decades. First was the wave of hostile takeovers and leveraged buyouts that dominated the financial landscape of the 1980s. Underperforming companies—those generating insufficient profits to satisfy shareholders—were taken over, either by allegedly more competent rivals or by corporate raiders (or, as Alan Greenspan dubbed them at the time, "unaffiliated corporate restructurers"), or they were taken private by a management team in partnership with outside investors using lots of borrowed money. Regardless of the financial maneuver, the operational strategy was similar: shut or sell weak divisions, lay off workers, cut wages, break unions (where they existed), speed up the line, get the profit rate up. The moral philosophy of this period was nicely summed up by Oliver Stone's Gordon Gekko, channeling the most famous inside trader of all time, Ivan Boesky: "Greed is good."

Unfortunately, these maneuvers usually involved lots of debt, and the debt load proved crippling by decade's end. So there was a shift of strategy toward shareholder activism. Led by large pension funds, particularly the California Public Employees Retirement System (Calpers), institutional investors drew up hit lists of saggy companies, and pressed management to shape up or ship out. At the same time, managers' pay was shifted from straight salaries to stock options—the idea was to make managers think not like pampered employees, but like stockholders, whose income was directly tied to the stock price. The operational strategy was similar to that of the 1980s, however—downsizing, outsourcing, and speedup—whatever was necessary to get profits, and with them, stock prices, up.

The micro-record of "restructurings"—the mix of downsizings, the closure or sale of weaker divisions, and big accounting writeoffs—isn't always as good as theorists promise. Restructurings are usually thought to boost profits, and therefore stock prices. Certainly that's the popular perception in the business press and among workers. Rigorous studies are far less certain of this conclusion: the effect of restructuring announcements on stock prices is positive in some studies, negative in others, but hardly conclusive either way. And the effect on profitability seems to be negative, not positive, in the five years following the announcement (Lopez et al. 2000).

Lopez and his colleagues don't speculate on the reason for this disappointing performance. It may be that restructuring firms are wounded animals to begin with—the ones in this study were less profitable on average than their industry peers going into the restructuring—and a round of bloodletting does nothing to restore corporate health. Downsizings may damage morale among surviving workers, who may concentrate more on looking good than working well. Better workers—those with the brightest reemployment prospects—may be the ones who volunteer to leave when buyout packages are offered, leaving behind the timeservers. Or it may be that since workers, not portfolio managers and CEOs, are the actual producers of value, reducing their numbers may hurt the bottom line over the long term.

At the macro level, it's a different story, where the effects can be bracing, since they help induce a climate of fear and deference. Workers who read stories of massive layoffs at brand-name firms may be more inclined to do whatever the boss asks—toil harder, longer, cheaper—than they would otherwise be. Persistent and high levels of worker anxiety, so cheerfully noted by Alan Greenspan, well into the 1990s expansion may be the successful general result of policies that are less successful at the firm level. Restructuring CEOs may not be expanding their own bottom lines, but they're doing a favor to their class when they announce 5,000 layoffs; it sends a salutary message through the system.

The experiment in compensation looks less successful at any level. Tying managerial pay to stock prices was supposed to solve at least two problems. Aligning managers' incentives with those of shareholders was supposed to end the owner–manager conflict that Berle/Means and Jensen whined about. And since efficient market theory assured that the stock market's judgments were as good as you could get, managers were held to an objective and pitiless discipline. But things didn't work out according to plan. Managers good and bad profited from the bull market, which drove most share prices relentlessly higher with little distinction. *Business Week*'s annual surveys of executive pay prove year after year that there's no relation at all between compensation and corporate performance. And in seriously troubled companies, where profits were invented by clever accountants, there was no incentive to blow the whistle. Instead, the incentive was the opposite, to experiment more aggressively with creative accounting and keep it quiet.

Not that the options game was wholly without payoff. For companies, options have several charms: they substitute for cash salaries, offer big tax deductions, and allow heavy users to overstate their profits, since options need not be accounted for as an expense. Such 1990s highfliers as AOL, Viacom, Lucent, and Cisco would have reported earnings 25–75% lower than they did in the late 1990s had accounting standards required honesty.

And options helped reduce the IRS bill: Microsoft saved more than $2 billion on taxes in 2000 thanks to options; Cisco, $1.4 billion; Enron, $390 million (Henry and Conlin 2002).

And options offered gigantic payoffs to senior execs (and, democratic rhetoric to the contrary, options were overwhelmingly concentrated among senior execs, not ordinary employees, as we saw at the end of chapter 3). When *Business Week* started doing its annual compensation survey in 1950, the highest-paid CEO was GM's Charles Wilson, who took home $652,156 (before taxes), or 229 times as much as the average worker. In 2001, the pay champ was Oracle's Larry Ellison, who exercised some long-held options, netting himself $706 million (even though the company and its stock was doing rather badly)—or 28,193 times as much as the average worker. Those are extreme cases compared over the very long term, but even nonextreme comparisons are stunning: the average CEO pulled down more than 400 times as much as the average hourly worker in 2001, up from a mere 42 times in 1980 (Borrus and Foust 2003). It'd be very hard to argue that the economy of 2001 was 123 times as good as that of 1950, or almost ten times as good as that of 1980. Unless you're a CEO, that is.

Most egregiously, execs profited handsomely even among companies that went under. A *Financial Times* survey of the twenty-five biggest bankruptcies of 2001 and early 2002 found that executives and directors took home $3.3 billion, almost all of it from stock options (Cheng 2002). Many of the Barons of Bankruptcy, as the *FT* dubbed them, showed uncanny timing, exercising their options just before the stocks fell from grace.

The Americanization of global finance

Though it remains to be seen whether the trend will survive the homeland meltdown, the 1990s saw the spread of U.S.-style financial markets around the globe. As national barriers to capital mobility have largely disappeared over the last twenty years—thanks importantly to U.S. lobbying—the global financial scene has come to resemble the domestic American one: vast, complex, freewheeling, polarizing, volatile, and accident-prone.

To anyone who's been following the economic news over the last few years, this will all seem familiar. But behind the highly visible melodramas—the manias, the panics, the bailouts—lies a reconfiguration of power between richer and poorer countries and between owners and workers nationally and internationally.

As the *New York Times* put it, Clinton, and his Treasury Secretary and former Goldman Sachs co-chair Robert Rubin, "took the American passion for free trade and carried it further to press for freer movement of capital" (Kristof and Sanger 1999). That's not exactly true; the U.S. has been pressing for the freer movement of capital since the early 1970s, and the Organization for Economic Cooperation and Development (OECD) set up a Code of Liberalization of Capital Movements at the time of the organization's birth in 1961 (Helleiner 1994, pp. 94, 111). But there's little question that the passion for freer international money flows accelerated in the Clinton-Rubin years. As former Commerce Department negotiator Jeffrey Garten put it, "I never went on a trip when my brief didn't include either advice or congratulations on liberalization.... We were convinced we were moving with the stream, and that our job was to make the stream move faster.... Wall Street was delighted" (Kristof and Sanger 1999).

What are some of the features of U.S. finance that the rest of the world has been encouraged to adopt? Perhaps the broadest taxonomical distinction is that between stock-market and bank-centered systems. In most Asian and continental European countries, stock markets have historically been relatively small and sleepy, and they aren't terribly relevant to how corporations are run. In the U.S. and most of the other predominantly

English-speaking countries, stock markets are large and busy, and they have a great influence on corporate life. This ideal typology has blurred in recent years, as stock and other financial markets have grown—and it's virtually certain that the creation of the euro will greatly Americanize European finance. But it's still a useful way to start thinking about the relations between finance and the real world. And there's been enormous pressure, through the IMF and the World Bank, on poorer countries to adopt U.S.-style financial structures.

It's fairly simple to draw parallels from the brief financial history of the U.S. to a global scale. At the end of World War II, the international monetary system, known as Bretton Woods, was based on fixed exchange rates—the value of currencies were set relative to the U.S. dollar, and the U.S. dollar was set to a gold price of $35. The designers of the Bretton Woods system knew that fixed exchange rates were incompatible with free capital flows. International trade was encouraged by policy, but cross-border money flows weren't.

Strains began building on this fixed arrangement in the 1960s. Inflation rose, meaning that the dollar was effectively no longer worth the $35 an ounce that it was declared to be. Also, Western Europe and Japan were busily catching up to U.S. productivity levels, meaning that their currencies were chronically undervalued relative to the dollar.[7]

Starting in the 1970s, the U.S. began pressing for liberalization of capital accounts worldwide. The classic Bretton Woods system encouraged trade flows, as did repeated tariff reductions agreed on through the mechanism of the General Agreement on Tariffs and Trade (GATT). But capital flows had been pretty tightly restricted. The lead designers of the fixed exchange rate system, John Maynard Keynes from Britain and Harry Dexter White from the United States, thought it important to insulate countries from the pressures of international capital markets. Quaintly, the point of national economic policy was thought to be the encouragement of full employment, and, in the eyes of Keynes and White, free international capital movements would undermine such policies. To financiers, the full employment policies are frequently equated with inflation, and any country pursuing such policies in a world of liberalized finance would be punished with capital flight.

There was intellectual opposition to the system from the free-market right, which hated the idea of state-specified exchange rates taking precedence over market-determined ones, and some grumbling from Wall Street and the City of London, but those forces were pretty marginal in the 1950s and early 1960s. As pressures on the system grew, however, liberalization appeared to be a solution, especially to the U.S.

The first steps in the early 1970s were crucial—breaking apart the fixed exchange rate system and severing the dollar's link to gold. For the last twenty-five years, currency values have been increasingly set by the foreign exchange markets, not governments. One by one, countries abandoned their attempts to fix the value of their currencies and surrendered to the whims of foreign exchange traders in New York and London.

At first, liberalization concerned mainly the rich countries; the 1970s were not yet the era of "emerging markets." With the onset of the debt crisis in 1982, however, capital accounts were liberalized as part of the solution to the crisis. Nationalist development policies, which had insulated countries from outside capital and trade flows, were dismantled wholesale. Economists and bankers assured everyone that bringing the debtor countries into the world product and financial markets would be best for everyone over the long term. Just as protectionist trade policies were said to "distort" prices and other economic relationships, restrictions on capital movements were said to inhibit the optimal global allocation of capital. If capital were free to seek its highest, best purposes—defined, of course, by its maximum profit opportunities—efficiency would rule and growth would accelerate. It may surprise readers to learn that that's a description of the world we've been living in for the past twenty years, a world of maldistribution and waste, but that's the theory.

The "resolution" of the debt crisis contributed directly to the Americanization of global finance in several ways. Debtor countries privatized state firms, often turning them over to foreign owners; debts were transformed into equity holdings (that is, creditors were given ownership shares to replace debts that would never be fully paid off); and bank debts were transformed into so-called Brady bonds (that is, instead of a bank holding a credit until it matured, the newly minted bond could be sold on world financial markets; the instrument is named after Bush 41's treasury secretary, Nicholas Brady). Official finance—loans from governments and from public entities like the World Bank—dwindled, and private finance took its place, and within the realm of private finance, loans from banks dwindled, and they were replaced by funds coming from bond and stock markets.

And, along with the growth of so-called portfolio investment (flows from stock and bond markets), foreign direct investment (FDI) played an increasing role. FDI—cross-border investment by multinational corporations—is usually thought of as "real," as opposed to purely financial investment. And certainly there's been plenty of creation of new plants and production networks by multinationals all across Latin America and Asia. But by official definitions, FDI also includes the purchase of existing corporate assets—for example, the purchase of a privatized national telephone company by a foreign company would count as FDI, even though no new physical assets are created in the process. Indeed, by U.S. definitions, the purchase of as little as 10% of the stock of an existing company by a foreign investor counts as direct investment, even though it resembles a portfolio transaction. The logic is that a purchase of a stake that large isn't really a short-term trade, but part of a longer-term business strategy. But it's worth emphasizing again that financial flows are at least as much about arranging ownership as they are about providing funds for real economic activity.

To put it bluntly but not inaccurately, twenty years ago, the bulk of foreign finance for so-called middle-income countries like Mexico and Brazil came from commercial bank loans and official institutions; now, the bulk comes from the bond and stock markets and FDI by foreign multi-nationals. This has several important consequences. While FDI flows are relatively stable, purely financial flows are anything but. Financial markets are notoriously volatile, given to extremes of optimism and despair. Minor shocks can get magnified into major disasters, and innocent bystanders can get punished by the so-called "contagion" effect. Countries can get punished in a financial panic merely for speaking the same language as or being next door to a country in crisis. Trouble in Mexico can be bad news for Argentina. During the 1980s debt crisis, the fact that the prominent creditors were banks meant that things were worked out by a relatively small group of negotiators over the course of years. Since the 1990s, with widely dispersed bondholders and stockholders as the principal source of foreign funds, a crisis can be precipitated practically overnight, and you'd need a soccer stadium to house all the creditors (though of course the U.S. Treasury and the IMF always take a leading role in acting on the creditors' behalf).

The Mexican boom-and-bust cycle of the early 1990s and the Asian boom-and-bust cycle of the mid-1990s are textbook examples of the contagious volatility characteristic of this Americanized global system. In both cases, the foreign inflows created a speculative bubble followed by a dramatic bursting. In Mexico's case, the bubble was largely financial; there was relatively little real-world investment financed by the inflow. In the Asian case, a lot of the inflow did find its way into real investment, ranging from factories to office buildings, which turned out to be worthless when the bubble burst. In the Mexican case, ordinary people felt little benefit during the inflow; in the Asian case, real jobs (hardly dream jobs, for sure) were created and incomes rose. In both cases, though, the consequences for Mexican and Asian workers when the bubble burst were savage, with jobs disappearing and incomes collapsing.

Besides the volatility of capital flows in this privatized, Americanized world, there's another serious problem—concentration. Both portfolio and direct investment tends to be concentrated in a few countries, mainly the larger Latin American countries, a few Asian ones (China especially), and a few "transition" countries (Poland, Russia). Portfolio flows are also highly concentrated, confined mainly to countries that provincial U.S.-based portfolio managers have heard of. Smaller and poorer countries, like those of the Caribbean, Africa, or South Asia, are largely excluded from this circuit of private capital flows.

It's not just American financial structures that Washington has been promoting—it's the corporate governance model as well. Though it now seems hilarious after Ken Lay and Gary Winnick, the U.S. Treasury and its effective subsidiary, the IMF, blamed the 1997–98 Asian crisis on poor corporate governance practices and a lack of transparency. U.S. pundits also trace Japan's troubles to similar faults. What this means is that Asian corporations typically have intimate ties to one another, to banks, and to governments that are profoundly different from the system prevailing in the U.S., where stockholdings are widely dispersed among thousands, even millions, of holders, and governments are much less involved in corporate affairs. Instead of listening to colleagues (or "cronies," in the pejorative voice), bankers, and bureaucrats, U.S. managers are guided by the stock market in the ways we've seen. Now we know that cronyism can thrive in a stock-centered system too. Meanwhile, most of the Asian economies have recovered, and the healthier ones, like South Korea, did their best to ignore the IMF's advice.

Whatever you think of the stock-centered system in its homeland, it has little to recommend itself to "developing" countries. Poorer countries need to invest in extremely long-term projects, but stock markets are notorious for tolerating only the surest, quickest-payback investments. Historically, countries aiming to catch up to richer rivals—Germany in the late nineteenth century, Japan in the mid–twentieth century, Korea a bit later than Japan—have controlled finance tightly, ceding a large hand to the state, with firms mainly owned and/or controlled by banks and not by impatient, volatile shareholders. That arrangement is no guarantee of success, of course, but it's a formula that's proved workable.

To U.S. and British pundits, these systems are ossified and prone to "cronyism." It's no matter that Japan and Korea were once touted in the same circles as models of development; that was last decade's truth.

Despite the liberalization of international markets, many domestic systems have a very long way to go before being fully Americanized. Asia has the longest way; Japan and China have barely started. Continental Europe is a major nut to crack; the creation of a single giant financial market with the evolution of the euro will almost certainly bring a more U.S.-like style to finance, but there's a lot of work to do, and political resistance to the social sequelae of Americanization—instability, impoverishment, marginalization—is strong, and strengthened by the course of the NASDAQ after the spring of 2000. Liberalization has been deeply discredited by the Asian smash-up, though not all that much in the U.S., which strenuously objects to any attempt to reregulate global finance.

The Americanized system has proved remarkably unreliable at promoting prosperity. Much of the world has done poorly by this restructuring. Latin America has gone in and out of crisis for the last twenty years. East Asia did well until its crisis of 1997—a crisis that occurred mainly because of the destabilizing effects of financial capital flows, which magnify both boom and bust; the capital started flowing because of American pressure for liberalization. Another exception, China, which is pretty deep into one of the greatest booms ever known, has almost no exposure to capital flows (of the purely financial kind), and survived the crisis nicely. Russia and much of the rest of the former socialist bloc were liberalized under American pressure, and they enjoyed a great collapse.

But mass prosperity is probably the last thing to expect from Americanization; it's a system designed to drive down costs and maximize the flow of profits to shareholders. Besides polarization, the Americanized system has shown a great propensity for destructive crises. It may destroy itself one of these days, though the system's powers of recovery should never be written off. Catastrophists' hopes to the contrary, though, self-immolation is hardly a safe bet. Thankfully, there are signs that many of the world's people, even a few Americans, are getting annoyed with it.

Conclusion

What comes after the New Economy?

Of course, there's always some new economy. But the intoxicating miracles of the late 1990s—20% annual stock returns, the democratization of ownership and work, fantasies of the end of the business cycle—are gone. Barring a not-at-all-unlikely environmental catastrophe or some presently unimaginable political upheaval, we may see another fantastic boom ten or twenty years from now that produces fantasies similar to those of the late 1990s; certainly that's the historical pattern. But Gen Xers are likely to be drawing Social Security checks when that happens, assuming Social Security still exists.

That's not to say we're in the early stages of another Great Depression. There will be expansions. But it is to say that it looks like the U.S. economy has entered a period of troubles on the order of those of the 1970s. Not in the literal sense, of course: we're not likely to see a return of wildcat strikes and double-digit inflation rates. Those marked the flameout of a very different economic expansion, one founded on broadly rising living standards, a lessening of inequality, high levels of investment, and relatively subdued levels of financial speculation—not just in the U.S., but worldwide. All that was too good to be true for very long, and it came to a bad end. The inflation of the 1970s was "cured" by a massive and successful one-sided class war, as austerity programs, first tested out in the

New York City fiscal crisis of the mid-1970s, were generalized to much of the world.

Austerity largely succeeded on its own terms. Third World rebellions were subdued, and people were convinced by the billions that there was no alternative to economic orthodoxy. But for many parts of the world, the gain promised as the dividend for all this imposed pain never materialized. There were exceptions; hundreds of millions of Chinese, for example, have seen rising incomes—but many millions have also been thrown into unemployment and insecurity. Japan and Western Europe have spent the last decade in the grip of economic stagnation—not miserable, by any means, but certainly not prospering. Latin America has been in and out of recession since the onset of the debt crisis in 1982, and Africa has been sinking deeper into despair.

Japan's former vice–finance minister Eisuke Sakakibara, known around the world as Mr. Yen, has said that the world has entered a new era of deflation, with Japan having led the way. "Alan Greenspan never used the word deflation. He called it an increase in productivity. But it's the same thing" (Pilling 2003). This book has argued that the increase in productivity is a lot more problematic than Greenspan or Sakakibara would have it, but Mr. Yen was right to point to the connection. Just as inflation was an economic symptom of systemic indiscipline (an argument made in chapter 4), deflation is the sickness that comes with excessive discipline—the intensification of competition and savaging of social protections of the last twenty-five years.

It's tempting to read the New Economy era as the ecstatic climax of neoliberalism—that political restructuring of the world that began with the onset of the Thatcher and Volcker regimes in 1979 (though Carter-era transport deregulation was a strong overture), which was further intensified by the Reagan revolution, and was secured with the transformation of most left-of-center political parties into market-friendly entities. It had many triumphs—the use of debt crises to restructure scores of Southern economies, attacks on the welfare state in the North, the apparent death of any substantial ideological or political alternative to the rule of capital.

The New Economy was supposed to be the prosperous payoff of the neocapitalist revolution. It worked in the U.S. for a while, but now several dividend payments had to be omitted. Outside the U.S., global economic prospects don't look brilliant.

Current economic policy looks unlikely to remedy the situation. Massive tax cuts for the very rich—pretty much the Bush administration's only approach—may provide a little fiscal boost. But they won't do anything to address the long-term pathologies of the U.S. economy, like polarization, insecurity, and a massive dependence on foreign capital inflows. Yet things are hardly hopeless.

Four or five years ago, the ideological/political case looked pretty much closed. But in the last few years, a global movement that sometimes calls itself anticapitalist has developed. In the months leading to the U.S. war on Iraq, millions of people filled streets worldwide to object, in a movement that sometimes calls itself anti-imperialist. That's a pretty big deal.

And while this book has been rather unfriendly to New Economy dogma, it's still worth examining its utopian bits. Arising in the midst of what looked like a period of unrestrained capitalist triumphalism, New Economy discourse expressed hopes for something rather different from our predominant economic reality. In a time of massive wealth polarization, it talked about the democratization of ownership. In a time of mass overwork, it dreamt of meaningful, enjoyable work, self-management, and flattened hierarchies. In what seemed like a profoundly conservative time, it appropriated language of revolution (the image of Lenin was even used to advertise a cable-TV company). Amidst a vast speedup of the social factory's assembly line, it evoked fantasies of abundance. And amidst aggressive attempts to privatize information, tighten up intellectual property restrictions, and put a meter on almost everything but the air, it stoked hopes for global linkages. "Information wants to be free," the saying goes, but not as long as AOL Time Warner has its say.

But why did The System's publicists need the utopian story? If all challenges to capitalism were dead, why did we hear so much about democratization and the overturning of hierarchy? Evidently the message has appeal, even in apparently conservative times.

Fine. If a little hierarchy-overturning economic democratization is such a good thing, then why not more? As Jack Kemp once said in a very different context, if you're going to go for it, you should really go for it.

Notes

1 Novelty

1. Though it's sobering to learn that, according to a Scudder Kemper Investments poll, over 80% of Americans have neither heard nor read of a New Economy (reported in *Business 2.0,* September 12, 2000, p. 36).

2. For a classic statement, see *Wired*'s "Encyclopedia of the New Economy" at <hotwired.lycos.com/special/ene/>. There's also former *Wired* editor Kevin Kelly's "New Rules of the New Economy," <www.wired.com/5.09/networkeconomy/>, as well as his exuberant but thinly argued expansion of that article into a book, *New Rules for the New Economy* (Kelly 1999). Kelly—now deposed as editor of *Wired,* a magazine long past its prime—combines born-again Christianity, Social Darwinism, and classic American hucksterish optimism into a single package.

3. Summers is no slouch at selective memory. In the wake of the Mexican crisis of 1994–95, Summers enthused to a House committee about how "the dollar value of annual Mexican exports had nearly doubled from 1980 to 1993"—forgetting to mention that they'd nearly tripled between 1960 and 1973, and that they increased nearly seventeen-fold between 1970 and 1983. Further, Summers kvelled, "real annual GDP growth averaged 3.0% between 1989 and 1994 compared to an average of 0.1% between 1982 and 1988"—comparing a modest recovery with the worst of the debt crisis, and neglecting to say that growth averaged 7.5% a year in the 1960s and 6.6% in the 1970s, a period Summers & Co. dismiss as one of hopelessly backward economic policies.

4. With the increased privatization of high-tech research, the relative openness of work in the public sector and noncorporate academia has been replaced by a regime of corporate secrecy, governed by nondisclosure agreements and the lust for competitive advantage, and enforced by intellectual property lawyers. Whether this will be good for scientific and technical progress over the long term remains to be seen; it is clear, however, that the openness didn't impede progress, privateers' claims to the contrary.

5. A few months later, in September 1965, the same magazine cited several reasons why a pickup in inflation was unlikely, among them small wage gains, high productivity gains, well-behaved unit labor costs, and the absence of supply bottlenecks (quoted in Grant 2000b). This list also looks quite familiar to the student of the most recent New Economy.

6. Not only did the Gipper hand out copies of *Wealth and Poverty* by the boxful; he is even said to have read it, and his chief spook, the now-defunct Bill Casey, subsidized the author during the lean months of composition.

7. Gilder has evolved from the microcosm to the *Telecosm* and no doubt beyond, but it's hard to keep up with his speed-of-light travels towards earthly utopia. But his journey has been longer even than it might appear at first glance. After his father was killed in World War II, Gilder was adopted by David Rockefeller's family; that very symbol of established wealth was the elder Gilder's college roommate. A liberal Republican in the 1960s, Gilder once mocked Ronald Reagan and Barry Goldwater (Perlstein 2001, p. 183). One thing that has remained constant is his primitive sexual ethic. The whole story is wonderfully told by Susan Faludi (1992, pp. 283–90).

8. The Silicon Valley Toxics Coalition <www.svtc.org> has done excellent work bringing the disposal "problem to public attention, along with the broader issues of the impact of computer technology on worker, community, and environmental health."

9. Maybe he was just pandering to a popular audience in the *Fast Company* interview. In a paper posted on his website (Lev, n.d.) says that the announcement of a drug approval can result in up to a 2% pop in the stock price. After reporting this, Lev then asks himself a question, which he promptly answers: "Why not wait for the consequences of innovation activities to be realized in the form of products' revenues and earnings? In most cases, the interval between initiation or even maturation of product development and the ultimate realization of revenues extends over several years. In the meantime, selling shareholders and employees exercising stock options lose when the stock is undervalued, and new stock issued into an underpriced market dilutes shareholders' equity." If the revenues and earnings don't materialize, and thereby justify the 2% pop, then that's a kind of mispricing, but it's much more fun than waiting years!

10. Book value equals the sum of the value of a firm's physical and financial assets less its debts and other liabilities.

11. Specifically, the numbers come from the Fed's flow of funds accounts—market value of equity divided by value of assets, both for nonfinancial corporations.

12. He also included with it an email from his editor, who burbled that she hadn't done much with it "since it's simply wonderful :-)" [emoticon in original].

13. And not just finance: an August 2000 press kit touting Ian Schrager's new New York City hotel, the Hudson, enthused that it is "populist without sacrificing high-style, and refreshingly high-style without pretension, the Hudson is a bellwether for our time. It is an outgrowth of a new world order, one where ever-growing, instant access to global travel and the Internet, with its endless stream of real-time information, has led to a democratization of style, breaking down formerly sacred barriers, and returning it to the people." It is, the publicist declared, "Hotel as Lifestyle."

14. Literally so: the NASDAQ rose a mere 86% in 1999; tulip prices tripled in weeks, and increased tenfold over a matter of months in the mid-1630s.

15. New Economy companies, it seems, didn't perform very well at diversifying their boards of directors. The headhunting firm Spencer Stuart found in a study of a hundred net-related companies that the boards were generally smaller than normal big-company boards, and with all but 3% of them men (Ridge 2000a).

16. n ideological aside: many on the left and right blame the culture industries for our various failures; for the left, if it weren't for Hollywood, the masses would be revolutionary; for the right, the masses would be moral.

17. That's actually a low estimate. Manufacturers are heavy users of temporary workers, but temps working in factories are classified as working for "help supply" firms, which are in the service sector.

18. In fact, that was exactly the reaction of former Treasury Secretary Paul O'Neill, who, when asked to comment on the collapse of Enron, described it as "part of the genius of capitalism."

2 Work

1. The family is the unit here rather than the household, and the manufacturing worker rather than all private-sector workers, because figures for the broader categories are available starting only in the 1960s.

2. These issues were prominent in the recent controversy over the U.S. consumer price index. Critics, ranging from professional economists to Alan Greenspan, argued that the official

CPI measure was overstating inflation, in part because of insufficient adjustment for quality improvements. A commission led by Michael Boskin, George H.W. Bush's chief economic advisor, investigated and decided in 1996 that the CPI overstated inflation by 1.1 percentage points per year. The Bureau of Labor Statistics, which produces the CPI, incorporated many of the changes suggested by the Boskin commission, but many economists (and Greenspan) still think inflation is overstated. Marking down reported inflation has the delightful fringe benefit of reducing cost of living adjustments in wages and pension benefits; it also lowers the poverty rate over time, since the poverty line is adjusted every year using the CPI. The Boskin commission was stacked with economists already on record as believing in a large overstatement, and absolutely no attention was paid to the possibility of understatement, either by the commission or the pundit community.

3. These estimates are derived as follows: real output in manufacturing is about 20% of all real nonfarm output, and has been for a long time. (Nominal manufacturing has shrunk as a percentage of the whole, but since service prices have increased nearly twice as fast as have goods prices, the inflation-corrected manufacturing share has stayed remarkably stable.) Knowing this output mix, and having the separate productivity figures for manufacturing and all private nonfarm business, we can consequently estimate the nonmanufacturing rate. This is emphatically not rocket science; it's the silicon equivalent of back-of-the-envelope work.

4. The assumption is that profit rates are equalized because capital will leave less profitable sectors (driving down the price of those sectors' capital stock, thereby raising the rate of return) in favor of more profitable sectors (driving up the prices of their capital stock, depressing rates of return). It's hard to imagine how, say, $10,000 invested in a taco stand could be easily redeployed in semiconductor manufacture.

5. eBay is new. What contribution the ability to buy and sell used panties and Saddam dinars on the web makes to productivity stats or the richness of life is hard to specify.

6. These full-time-equivalent numbers come from the national income accounts, and don't account for part-time work and the mix of management and line workers. Nonsupervisory workers in wholesale trade are paid an hourly wage 13% above the national average.

7. Barber and Odean (2000) attribute this to "overconfidence augmented by self-attribution bias, the illusion of knowledge, and the illusion of control." Self-attribution bias is an academic way of saying successful traders come to think they're geniuses. And, by the way, men, being more likely to puff and swagger, trade more than women and hold more aggressive stocks—and do that much the worse for it.

8. With that in mind, it's not reassuring to learn that ad agencies are now joining in drug de-

velopment—"an emerging convergence between the clinical development and the commercialization of drugs," as one adman put it. Agencies are running their own labs (O'Connell 2002). The whole practice of drug firms advertising directly to consumers—"ask your doctor" ads—has no doubt contributed to the fortunate shift to higher-priced drugs. Apparently this is good for the productivity stats. Health effects are yet unproved.

9. His publisher's publicity material for the new book isn't so modest: it boasts that Rifkin's "*The End of Work* is widely credited with helping shape the current global debate on technology displacement, corporate downsizing, and the future of jobs." So much the worse for the debate then.

10. That closing quip is an unacknowledged quote from Joan Robinson, who deserves better. The original: "The misery of being exploited by capitalists is nothing compared to the misery of not being exploited at all."

11. These are from the 2001 projections, available at <www.bls.gov/news.release/ecopro.toc.htm>.

12. David R. Howell and Edward N. Wolff, "Trends in the Growth and Distribution of Skills in the U.S. Workplace, 1960–1985," *Industrial and Labor Relations Review* 44 (April 1991), pp. 486–502.

13. During the late 1990s, these characteristics were sought in the cool industries, but the bursting of the bubble ended that and brought a return to traditional values.

3 Income

1. In addition to the fortunes created directly by industrialization, landlords and developers enjoyed great windfalls from the explosion in urban real estate values.

2. These figures come from an unpublished spreadsheet provided by Branko Milanovic of the World Bank.

3. Unemployment averaged 4.8% from 1950 to 1973; 6.9%, 1974–95; and 4.6% from 1996 through the first half of 2000.

4. Details on the CPS are available at <www.bls.census.gov/cps/cpsmain.htm>.

5. Note that the CBO/CBPP figures are after federal taxes; the Census figures are before taxes.

6. For a web overview of discrimination, see the report and background studies for the federal Glass Ceiling report, at <www.ilr.cornell.edu/GlassCeiling/>.

7. But within this subfield, the same gender structures replicate themselves: in the mid-1990s, women were 45% of assistant professors, 31% of associate, and 16% of full (Blau and Kahn 2000). All those figures are up substantially from their levels a decade earlier, but still, there's a long way to go.

8. Waldfogel (1998) reports that the motherhood penalty accounted for 56% of the overall gender gap in 1991, compared to 35% in 1980.

9. That is, to take an example, the black offspring of parents who have only a high school diploma are more likely to graduate from college than white offspring of parents who have only a high school diploma. And so on, across the educational spectrum.

10. Darity and Mason also cite research from Brazil—a place where race is often said not to matter—showing a strong correlation between skin shade and income.

11. IT's share of *growth* in employment is a bit more impressive than its share of total employment in either 1998 or 2008: the five core occupations are expected to account for almost 9% of total employment growth over the decade. Still, that's less than the share of growth claimed by three considerably less stylish professions: retail salespersons, cashiers, and truck drivers.

12. The CEA report also cites surveys showing that many women leave IT and other technical fields because they're such an unfriendly place for them to work.

13. Jacobs's study relies on tax data, which has the virtue of capturing upper-income filers who are overlooked by Census household surveys. But using tax data overlooks low-income filers, who are often too poor or too illegal to file a tax return (which isn't to blame Jacobs for anything—he had to use the data that was available). Also, the increase in the share of low-income households among total filers may have been influenced by the establishment of a state version of the Earned Income Tax Credit (EITC); it's possible, though no one really knows, that many poorer New Yorkers filed for the first time to claim the EITC, which they can get even if they owe no taxes.

14. The CSS study covers only families with children, a bias that mars a lot of liberal income and poverty research. Presumably the idea is to appeal to family-values types, but many people don't live in families, and those who don't are poorer than those who do.

15. The phrase "poverty line" was coined by the nineteenth-century British shipowner and sociologist Charles Booth.

16. Fisher reports one study showing that male researchers were more likely to favor moral explanations, and women, structural ones.

17. The U.S. Department of Agriculture's 1999 version of the "economy" food plan <www.wip.usda.gov:80/cnpp/FENR/fenrv12n2/fenrv12n2p66.PDF>, since renamed the "thrifty" food plan, posits that two adults between 20 and 50 can eat on $59.10 per week, or $1.41 per meal. After age fifty, they need a mere $1.31. This is what Food Stamp recipients are expected to live on. The more generous "low-cost" plan allows $1.78 and $1.72, respectively.

18. Ironically, Smith's self-identified intellectual descendants, who generally prefer wearing images of him on their neckties to reading his words, almost always reject this in favor of absolute definitions.

19. A problem with defining poverty lines through public opinion surveys is that while the averages may hug close to the half-the-median line, there's an immense variation around those averages, and responses are very sensitive to how the questions are worded (Citro and Michael 1995, p. 135, 137).

20. "Household" is a broader concept than "family"; it includes singles living alone and "unrelated" individuals sharing living quarters. In 1998, the average household had 2.6 members; the average family, 3.2.

21. In 1998, 21.5% of Americans lived in households with incomes less than 150% of the poverty threshold; 26.0% less than 175% of the threshold (U.S. Bureau of the Census 1999, table 2, p. 2).

22. Statistically speaking, there was a break in the downtrend in the mid-1970s, and there's been no trend in the rate since—two statements which pass tests of statistical significance.

23. The SCF calls the household units it looks at "families," but these include individuals and same-sex couples, as well as more conventionally defined families (Kennickell, Starr-McCluer, and Surette 2000). For links to a broad array of information from and about the Survey, see <www.federalreserve.gov/pubs/oss/oss2/scfindex.html>.

24. Another way of describing the skew. Median wealth (including principal residence) was $86,100 in 2001, but mean was $395,500—an impressively high ratio of 4.6. In 1992, the skew was only 3.8 (Aizcorbe et al. 2003).

25. The stock numbers come from the 1998 SCF; the overall wealth numbers from the 2001 survey. Though the numbers would undoubtedly have changed in the three-year interval, but not enough to matter.

26. According to the World Bank's *World Development Indicators 2000*, the poorest 20% of Brazilians claim 0.9% of national income; the richest 10%, 47.6%. The figures for Poland are 3.0% and 26.3%, respectively. Brazil's GNP per capita was $6,460 in 1998, 80th in the world ranking; Poland's, $7,543, 74 in the league tables.

27. To take an extreme example, when the U.S. dollar was at the peak of its strength in February 1985, it bought 260 Japanese yen; three years later, in May 1988, the dollar's value had been halved, to ¥125. If Japanese incomes had been converted to dollars at market rates of exchange they would have more than doubled in the space of three years. According to World Bank PPP estimates, Japanese real incomes grew by 40%—still hefty, but a lot less than a doubling.

28. China is a complex case. Chinese domestic income distribution has been growing more unequal since the end of the Maoist era and the embrace of capitalism (or "socialism with Chinese characteristics," if you prefer the euphemism). But the rapid growth in average incomes of over 1.2 billion Chinese has the effect of lowering world income inequality.

4 Globalization

1. Quoted in Engardio et al. (2003).

2. The report and supporting data can be gotten from <www.foreignpolicy.com/issue_jan-feb_2003/data.zip> and <www.atkearney.com/main.taf?site=1&a=5&b=4&c=1&d=64> (visited February 26, 2003).

3. The controversy is very nicely reviewed for the nonspecialist by Laura Secor (2003).

4. These measures use so-called purchasing power parity (PPP) exchange rates rather than market rates; PPP techniques attempt to estimate the actual living standards that money incomes can buy, which are often quite different from what happens on foreign exchange markets.

5. The precise measure used for labor costs is relative unit labor costs (RULC), the cost per unit of output valued in a common currency. What's measured is not the absolute level of costs, but the changes over time in each country's costs relative to all other members. So, a

10% appreciation in the currency, "a 10% slower rise in money wages, a 10% depreciation in the exchange rate or a 10% faster increase in labor productivity all have an identical impact" on the composite RULC index (Carlin et al. 2000).

6. Casarini is plagued by contradictions. The night after giving that talk, he was pied by the "Biotic Baking Brigade" before another appearance in New York, as punishment for his "authoritarianism"—claiming a mantle of leadership in a movement that's supposed to be leaderless. See the May 2003 archives of the nettime mailing list for an account <amsterdam.nettime.org/Lists-Archives/nettime-l-0305/threads.html>.

7. For a list of grantees, see <www.deepecology.org/gandmgrantees.html>.

8. Several sources close to Nader have told me this, though all crave anonymity; see also Lizza (2000). Milliken is intensely antiunion, and a big supporter of Pat Buchanan.

9. In his essay on the relations between racism and nationalism, Balibar writes, "[r]acism is not an 'expression' of nationalism, but a supplement of nationalism or more precisely a supplement internal to nationalism, always in excess of it, but always indispensable to its constitution and yet always still insufficient to achieve its project, just as nationalism is both indispensable and always insufficient to achieve the formation of the nation or the project of a 'nationalization' of society" (Balibar and Wallerstein 1991, p. 54). Nationalism, then, is not really a thing but an activity in need of constant renewal, and some kind of racism is generated in the process of keeping it alive.

10. The 2003 WEF, back in Davos, was no happier. It was even more deeply troubled by recession, war, and Bushite unilateralism.

5 Finance

1. The same researchers have also shown that because of overtrading bred by overconfidence, men generally show lower returns than women (Barber and Odean 2001).

2. Since the wording may be ambiguous, it's important to point out that financial assets are not part of GDP; GDP is used as a reference for comparisons over time.

3. For a fuller discussion of efficient market theory and related pathologies, see Henwood (1998), chap. 4. For a recent popular discussion of the theory and challenges to it, see Russel and Torbey (2002).

4. The profit rate shown in the chart is pretax profits for nonfinancial corporations, from the

national income accounts, divided by the value of the tangible capital stock, from the Fed's flow of funds accounts

5. Though many countries had explicit national industrial strategies in the pre-neoliberal era, the U.S. pretended not to. But of course the military budget was one, subsidizing the development of electronics and software. So too were much less glamorous farm subsidies.

6. Greenspan defined that pool as the sum of the officially unemployed, plus those not counted as unemployed who nonetheless say they want a job now. The second (and much smaller) group is considered not in the labor force because they weren't actively looking for work when the survey was taken.

7. As a nation's industry becomes more productive relative to its competitors, it's able to buy more of their goods and services than it was before—and its competitors are able to buy less. The currency adjustment corresponding to that changing set of facts is an appreciation—from the more productive country's point of view, other nations' produce has become less expensive, and from the less productive countries' point of view, the more productive country's produce has become more expensive. The exchange rate can be considered a country's price on world markets.

Bibliography

No references are given in the text for standard economic statistics. For the U.S., GDP and other national income accounting statistics come from the Bureau of Economic Analysis <www.bea.gov>. Income and poverty numbers come from the Bureau of the Census <www.census.gov>. Wage, employment, productivity, and price info comes from the Bureau of Labor Statistics <www.bls.gov>. Interest-rate data and the flow of funds accounts come from the Federal Reserve <www.federalreserve.gov>. World Bank income and social-indicator statistics come from the World Development Indicators database at <www.worldbank.org>.

Aaberge, Rolf, Anders Björklund, Markus Jäntti, Marten Palme, Peder J. Pedersen, Nina Smith, and Tom Wennemo (1996). "Income Inequality and Income Mobility in the Scandinavian Countries Compared to the United States," paper presented at the NEF Workshop on Income Distribution, September, Aarbus, Denmark <swopec.hhs.se/SWoPEc/hastef/papers/hastef0098.pdf>.

Aaronson, Daniel, and Daniel G. Sullivan (1998). "The Decline of Job Security in the 1990s: Displacement, Anxiety, and Their Effect on Wage Growth," Federal Reserve Bank of Chicago *Economic Perspectives,* First Quarter, pp. 17–43 <www.chicagofed.org/publications/economicperspectives/1998/ep1Q98_b.pdf>.

Acemoglu, Daron, Simon Johnson, and James A. Robinson, "The Rise of Europe: Atlantic Trade, Institutional Change and Economic Growth," Centre for Economic Policy Research discussion paper 3712 <www.cepr.org/pubs/new-dps/showdp.asp?dpno=3712>.

Aizcorbe, Ana M., Arthur B. Kennickell, and Kevin B. Moore (2003). "Recent Changes in U.S. Family Finances: Evidence from the 1998 and 2001 Survey of Consumer Finances," *Federal Reserve Bulletin,* January, pp. 1–32 <www.federalreserve.gov/pubs/bulletin/2003/0103lead.pdf>.

Anders, George (1999). "Virtual Realty: Web Firms Go On Warehouse Building Boom," *Wall Street Journal,* September 5, 1999.

Anderson, Joseph M. (1999). "American Family Wealth: Analysis of Recent Census Data," unpublished paper prepared by Capital Research Associates for the Consumer Federation of America and Primerica (Chevy Chase: Capital Research Associates, October 25) [earlier version, prepared for Merrill Lynch, available at <www.ml.com/woml/forum/wealth1.htm>].

Anonymous (2000). "Précis: Telecommuting or work invasion?," *Monthly Labor Review* 123 (March) <stats.bls.gov/opub/mlr/2000/03/precis.htm>.

Antolín, Pablo, Thai-Thanh Dang, and Howard Oxley (1999). " Poverty Dynamics in Four OECD Countries," Organisation for Economic Cooperation and Development Economics Department Working Paper 212 (Paris: OECD), April <www.olis.oecd.org/olis/1999doc.nsf/linkto/eco-wkp(99)4>.

Aronowitz, Stanley, and Jonathan Cutler (1997). *Post-Work* (New York: Routledge).

Aronowitz, Stanley, and William DiFazio (1995). *The Jobless Future: Sci-Tech and the Dogma of Work* (Minneapolis: University of Minnesota Press).

Arrighi, Giovanni (1994). *The Long Twentieth Century* (New York and London: Verso).

Atkinson, Robert D. (2001). "Alive and Kicking," *Blueprint Magazine* (Democratic Leadership Council), April 25 <www.ndol.org/print.cfm?contentid=3298>.

Badgett, M.V. Lee (1995). "The Wage Effects of Sexual Orientation Discrimination," *Industrial and Labor Relations Review* 48 (July).

——— (1998). "Income Inflation: The Myth of Affluence Among Gay, Lesbian, and Bisexual Americans (Amherst: Institute for Gay and Lesbian Strategic Studies) <www.iglss.org/media/files/income.pdf>.

Balibar, Etienne, and Immanuel Walerstein (1991). *Race, Nation, Class: Ambiguous Identities* (London and New York: Verso).

Barber, Brad M., and Terrance Odean (2000a). "Trading Is Hazardous to Your Wealth: The Common Stock Investment Performance of Individual Investors," *Journal of Finance* 45 (April), pp. 773–806 (also at <faculty.gsm.ucdavis.edu/~bmbarber/Individual_Investor_Performance_4-99.pdf>).

——— (2000b). "Online Investors: Do the Slow Die First?" University of California at Davis, October <faculty.gsm.ucdavis.edu/~bmbarber/online.pdf>.

——— (2001). "Boys Will Be Boys: Gender, Overconfidence, and Common Stock Investment," *Quarterly Journal of Economics,* October, pp. 261–292 (also at <faculty.gsm.ucdavis.edu/~bmbarber/BoysWillBeBoys.pdf>).

Barko, Naomi (2000). "The Other Gender Gap," *The American Prospect,* June 19–July 3, pp. 61–63 <www.prospect.org/archives/V11-15/barko-n.html>.

Barrington, Linda (2000). *Does a Rising Tide Lift All Boats?* (New York: The Conference Board).

Bateman, Thomas S., and Dennis W. Organ (1983). "Job Satisfaction and the Good Soldier: The Relationship Between Affect and Employee 'Citizenship,'" *Academy of Management Journal* 26, pp. 587–95.

Baudrillard, Jean (1993). *The Tranparency of Evil,* translated by James Benedict (New York and London: Verso).

Bayard, Kimberly, Judith Hellerstein, David Neumark, and Kenneth Troske (1999). "New Evidence on Sex Segregation and Sex Differences in Wages from Matched Employee-Employer Data," National Bureau of Economic Research Working Paper 7003, March <www.nber.org/papers/w7003>.

Bennehum, David (1996). Interview with Robert Reich, *Meme* 2.02 <memex.org/meme2-02.html>.

Benner, Chris (1998). *Growing Together or Drifting Apart: Working Families and Business in the New Economy, A Status Report on Social and Economic Well Being in Silicon Valley* (San Jose: Working Partnerships USA) <www.atwork.org/wp/cei/gtda.pdf>.

Berman, Dennis K. (2001). "'Lousy' Sales Forecasts Helped Fuel the Telecom Mess," *Wall Street Journal,* July 9, p. B1.

Bjorhus, Jennifer (2000). "Productivity Is at Center of New Economy Debate," *San Jose Mercury News,* July 3, 2000.

Blanchflower, David G., and Andrew J. Oswald, "Well-Being Over Time in Britain and the USA," National Bureau of Economic Research Working Paper 7487, January <www.nber.org/papers/w7487>.

Blau, Francine D. (1996). "Where Are We In the Economics of Gender? The Gender Pay Gap," National Bureau of Economic Research Working Paper 5664, July <www.nber.org/papers/w5664>.

Blau, Francine D., and Lawrence M. Kahn (1992). "Race and Gender Pay Differentials," National Bureau of Economic Research Working Paper 4120, July <www.nber.org/papers/w4120>.

——— (2000). "Gender Differences in Pay," National Bureau of Economic Research Working Paper 7732, June <www.nber.org/papers/w7732>.

Borrus, Amy, and Dean Foust (2003). "A Battle Royal against Regal Paychecks," *Business Week,* February 24.

Bourguignon, François, and Christian Morrisson (1999). "The Size Distribution of Income Among World Citizens: 1820–1990," unpublished paper, World Bank [available from Bourguignon at <Fbourguignon@worldbank.org>].

Boushey, Heather (1999). "Life After Wellfare," *Left Business Observer* 90, June.

Bowles, Samuel, and Herbert Gintis (1995). "Why Do the Educated Earn More? Productive Skills, Labor Discipline, and the Returns to Schooling," unpublished paper, University of Massachusetts Department of Economics, November 28.

Brady, Diane (2000). "Why Service Stinks," *Business Week,* October 23, pp. 118–28.

Brief, Arthur P. (1986). "Prosocial Organizational Behaviors," *Academy of Management Review* 11 (1986), pp. 710–25

Brill, Harry (1999). "Partners in Deceit: The Bureau of Labor Statistics (BLS) and the Census Bureau," *Z Magazine,* September, pp. 39–44.

Bronson, Po (1996). "George Gilder," *Wired* 4.03 (March) <www.wired.com/wired/archive/4.03/gilder_pr.html>.

Buchinsky, Moshe, and Jennifer Hunt (1996). "Wage Mobility in the United States," National Bureau of Economic Research working paper 5455 <www.nber.org/papers/w5455>.

Burbury, Rochelle (2001). "Mind Games," *The Fin,* supplement to the weekend *Australian Financial Review,* July 21–22, p. 5.

Callow, Julian (2003). "Getting Europe to Work," Credit Suisse First Boston (London), April 10.

Cappelli, Peter (1992). "College Students and the Workplace: Assessing Performance to Improve the Fit," *Change,* November/December, pp. 55–61

——— (1995). "Is the 'Skills Gap' Really About Attitudes?" *California Management Review* 37 (Summer), pp. 108–24.

Carlin, Wendy, Andrew Glyn, and John Van Reenen (2001). "Export Market Performance of OECD Countries: An Empirical Examination of the Role of Cost Competitiveness," *Economic Journal* 111 (January), pp. 128–62.

Castells, Manuel (1994). "European Cities, the Informational Society and the Global Economy," *New Left Review* 204, pp. 18–32.

—— (1996). *The Rise of the Network Society* (*The Information Age, Economy, Society, and Culture,* vol. 1), Oxford and Cambridge, Mass.: Blackwell Publishers.

Cato, Molly-Scott (2000). "Do Workers in the Caring Sector Face Wage Discrimination?," paper delivered at the annual conference of the International Association for Feminist Economics, Istanbul, August.

Chandler, Alfred D., Jr. (1977). *The Visible Hand* (Cambridge: Harvard University Press).

Cheng, Ien (2002). "Survivors Who Laughed All the Way to the Bank," *Financial Times,* July 30.

Citro, Constance F., and Robert T. Michael, eds. (1995). *Measuring Poverty: A New Approach* (Washington: National Academy Press) <www.census.gov/hhes/poverty/povmeas/toc.html>.

Click, Reid W., and Paul Harrison (2000). "Does Multinationality Matter? Evidence of Value Destruction in U.S. Multinational Corporations," Federal Reserve Board FEDS paper 2000-21 (March) <www.bog.frb.fed.us/pubs/feds/2000/200021/200021pap.pdf>.

Collins, Doug (1999). "On the Line at Amazon.com," Seattle Weekly, March 11–17 <www.seattleweekly.com/features/9910/tech-collins.shtml>.

Community Service Society (2000). "More Work, More School...More Poverty?: The Changing Face of Poor Families in New York City," CSS Data Brief 2, April <www.cssny.org/reports/databrief/databrief4_7_00.htm>.

Conlin, Michelle (1999). "Hey, What About Us?," *Business Week,* December 27, pp. 52–5.

Council of Economic Advisors (1999). *Families and the Labor Market, 1969–1999: Analyzing the 'Time Crunch,'"* May <www.whitehouse.gov/WH/EOP/CEA/html/famfinal.pdf>.

—— (2000). *Opportunities and Gender Pay Equity in New Economy Occupations,* May 11 <www.whitehouse.gov/WH/EOP/CEA/html/Pay_Equity.pdf>.

Cowell, Alan (1997). "Workers in Germany Fear the Miracle Is Over ," *New York Times,* July 30, p. A1.

Cox, W. Michael, and Richard Alm (1996). "By Our Own Bootstraps," Federal Reserve Bank of Dallas, 1995 annual report <www.dallasfed.org/publications/ar/pdf/ar_95.pdf>.

—— (1999). *Myths of Rich and Poor: Why We're Better Off Than We Think* (New York: Basic Books).

Crafts, Nicholas (1999). "East Asian Growth Before and After the Crisis," *IMF Staff Papers,* Vol. 46, No. 2 (June) <www.imf.org/external/pubs/ft/staffp/1999/06-99/pdf/crafts.pdf>.

Cramer, James J. (1999). "Wrong! Take Two: Cramer's Rewrite of His 'The Top 10 Internet Myths' Piece," *TheStreet.com*, September 25 <www.thestreet.com/comment/rewrite/787533.html>.

Daly, Mary C., and Greg J. Duncan (1997). "Earnings Mobility and Instability, 1969-1995," Federal Reserve Bank of San Francisco working paper 97-12 <www.frbsf.org/econrsrch/workingp/wp97-12.pdf>.

—— (1998). "Income Inequality and Mortality Risk in the United States: Is There a Link?," Federal Reserve Bank of San Francisco *Economic Letter*, 98-29, October 2 <www.frbsf.org/econrsrch/workingp/wp98-29.pdf>.

Darity, William A., Jr., and Patrick L. Mason (1998). "Evidence on Discrimination in Employment: Codes of Color, Codes of Gender," *Journal of Economic Perspectives* 12 (Spring), pp. 63–90.

Darity, William A., Jr., Patrick L. Mason, and James B. Stewart (1998). "Race, Class, and the Economics of Identity: A Theory of Racism," unpublished paper.

De Nardi, Mariacristina, Liqian Ren, and Chao Wei (2000). "Income Inequality and Redistribution in Five Countries, Federal Reserve Bank of Chicago *Economic Perspectives*, Second Quarter, pp. 2–20 <www.frbchi.org/pubs-speech/publications/periodicals/ep/2000/2qep1.pdf>.

Dobrzynski, Judith H. (2000a). "Online Bid Soars to $135,805, Provenance Not Guaranteed," *New York Times*, May 9, p. A1.

—— (2000b). "Online Seller of Abstract Work Adds a Money-Back Guarantee," *New York Times*, May 10, p. A1.

Dorman, Peter, and Paul Hagstrom (1997). "Wage Compensation for Dangerous Work Revisited," unpublished paper, Michigan State University, November.

Dornbusch, Rudi (1998). "Growth Forever," *Wall Street Journal*, July 30, p. A18.

Douglas, Ian (1997). "Globalization and the End of the State," *New Political Economy* 2, pp. 165–77.

Duncan, Greg J., Johanne Boisjoly, and Timothy Smeeding (1995). "Slow Motion: Economic Mobility of Young Workers in the 1970s and 1980s," Northwestern University Center for Urban Affairs and Policy Research, Working Paper 95-18 (June 23).

Easterlin, Richard (1974). "Does Economic Growth Improve the Human Lot?," in P.A. David and M.W. Reder, eds., *Nations and Households in Economic Growth* (New York and London: Academic Press, 1974).

Edgecliffe-Johnson, Andrew (2001). "Trendies Go From Dotcom to Garçon," *Financial Times,* March 14, p. 1.

Edwards, Richard C. (1977). "Personal Traits and 'Success' in Schooling and Work," *Educational and Psychological Measurement* 37, pp. 125–38

Ehrenreich, Barbara (2000). "Maid To Order: The Politics of Other Women's Work," *Harper's* (April), pp. 59-70.

Eichenwald, Kurt (2003). "Company Man to the End, After All," *New York Times,* February 9.

Elkind, Peter (2001). "Where Mary Meeker Went Wrong," *Fortune,* May 14.

Ellis, Richard (2000). "The IT Labor Shortage: Fact or Fiction," *Dr. Dobb's Journal* (April) <www.ddj.com/articles/2000/0004/0004k/0004k.htm>.

Elmstrom, Peter (2000). "Jack Grubman: The Power Broker," *Business Week,* May 15.

Engardio, Pete, Aaron Bernstein, and Manjeet Kripalani (2003). "Is Your Job Next?," *Business Week,* February 3, pp. 50–60.

England, Paula, and Nancy Folbre (1998). "The Cost of Caring," *Annals of the American Academy of Political and Social Science,* special issue on emotional labor [also at <www.olin.wustl.edu/macarthur/working papers/wp-englandfolbre.htm>].

Evans, John P., and James A. Gentry (2000). "Do Strategic Share Repurchase Programs Create Long-Run Firm Value?," unpublished paper, University of Illinois, Department of Finance.

Faludi, Susan (1992). *Backlash: The Undeclared War Against American Women* (New York: Anchor Books).

Featherstone, Liza (2003). "Wal-Mart Values," *The Nation,* December 16 <www.thenation.com/doc.mhtml?i=20021216&c=1&s=featherstone>.

——— (2004). *Women's Work* (New York: Basic Books) [forthcoming].

Fefer, Mark D. (1999). "Outing the Amazonians," *Seattle Weekly,* September 2–8 <www.seattleweekly.com/features/9935/tech-fefer.shtml>.

Fidler, Stephen (2000). "Summers Hits at Congress Over Debt Relief Level," *Financial Times,* July 13.

Fisher, Gordon M. (1997a). "From Hunter to Orshansky: An Overview of (Unofficial) Poverty Lines in the United states from 1904 to 1965," U.S. Census Bureau Poverty Measurement

Working   Paper   <www.census.gov/hhes/poverty/povmeas/papers/hstorsp4.html>;
summary at <aspe.os.dhhs.gov/poverty/papers/htrssmiv.htm>.

——— (1997b)."The Development of the Orshansky Poverty Thresholds and Their Subsequent
History as the Official U.S. Poverty Measure," U.S. Census Bureau Poverty Measurement
Working Paper <www.census.gov/hhes/poverty/povmeas/papers/orshansky.html>.

Forrester, Viviane (1999). *The Economic Horror* (Cambridge, UK: Polity Press).

Frankel, Richard M., Marilyn F. Johnson, and Karen K. Nelson (2002). "The Relation Between
Auditors' Fees for Non-Audit Services and Earnings Quality," MIT Sloan School of Management Working Paper 4330-02 (January) <papers.ssrn.com/abstract_id=296557>.

Freeman, Richard B., and Wiliam M. Rodgers III (1999). "Area Economic Conditions and the
Labor Market Outcomes of Young Men in the 1990s Expansion," National Bureau of
Economic Research Working Paper 7073, April <www.nber.org/papers/w7073>.

Ghemawat, Pankaj, and Fariborz Ghadar (2000). "The Dubious Logic of Global Megamerg-
ers," *Harvard Business Review,* July–August, pp. 65–72.

Gilder, George (1995). *Visible Man* (San Francisco: Institute for Contemporary Studies) [reissue
of 1978 edition published by Basic Books]

——— (1986). *Men and Marriage,* (Gretna, Louisian: Pelican).

——— (1990). *Microcosm: The Quantum Revolution in Economics and Technology* (New York:
Touchstone Books).

——— (2002). "The Confidence Game," *Forbes,* December 23 <www.forbes.com/free_
forbes/2002/1223/234.html>.

Ginsky, Jake (1999). "High-Income Poverty," *MoJo Wire,* December 17 <www.motherjones.
com/news_wire/poverty.html>.

Gittleman, Maury, and Mary Joyce (1996). "Earnings Mobility and Long-Run Inequality: An
Analysis Using Matched CPS Data," *Industrial Relations* 35 (April), pp. 180-196.

Glasner, Joanna (2000). "About Those Debt Offerings…," *Wired News,* July 3 <www.wired.com/
news/business/0,1367,37284,00.html?tw=wn20000703>.

Goldman, Henry (2000). "The Expansion That Won't Quit," *Bloomberg,* January, pp. 31–6.

Gordon, Robert J. (1999). "Has the 'New Economy' Rendered the Productivity Slowdown
Obsolete?," mimeo (June 14) <faculty-web.at.nwu.edu/economics/gordon/334.html>.

———— (2000). "Does the 'New Economy' Measure Up to the Great Inventions of the Past?," *Journal of Economic Perspectives* 14 (Fall), pp. 49-74. [also available at <faculty-web.at.nwu.edu/economics/gordon/351.html>].

———— (2001). "The Wrap-Up," conference, Brookings Institution, Washington, DC, February 23 (rev. June 15) <www.brook.edu/es/research/projects/productivity/workshops/20010223/07_wrapup.pdf>.

———— (2002). "Recent Productivity Puzzles in the Context of Zvi Griliches' Research," paper presented at the American Economics Association meeting, New York, January 5 <faculty-web.at.nwu.edu/economics/gordon/Aeazg.pdf>.

Gottschalk, Peter (1996). "Notes on 'By Our Own Bootstraps: Economic Opportunity and the Dynamics of Income Distribution' by Cox and Alm," unpublished paper, Boston College, April 22.

———— (1997). "Inequality, Income Growth, and Mobility: The Basic Facts," *Journal of Economic Perspectives* 11 (1997), pp. 21-40.

Gottschalk, Peter, and Sheldon Danziger (1997). "Family Income Mobility—How Much Is There and Has It Changed?" Boston College economics department working paper 398 <fmwww.bc.edu/ec-p/wp398.pdf>.

Gottschalk, Peter, and Robert Moffitt (1994). "The Growth of Earnings Instability in the U.S. Labor Market," *Brookings Papers on Economic Activity* 2, pp. 217-72.

Grant, James (2000a). "The Great Productivity Delusion," *Grant's Interest Rate Observer* 18, March 31, pp. 1–2.

———— (2000b). "Unproductivity," *Grant's Interest Rate Observer* 18, May 12, pp. 4–8.

Greenhouse, Steven (2000). "Phone Workers Fight for Place in Wireless Era," *New York Times,* July 31, p. A1.

———— (2002). "Suits Say Wal-Mart Forces Workers to Toil Off the Clock," *New York Times,* June 25.

Greenspan, Alan (1988). "Goods Shrink and Trade Grows," *Wall Street Journal,* October 24, p. 12.

———— (2000). "Structural change in the new economy," speech to the National Governors' Association, 92nd Annual Meeting, State College, Pennsylvania, July 11 <www.bog.frb.fed.us/BoardDocs/Speeches/2000/20000711.htm>.

Greif, Mark (2001). "Learning to Love Globalization," *The American Prospect,* May 21 <www.prospect.org/print/V12/9/greif-m.html>.

Hansell, Saul, and Judith H. Dobrzynski (2000). "eBay Cancels Sale in Auction of Abstract Painting," *New York Times*, May 11, p. A1.

Helleiner, Erich (1994). *States and the Reemergence of Global Finance: From Bretton Woods to the 1990s* (Ithaca: Cornell University Press).

Henderson, David (1999). *The MAI Affair: A Story and Its Lessons* (London: Royal Institute of International Affairs).

Henry, David, and Michelle Conlin (2002). "Too Much of a Good Incentive," *Business Week*, March 4, pp. 38–9.

Henwood, Doug (1998). *Wall Street: How It Works and for Whom* (New York: Verso).

——— (2002). "Stiglitz: time to snuff the IMF?" (interview with Joseph Stiglitz), *Left Business Observer* 102 (September) <www.leftbusinessobserver.com/Stiglitz.html>.

Herman, Edward S., and Ceceilia Zarate-Laun (1999). "Globalization & Instability: The Case of Colombia," *Z Magazine*, September, pp. 30–4.

Herman, Tom (2000). "Tax Report," *Wall Street Journal*, July 5, p. A1.

Herrnstein, Richard J., and Charles Murray (1994). *The Bell Curve: Intelligence and Class Structure in American Life* (New York: The Free Press).

Hirst, Paul, and Grahame Thompson (1996). *Globalization in Question* (Cambridge, UK.: Polity Press).

Hoogvelt, Ankie (1997). *Globalization and the Postcolonial World: The New Political Economy of Development* (Baltimore: Johns Hopkins University Press).

Howard, Richard (1998). "How I "Escaped" From Amazon.cult," July 16–22 <www.seattleweekly.com/features/9828/features-howard.shtml>.

Howell, David (2000). "Skills and the Wage Collapse," *The American Prospect*, June 19–July 3, pp. 74–7 <www.prospect.org/archives/V11-15/howell-d.html>.

Hunt, Albert R. (2000). "Major Progress, Inequities Cross 3 Generations," *Wall Street Journal*, June 22, p. A9.

Huws, Ursula (1999). "Material World: The Myth of the 'Weightless Economy,'" in Leo Panitch and Colin Leys, eds., *Socialist Register 1999*, pp. 29–55.

InfoWorld (2001). "Offline: Spending Spree," *InfoWorld*, May 14, p. 21.

Institute for Public Accuracy (1999). "Responses to Clinton's WTO Protest Welcome," press release, October 14.

Ip, Greg, Susan Pulliam, Scott Thurm, and Ruth Simon (2000). "How the Internet Bubble Broke Records, Rules, Bank Accounts," *Wall Street Journal*, July 14, p. A1.

Jacobs, Michael P. (2000). "Big City, Big Bucks: NYC's Changing Income Distribution," New York City Independent Budget Office, June <www.ibo.nyc.ny.us/iboreports/IncDistJune00.pdf>.

Jameson, Fredric (1998). "Culture and Finance Capital," in *The Cultural Turn: Selected Writings on the Postmodern, 1983–1998* (New York and London: Verso), pp. 136–61.

Jensen, Michael (1989). "The Evidence Speaks Loud and Clear," *Harvard Business Review* 89 (November–December), pp. 12–14.

Jessop, Bob (2001). "On the Spatio-Temporal Logics of Capital's Globalization and their Manifold Implications for State Power," working paper, Lancaster University, Department of Sociology <www.comp.lancs.ac.uk/sociology/soc072rj.html>.

Jorgenson, Dale W., and Kevin J. Stiroh (2000). "U.S. Economic Growth in the Information Age," *Brookings Papers on Economic Activity* 1, pp. 125-212 [also available at <www.economics.harvard.edu/faculty/jorgenson/papers/dj_ks5.pdf>].

Juhn, Chinhui, Kevin M. Murphy, and Brooks Pierce (1993). "Wage Inequality and the Rise in Returns to Skill," *Journal of Political Economy* 101, pp. 410–42.

Kaldor, Nicholas (1978). "The Effect of Devaluation on Trade In Manufactures," in *Further Essays in Applied Economics*, pp. 99–116.

Kaplan, George A., and John W. Lynch (1997). "Editorial: Whither Studies on the Socioeconomic Foundations of Population Health," *American Journal of Public Health* 87, pp. 1409–1411.

Kaplan, George A., Elsie R. Pamuk, John W. Lynch, Richard D. Cohen, and Jennifer I. Balfour (1996). "Inequality in Income and Mortality in the United States: Analysis of Mortality and Potential Pathways," *British Medical Journal* 312 (April 20), p. 999–1003.

Kawachi, Ichiro, Bruce P. Kennedy, Kimberly Lochner, and Deborah Prothrow-Stith (1997). "Social Capital, Income Inequality, and Mortality," *American Journal of Public Health* 87, pp. 1491–1498.

Kelly, Kevin (1995). "Interview with the Luddite" (interview with Kirkpatrick Sale), *Wired* 3.06 (June) <www.wired.com/wired/archive/3.06/saleskelly.html>.

——— (1999). *New Rules for the New Economy: 10 Radical Strategies for a Connected*

World (New York: Penguin USA).

Kennedy, Bruce P., Ichiro Kawachi, and Deborah Prothrow-Stith (1996). "Income Distribution and Mortality: Cross Sectional Ecological Study of the Robin Hood Index in the United States," *British Medical Journal* 312 (April 20), pp. 1004–7.

Kennickell, Arthur (2000). "An Examination of Changes in the Distribution of Wealth From 1989 to 1998: Evidence from the Survey of Consumer Finances," working paper, February 29 <www.federalreserve.gov/pubs/oss/oss2/papers/concent.1.pdf>.

——— (2003). "A Rolling Tide: Changes in the Distribution of Wealth in the U.S., 1989–2001," working paper, March 3 <www.federalreserve.gov/pubs/oss/oss2/papers/conc entration.2001.6.pdf>.

Kennickell, Arthur B., Martha Starr-McCluer, and Brian J. Surette (2000). "Recent Changes in U.S. Family Finances: Results from the 1998 Survey of Consumer Finances," *Federal Reserve Bulletin* 86 (January), pp. 1–29 <www.federalreserve.gov/pubs/oss/oss2/98/bull0100.pdf>.

Kenworthy, Lane (1998), "Do Social-Welfare Policies Reduce Poverty? A Cross-National Assessment," Luxembourg Income Study working paper 188 <www.lisproject.org/publications/liswps/188.pdf>.

Keynes, John Maynard (1973). *The Collected Writings of John Maynard Keynes,* Donald Moggridge, ed. (Cambridge, UK: Cambridge University Press).

Kiley, Michael T. (1999). "Computers and Growth with Costs of Adjustment: Will the Future Look Like the Past?," Federal Reserve Board FEDS paper 1999–36 (July) <www.bog.frb.fed.us/pubs/feds/1999/199936/199936pap.pdf>.

Klein, Naomi (1999). *No Logo: Taking Aim at the Brand Bullies* (New York: Picador USA).

Korpi, Walter, and Joakim Palme (1998). "The Paradox of Redistribution and Strategies of Equality: Welfare State Institutions, Inequality and Poverty in the Western Countries," Luxembourg Income Study working paper 174 <www.lisproject.org/publications/liswps/174.pdf>.

Korten, David (1999). *Yes!: A Journal of Positive Futures,* Spring <www.futurenet.org/9economics/kortendave.html>.

Krieger, Nancy, and Stephen Sidney (1996). "Racial Discrimination and Blood Pressure: The CARDIA Study of Young Black and White Adults," *American Journal of Public Health* 86 (October), pp. 1370–8.

Kristof, Nicholas D., and David E. Sanger (1999). "How U.S. Wooed Asia to Let Cash Flow In," *New York Times,* February 16.

Krueger, Anne O. (2002). "The Evolution of Emerging Market Capital Flows," speech given in Melbourne, Australia, January 21 <www.imf.org/external/np/speeches/2002/012102.htm>.

Krugman, Paul (1994). "The Myth of Asia's Miracle," *Foreign Affairs,* November <web.mit.edu/krugman/www/myth.html>.

Landefeld, J. Steven, and Bruce T. Grimm (2000). "A Note on the Impact of Hedonics and Computers on Real GDP," *Survey of Current Business,* December, pp. 17–22 <www.bea.doc.gov/bea/articles/beawide/2000/1200hm.pdf>.

Lev, Baruch (n.d.). "Communicating Knowledge Capabilities," unpublished paper <www.stern.nyu.edu/~blev/communicating.doc>.

——— (2000). "Knowledge and Shareholder Value," unpublished paper <www.stern.nyu.edu/~blev/knowledge&shareholdervalue.doc>.

——— (2001). *Intangibles: Management, Measurement, and Reporting* (Washington: Brookings Institution), forthcoming.

Lewis, Peter H. (2000). "Wireless Valhalla: Hints of the Cellular Future," *New York Times,* July 13, p. G1.

Lex (2003). "AT&T Wireless," *Financial Times,* January 28.

Linder, Marc (2000). *Moments Are the Elements of Profit: Overtime and the Deregulation of Labor Under the Fair Labor Standards Act* (Iowa City: Fanpihua Press).

Lizza, Ryan (2000). "The Man Behind the Anti-Free-Trade Revolt," *The New Republic,* January 10 < <www.tnr.com/011000/lizza011000.html>.

Lopez, Thomas J., Philip R. Regier, and Lori Holder Webb (2000). "Do Restructurings Improve Operating Performance?," unpublished paper, Texas A&M Business School (January).

Lynch, John W., George A. Kaplan, and Sarah J. Shema (1997). "Cumulative Impact of Sustained Economic Hardship on Physical, Cognitive, Psychological, and Social Functioning," *New England Journal of Medicine* 337 (December 25), pp. 1889–95.

Macpherson, David A., and Barry T. Hirsch (1995). "Wages and Gender Composition: Why Do Women's Jobs Pay Less?," *Journal of Labor Economics* 13, pp. 426–71.

Maddison, Angus (1995). *Monitoring the World Economy, 1829–1992* (Paris: Organisation for Economic Cooperation and Development).

Marx, Karl (1977). *Capital*, vol. 1, translated by Ben Fowkes (New York: Vintage).

Mason, Patrick L. (1998a). "Race, Culture, and Skill: Interracial Wage Differences Among African Americans, Latinos, and Whites," *Review of Black Political Economy* <www.nd.edu/~pmason/papers/rbpe1998.pdf>.

——— (1998b). "Race, Cognitive Ability, and Rising Wage Inequality: 1968–1991," unpublished working paper <www.nd.edu/~pmason/papers/challenge.pdf>.

——— (2000). "Persistent Discrimiantion: Racial Disparity in the United States, 1967–1988," *AEA Papers and Proceedings* 90, pp. 312–6.

McKinsey Global Institute (2001). "U.S. Productivity Growth, 1995–2000,"Washington: MGI, October <www.mckinsey.com/knowledge/mgi/productivity/index.asp>.

Mason, Patrick L., and Philip R. Martinez (1998). "Is Race Endogenous? Some Preliminary Evidence on Latinos," unpublished paper <www.nd.edu/~pmason/papers/MasnMart.pdf>.

Mattey, Joe (2000). "California's IPO Gold Rush," *FRBSF Economic Letter,* 2000-07, March 10 <www.frbsf.org/econrsrch/wklyltr/2000/el2000-07.html>.

Milanovic, Branko (1999). "True World Income Distribution, 1988 and 1993: First Calculations, Based on Household Surveys Alone," World Bank working paper WPS 2244, November <www.worldbank.org/research/workingpapers>.

Mitter, Swasti (1994). "What Women Demand of Technology", *New Left Review* 205, pp. 100-110.

Moffett, George D. III (1991). "Democracy: Today's calls for Liberty Echo the Popular Revolts of the Mid-19th Century," *Los Angeles Times,* June 23, p. A23.

Moïsi, Dominique (2001). "The West Must Temper Strength with Generosity," *Financial Times,* October 22, p. 13.

Moosmüller, Alois (2002). "Coping With Cultural Differences: American and German Companies Compared," paper presented at the conference Cultures of Economy/Economics of Cultures, Bavarian American Academy, Munich, June 22.

Morgenson, Gretchen (2001). "Market Place," *New York Times,* January 18, p. C14.

Morrissey, Monique (2000). *Employee Stock Options* (Philomont,Va.: Financial Markets Center), April <www.fmcenter.org/fmc_superpage.asp?ID=369>.

Morris-Suzuki, Tessa (2000). "For and Against NGOs," *New Left Review* 2 (second series), March/April, pp. 63–84.

Mowrey, Mark A. (2000). "Wall Street Impatient With Runaway Dot-Com Marketing Spending," *The Industry Standard,* email Metrics Report, March 8.

Muntaner, Carles, W.W. Eaton, C. Diala, R.C. Kessler, and P.D. Sorlie (1998). "Social Class, Assets, Organizational Control, and the Prevalence of Common Groups of Psychiatric Disorders," *Social Science and Medicine* 47, pp. 2043–53.

Muntaner, Carles, F. Javier Nieto, and Patricia O'Campo (1997). "Race, Social Class, and Epidemiologic Research," *Journal of Public Health Policy* 18 (Autumn), pp. 261–4.

Nasar, Sylvia (1999). "Economic View: Is the U.S. Income Gap Really a Big Problem?," *New York Times,* April 4.

National Center for Employee Ownership (1998). "Study Reveals That Nonmanagement Employees are Developing Significant Wealth Through Stock Options" (n.d.) <www.nceo.org/library/option_survey98_1.html> .

——— (2000). "A Growing Number of U.S. Employees Receive Stock Options: New Estimates from the NCEO," press release (n.d.) <www.nceo.org/library/option_growth_feb2000.html>.

Oaxaca, Ronald L., and Michael R. Ransom (1994). "On Discrimination and the Decomposition of Wage Differentials," *Journal of Econometrics* 61, pp. 5–21.

O'Connell, Vanessa (2002). "Agencies Join in Drug Development," *Wall Street Journal,* March 13, p. B1.

Oliner, Stephen D., and Daniel E. Sichel (2000a). "The Resurgence of Growth in the Late 1990s: Is Information Technology the Story?," Federal Reserve Finance and Economics Discussion Series working paper 2000-20 (March) <www.federalreserve.gov/pubs/feds/2000/200020/200020pap.pdf>.

——— (2000b). "The Resurgence of Growth in the Late 1990s: Is Information Technology the Story?," *Journal of Economic Perspectives* 14 (Fall), pp. 3–22.

——— (2002). "Information Technololgy and Productivity: Where Are We Now and Where Are We Going?," Conference on Technololgy, Growth, and the Labor Market, Atlanta, January 7 <www.frbatlanta.org/news/conferen/techconf/OlinerSichel.pdf>.

Oliver, Melvin L., and Thomas M. Shapiro (1995). Black Wealth/White Wealth: A New Perspective on Racial Inequality (New York and London: Routledge).

Organisation for Economic Cooperation and Development (1996)."Earnings Inequality, Low-Paid Employment and Earnings Mobility," *Employment Outlook* , pp. 59-108.

———— (1997). "Earnings Mobility: Taking a Longer-Run View," *Employment Outlook*, pp. 27-61.

Parenti, Christian (2003). *The Soft Cage: Surveillance in America from Slavery to the War on Terror* (New York: Basic Books).

Patkin, Ruth (2000). "Maria Bartiromo," *WorkingWoman.com* <www.workingwoman.com/wwn/article.jsp?contentId=4190&ChannelId=208>.

Paulin, Geoffrey, and Brian Riordan (1998). "Making It on Their Own: The Baby-Boom Meets Generation X," *Monthly Labor Review* 121 (February), pp. 10-21 <www.bls.gov/opub/mlr/1998/02/art2full.pdf>.

Perlstein, Rick (2001). *Before the Storm: Barry Goldwater and the Unmaking of the American Consensus* (New York: Hill and Wang).

Petras, James (1999). "Globalization: A Critical Analysis," *Journal of Contemporary Asia* 29 (1), pp. 3–37.

Pilling, David (2003). "'Mr Yen' Proclaims a New Era of Deflation," *Financial Times,* May 14, 2003.

Platt's Global Water Report (2002). "Azurix: The Roller-Coaster Years," January 25 <www.platts.com/features/enron/azurix.shtml>.

Plender, John (2002). "The Great Stock Hijack," *Financial Times,* January 22.

Poterba, James M. (2000)."Stock Market Wealth and Consumption," *Journal of Economic Perspectives* 14 (Spring), pp. 99–118.

Prasso, Sheridan (2003). "Up Front: Early Returns for Venture Capital," *Business Week,* February 24.

Prins, Nomi (2002). "The Telecoms Disaster," *Left Business Observer* 101 (July) <www.leftbusinessobserver.com/Telecoms.html>.

Pulliam, Susan, and Randall Smith (2001). "As Banker and Investor, Quattrone Found A Gold Mine in IPOs, Venture-Capital Ties," *Wall Street Journal,* May 3.

Rattner, Steven (1979). "Volcker Asserts U.S. Must Trim Living Standards," *New York Times,* October 18, p. A1.

Reddy, Sanjay G., and Thomas W. Pogge (2003). "How Not To Count the Poor," working paper, Columbia University <www.columbia.edu/~sr793/count.pdf>.

Ridge, Pamela Sebastian (2000a). "Business Bulletin," *Wall Street Journal,* April 27, p. A1.

―――― (2000b). "Business Bulletin," *Wall Street Journal,* July 13, p. A1.

Rifkin, Jeremy (1995). *The End of Work: The Decline of the Global Labor Force and the Dawn of the Post-Market Era* (New York: Putnam).

―――― (2000). *The Age of Access: The New Culture of Hypercapitalism Where All of Life Is a Paid-For Experience* (New York: Jeremy P. Tarcher/Putnam).

Rivlin, Gary (2002). "The Madness of King George," *Wired* 10.07 (July) <www.wired.com/wired/archive/10.07/gilder_pr.html>.

Robinson, William I., and Jerry Harris (2000) "Towards a Global Ruling Class? Globalization and the Transnational Capitalist Class", *Science & Society,* 64 (Spring), pp. 11–54 <www.geocities.com/CapitolHill/Senate/8908/transnational.html>.

Rogers, Wyatt M., Jr. (2000). *Third Millennium Capitalism: Convergence of Economic, Energy, and Environmental Forces* (Westport, Conn.: Quorum).

Rojas, Aurelio (2000). "E. Palo Alto Poor Driven Out By Boom: Home Prices Soar Out of Reach," *Sacramento Bee,* January 25 <www.sacbee.com/news/projects/leftbehind/daythree_side.html>.

Russell, Marta (1999). "Productive Bodies and the Market," *Left Business Observer* 92 (September).

―――― (2000). "Backlash, the Political Economy, and Structural Exclusion," *Berkeley Journal of Employment and Labor Law* 21, pp. 335–66.

Russell, Philip S., and Violet M. Torbey (2002) "The Efficient Market Hypothesis on Trial: A Survey," *Business Quest* (web only) <www.westga.edu/~bquest/2002/market.htm>.

Saigol, Lina (2002). "Bankers learn that sending the wrong e-mail could be terminal," *Financial Times,* December 28.

Sala-i-Martin, Xavier (2001). "The Disturbing 'Rise' In Global Income Inequality," Columbia University, Department of Economics, August <www.columbia.edu/~xs23/papers/GlobalIncomeInequality.htm>.

―――― (2002). "The World Distribution of Income," Columbia University, Department of Economics, April 17 < www.columbia.edu/~xs23/papers/WorldDistribution.htm>.

Schama, Simon (1987). *The Embarrassment of Riches: An Interpretation of Dutch Culture in the Golden Age* (New York: Vintage).

Schrammel, Kurt (1998). "Labor Market Success of Young Adults from Two Generations," *Monthly Labor Review* 121 (February), pp. 3–9 <www.bls.gov/opub/mlr/1998/02/art1full.pdf>.

Schwartz, Peter, and Peter Leyden (1997). "The Long Boom: A History of the Future, 1980–2020," *Wired*, July <www.wired.com/wired/5.07/longboom.html>.

Scigliano, Eric (1999). "Tech Pay Isn't What the *Times* Might Have You Think," *Seattle Weekly* September 9–15 <www.seattleweekly.com/features/9936/tech-scigliano.shtml>.

Secor, Laura (2003). "Mind the Gap: The Debate Over Global Inequality Heats Up," *Boston Globe*, January 5, p. D1.

Shapiro, Isaac, and Robert Greenstein (1999). "The Widening Income Gulf," Washington: Center on Budget and Policy Priorities <http://www.cbpp.org/9-4-99tax-rep.htm>.

Shiller, Robert J. (1981). "Do Stock Prices Move Too Much to Be Justified by Subsequent Changes in Dividends?," *American Economic Review* 71 pp. 421–35.

——— (2000). *Irrational Exuberance* (Princeton: Princeton University Press).

Sichel, Daniel E. (1997). *The Computer Revolution: An Economic Perspective* (Washington: Brookings Institution).

Sklar, Holly (1980). *Trilateralism* (Boston: South End Press).

Slocum, Tyson (2001). "Blind Faith: How Deregulation and Enron's Influence Over Government Looted Billions from Americans," Public Citizen, December <www.citizen.org/documents/Blind_Faith.pdf>.

Smith, Adam (1976). *An Inquiry Into the Nature and Causes of the Wealth of Nations,* edited by R.H. Campbell and A.S. Skinner (Oxford: The Clarendon Press) <socserv2.mcmaster.ca/~econ/ugcm/3ll3/smith/wealth/index.html>.

Smith, Paul (1996). *Millennial Dreams* (London and New York: Verso).

Smith, Roy, and Ingo Walter (2000). "The Death of Universal Banks," *Financial Times,* March 14, p. 17.

Smolensky, Eugene, and Robert Plotnick (1992). "Inequality and Poverty in the United States: 1900 to 1990," University of California, Berkeley, Graduate School of Public Policy, Working Paper 193, July 8.

Spiegel, Peter (2001). "FBI Taps Into Takeovers on Grounds of National Security," *Financial Times,* January 11, p. 20.

Standage, Tom (1999). *The Victorian Internet* (New York: Berkley).

Steckel, Richard H, and Carolyn M. Moehling (2000). "Wealth Inequality Trends in Industrializing New England: New Evidence and Tests of Competing Hypotheses," National Bureau of Economic Research Historical Paper 122 (February) <papers.nber.org/papers/H0122.pdf>.

Stone, Deborah A. (1994). "Making the Poor Count," *The American Prospect* 17 (Spring), <www.prospect.org/archives/17/17ston.html>.

Targett, Simon (2001). "Hermes Looks to Spread 'Activism' Across Europe," *Financial Times,* February 5, p. 15.

Tomkins, Richard (2001). "Brands Are the New Religion, Says Ad Agency," *Financial Times,* March 1, p. 4.

Triplett, Jack E. (1999). "Economic Statistics, the New Economy, and the Productivity Slowdown," *Business Economics,* April, pp. 13–17 <www.brookings.org/es/research/productivity/Trip4_99.pdf>.

Udesky, Laurie (1994). "The 'Social Responsibility' Gap: Sweatshops Behind the Labels," *The Nation,* May 16, p. 665.

U.S. Bureau of the Census (1998). *Voting and Registration in the Election of November 1996,* Current Population Reports P20-504 <www.census.gov/prod/3/98pubs/p20-504.pdf>, <www.census.gov/prod/3/98pubs/p20-504u.pdf>.

———— (1999). *Poverty in the United States, 1998,* Current Population Reports P60-207 <www.census.gov/prod/99pubs/p60-207.pdf>.

U.S. Bureau of Labor Statistics (2000). "When One Job Is Not Enough," *Issues in Labor Statistics,* Summary 00-15 (August).

———— (2001). "Characteristics and Spending Patterns of Consumer Units in the Lowest 10 Percent of the Expenditure Distribution," *Issues in Labor Statistics* 01–02 (May).

U.S. National Center for Health Statistics (1999).

Wachtel, Howard (2003). *Street of Dreams, Boulevard of Broken Hearts* (London: Pluto Press).

Waldfogel, Jane (1998). "Understanding the 'Family Gap' in Pay for Women with Children," *Journal of Economic Perspectives* 12 (Winter), pp. 137–56.

Webber, Alan M. (2000). "New Math for a New Economy" [Interview with Baruch Lev], *Fast Company* (January), pp. 217–24 <www.fastcompany.com/online/31/lev.html>.

Whelan, Karl (2000). "Computers, Obsolescence, and Productivity," Federal Reserve FEDS paper 2000-6 (January) <www.bog.frb.fed.us/pubs/feds/2000/200006/200006pap.pdf>.

White, Emily (1999). "Techno-tyrants," *Seattle Weekly*, October 14–20 <www.seattleweekly.com/features/9941/features-white.shtml>.

Wildcat (1999). "New World Order: The Rhetoric and the Reality," 18 <www.webcom.com/wildcat/NWORhetoricReality.html>.

Wilkinson, R.G. (1992). "Income Distribution and Life Expectancy," *British Medical Journal* 304 (January 18), pp. 165–68.

Williams, Raymond (1973). *The Country and the City* (New York: Oxford University Press).

Williams, Rhonda M. (2000). "If You're Black, Get Back; If You're Brown, Stick Around; If You're White, Hang Tight: A Primer on Race, Gender and Work in the Global Economy," Preamble Center working paper, May.

Williamson, Jeffrey G. (2002). "Winners and Losers over Two Centuries of Globalization" (WIDER Annual Lecture 6), World Institute for Development Economics Research <www.wider.unu.edu/publications/annual-lectures/annual-lecture-2002.pdf>.

Williamson, Jeffrey G., and Peter H. Lindert (1980). *American Inequality: A Macroeconomic History* (New York: Academic Press).

Wolff, Edward N. (2000). "Recent Trends in Wealth Ownership, 1983-1998," in Thomas M. Shapiro and Edward N. Wolff , eds., *Assets and the Disadvantaged: The Benefits of Spreading Asset Ownership* (New York: Russell Sage Foundation).

Wood, Winston (2000). "Work Week: Computer Gender Gap Threatens to Worsen High-Tech Labor Shortage," *Wall Street Journal*, July 11, p. A1.

World Bank (1999). *World Bank Poverty Update: Trends in Poverty* (Washington: World Bank) <www.worldbank.org/html/extdr/extme/2214-update.pdf>.

Zuckerman, Gregory (2000). "Debtor Nation: Borrowing Levels Reach a Record, Sparking Debate," *Wall Street Journal*, July 5, p. C1.

Index